REGISTERED

A MEMOIR

LIFE AFTER THE LABEL

N. BERNARD HARRIS

TABLE OF CONTENTS

APPENDICES

FOREWORD

In this memoir, N. Bernard Harris invites us into the intimate chambers of his life, its joys, struggles, revelations, quiet moments of reflection, and above all, his faith. To read these pages is to walk alongside the author, sharing in the experiences that shaped his will to persevere through the obstacles he faced in his younger years. What he learned along the way is that those choices helped build his character, fueled his desire to challenge the system, and strengthened his reliance on faith to overcome.

At its core, this story is about truth and timing. Silence learned early, practiced daily, and perfected out of necessity can create barriers that haunt the soul. The closet is not entered into lightly, nor exited the same way by everyone—and the fact that it is not a choice is the real burden.

This memoir is both a blessing and a testament to the power of faith, especially for those who may find themselves in difficult seasons. Facing criminal charges is one of the most disorienting experiences a person can endure. It places freedom, reputation, family, and future under a microscope, often at a moment when fear and uncertainty are at their peak. The process can feel impersonal and overwhelming, governed by unfamiliar rules, language, and life-changing consequences with every decision. With every turn of the page, we discover not only the person behind the words, but also ourselves, what resonates, what challenges us, and what calls us to greater empathy and compassion.

To fight is not merely to respond to a charge. It is to assert the right to be heard, to insist on fairness, and to engage fully in a process designed to test facts, credibility, and accountability. It means learning when to stand firm, when to seek guidance, and when to adapt in the face of new realities. Above all, it means refusing to be defined solely by a moment.

As you begin this book, I encourage you to read with an open mind and an empathetic heart. Allow yourself to be moved by the experiences, to learn from the lessons, and to find inspiration in the perseverance and hope that flow through these pages. Whether you are seeking understanding, comfort, or motivation, this memoir offers a reminder that our stories matter—and that sharing them can bring light to even the darkest places.

It is with great admiration that I invite you to embark on this journey. May it enrich your perspective, deepen your compassion, and remind you of the power we all hold to shape our own lives and the lives of those around us.

Lori Simmons
Stafford, VA

CHAPTER 1

I was born on June 9, 1981, right in the heart of Gemini season. Before I made my entrance, my parents had already welcomed my older sister, and just twenty-one months after me came my little brother, the baby of the bunch.

My childhood was a colorful patchwork of memories, some bittersweet, but mostly overflowing with joy. I was raised in a loving home, surrounded by both of my parents, a protective big sister who always had my back, and a younger brother who kept things lively. It wasn't perfect, but it was ours, and it gave me roots strong enough to grow, unabashedly.

My mom was a stay-at-home mom, and while I now see what a gift that was, I didn't always feel that way growing up. Back then, it embarrassed me a little. In our apartment complex, most of the other kids had working mothers, which meant that when school let out, they had the freedom to run wild, stay out late, and get into mischief. I used to envy that freedom. While they were outside playing hide-and-seek in the stairwells or sneaking into abandoned apartments, I was at home, washed up, loved on, and sitting at the dinner table with my family.

At school, they'd swap stories about their little adventures, while I sat there feeling like I'd missed out on something exciting, stuck in the safety and structure of a home that, at the time, felt a little *too* watched over. It wasn't until much later that I realized what a quiet privilege it was to have someone waiting for me every day, someone who kept the lights on, the food warm, and the chaos outside the door. What once felt like confinement now feels like care, and I carry that with me.

It wasn't exactly cool having your mom walk you to the bus stop every morning and wait for you after school. For years, I viewed it as something to be embarrassed about. I didn't appreciate it. However, with time and perspective, I came to understand the truth: what I once resented was something many of my friends longed for. Their mothers couldn't afford to be there because they were working multiple jobs to keep things afloat.

Now, as an adult, I thank God for the gift of a mother who was present, who watched over me, and who kept me grounded when I didn't even realize I needed it. She may not be perfect, but in my eyes, she's the living embodiment of the woman in Proverbs 31: strong, wise, nurturing, and deeply faithful. I'll admit I'm a mama's boy. I always have been. I was her shadow growing up, and to this day, her presence still brings me peace, comfort, laughter, and the kind of advice that only comes from someone who knows you intimately.

My dad was, and still is, a hard worker, deeply committed to providing for his family. I remember the season when he was laid off and humbly took a job at a toy store. One evening, my mom brought us to the mall to visit him at work. I'll never forget the pride that welled up in me as I watched him climb a ladder to stock shelves with toys. It wasn't about where he worked; it was about how he carried himself. No matter the circumstances, he always found a way to give us what we needed, and often, what we wanted.

One year, my brother and I asked for BB guns. A few days later, Dad checked us out of school and took us to pick them up. Mom took one look and put her foot down. Back they went. While we may have pouted about it at the time, moments like that reminded us that both of our parents were always looking out for our best.

Truthfully, I didn't grow up with many material wants. In my young eyes, we were rich, though my parents might have disagreed. What we had was presence, faith, and love, and that was more than enough.

Both of my parents are devoted Christians. Church wasn't just something we did; it was a lifestyle, a rhythm woven into our week. Sunday mornings. Sunday nights. Wednesday nights. Rain or shine, tired or not, we were in church. They didn't just show up. They lived the Word. They modeled it, breathed it, planted it deep in us. That foundation shaped who I became. To this day, my siblings and I still laugh when we remember Dad leading us in prayer walks through the apartment. He'd line us up in the living room, and we'd march behind him single file, praying out loud as we went from room to room. It may have seemed amusing back then, but it left a lasting impression. My parents weren't just Sunday morning Christians. They were the real thing, living their faith daily.

I genuinely loved going to church. The choir's harmonies, the energy of the band, the passion in the preaching; it all lit me up inside. I listened closely, whether in children's church or what we called "big church," always taking careful notes so I wouldn't miss a thing.

Then came Mondays, my personal pulpit. I'd line up my stuffed animals on top of my dresser and preach to them like they were a packed congregation. I used a can of air freshener as a microphone and stared into my reflection in the dresser mirror, as if it were a television camera. It wasn't just play. It was passion.

One Christmas, I unwrapped a karaoke machine with two real microphones. I was ecstatic. Dad, on the other hand, who probably missed the softer tones of the air freshener, used to joke that I was "the loudest child ever." He wasn't wrong.

I still remember the Sunday evening I was baptized. I wore my favorite red Ronald McDonald short set from Sears. As I stood in the baptismal pool with the deacon, my little brother snuck up the stairs to catch a better view and almost fell in with me. That memory still makes me smile.Like my parents, I fell in love with the Word of God. I was far from perfect, but even as a child, I tried to live by what I was taught. The lessons I learned at home, at church, and through my parents' example have built the foundation I still stand on today.

I recall a moment in fourth grade that shaped my self-perception. A classmate asked me, "Why don't you curse like everyone else?" Without flinching, I replied, "Because I don't want to." Looking back, it was more than just a bold statement; it was a reflection of the quiet conviction I carried even then.

By the time high school began, I had adjusted quickly. As a freshman, I was already thinking ahead to graduation, college, and a future beyond what I knew. I had a reputation as the class clown, but I kept my grades up and didn't give my parents much trouble. While many of my peers got caught up in drama, bad influences, or poor choices, I stayed on a steadier path. Most of my social life centered around band practice and Friday night football games.

As my friends and I grew older, our conversations began to shift. What once revolved around video games and cartoons slowly gave way to talk about girls and sex. At fourteen, sex wasn't something I'd given much thought to. All I really knew was that it was meant for making babies and was supposed to be reserved for marriage. I liked girls, and I was open to dating, but unlike many of the guys around me, I wasn't obsessed with the idea of seeing or touching a girl's body. Sex didn't dominate my thoughts the way it seemed to for others.

Instead, my attention began to drift in a different direction. I started to notice other boys, subtly at first. Things like the amount of hair on their legs or under their arms, the way their voices were changing, and how their bodies were filling out. At first, I didn't think much of it. I brushed it off as ordinary curiosity, but as time went on, those thoughts deepened, and I realized I was searching for something, answers to a growing sense of confusion I didn't know how to talk about.

My dad and I never had the "birds and the bees" talk, and I never brought it up. Even if we had, I doubt it would have addressed what I was feeling. The truth was, I wasn't interested in sex between a man and a woman. That narrative didn't apply to me. I recall visiting the library and discovering a book about puberty. It explained that boys sometimes compare their bodies to those of others during adolescence, and that this is normal. That gave me some relief. Maybe I wasn't so strange after all. Maybe other boys were having the same thoughts. I just didn't know who.

My sophomore year wasn't anything special on the surface. School was school, but inside, everything was shifting. I found myself noticing my male classmates more, especially the ones with pronounced masculine features. I still found some girls attractive, but it wasn't the same kind of pull. There was a detachment, a missing spark. I didn't question why I felt more at ease around the girls in my classes. I just assumed I connected with them more easily, and in many ways, I did.

Most afternoons, there was about a 45-minute gap between the end of school and the start of band practice. Since none of us had cars, we couldn't leave campus like the upperclassmen. However, we also didn't want to hang out in the band hall with the freshmen. So we'd walk to a friend's house nearby. We'd eat, watch movies, and talk, mostly about girls. When those conversations came up, I played along, nodding, laughing, doing what was expected, but inwardly, I was detached, pretending to be interested in things I didn't truly relate to.

One afternoon, the topic shifted to explicit content. To our surprise, our friend's older brother had a collection of adult tapes. We watched in silence, completely transfixed. I was stunned, not just by what I saw, but by how unfamiliar and raw it all felt. The body parts, the positions, the sounds, none of it resembled anything I'd been prepared for. Until then, the most I'd seen were glimpses of partial nudity on TV. This was something else entirely. Something overwhelming. Something I hadn't expected to affect me in the way that it did.

One afternoon, while we were watching the tapes, his mother came home unexpectedly. We scrambled, shoving everything out of sight, and bolted to the backyard, pretending we'd been on the trampoline the whole time. It was our usual routine: jumping, wrestling, bodies colliding mid-air, and laughter echoing through the yard, but this time, something felt different.

As we bounced and tumbled, I became aware, hyperaware of the physical closeness. I found myself intentionally falling so someone would land on me. I wanted the weight of their bodies against mine. The movements, the pressure, the friction, it awakened something in me that I didn't yet have the words to explain. My mind kept replaying the scenes we had just watched, layering sensation with fantasy. Their contact stirred something deep and unfamiliar.

It felt good. Too good. Sometimes, I could feel their bodies press into mine in ways that crossed an invisible line, though none of us said anything. To them, it was just fun, innocent roughhousing between friends, but for me, it was something else entirely. I realized, as I lay there laughing and pretending, that I was enjoying the trampoline for reasons I couldn't admit.

Looking back, I now understand that sophomore year was when things truly began to shift. By the end of that year, my thoughts were no longer vague curiosities. They were vivid, persistent, and focused. I found myself wanting to explore these feelings with another male, not just in thought, but in action.

The intensity of those desires only grew. At band practice, when we changed into our uniforms, I began watching my friends more closely, paying attention to every detail and every movement. Occasionally, someone would joke and say, "You're probably gay." I'd laugh it off, quick to change the subject or point the attention elsewhere. Even around the apartments, kids would tease me about having "sugar in my tank," half probing, never realizing how closely they brushed against the truth, but deep down, I was unsure. I didn't think I was gay, at least, not entirely. Maybe curious. Definitely confused. I didn't have a label; I only had questions and a quiet fear of being found out, that someone might notice my growing attraction and label me in a way I wasn't ready to claim.

Looking back now, with the perspective that only time can give, I understand more clearly what I was going through. I wasn't just a curious teenager with unanswered questions. I was quietly wrestling with identity, shame, and longing in a world that gave me very little room to do so.

At the time, I didn't have the language. I didn't know what it meant to be questioning, to explore feelings without being boxed in by a label. I just knew I was drawn to something, and someone, that didn't fit the mold I'd been handed.

I often wonder how different things might've been if someone, anyone, had sat me down and told me it was okay to feel what I was feeling, that I wasn't broken. That confusion doesn't equal guilt. That curiosity isn't a sin.

But no one did. So, I did what so many others do: I buried it. I performed. I laughed off the jokes. I silenced the parts of me that didn't feel safe. And in doing so, I created a quiet distance from myself, a distance I would spend years trying to close.

Sophomore year didn't just mark the beginning of my second year in high school. It marked the start of a journey, one filled with questions, contradictions, and the slow, aching work of becoming honest with myself.

CHAPTER 2

I never considered telling my parents about the thoughts I was having. The fear of their reaction kept me silent. Growing up in a Christian household, I knew exactly how they viewed homosexuality—sinful, unacceptable. I didn't need to hear their words to know what they would think. That fear wrapped itself around me like a second skin.

Though I had close friendships with classmates—both boys and girls—I never shared what I was feeling with anyone. I had seen how boys who were "out," or even just slightly feminine, were treated. I'd witnessed the teasing, the slurs, the sideways glances. I saw the hurt in their eyes. That was enough to convince me that my secret wasn't safe. So I kept it buried.

The school year ended, and summer arrived. I got my first job and spent the entire summer working. When junior year began, I kept working part-time, juggling shifts with band practice and school. My junior and senior years flew by in a blur. Most weekdays, I left the house before sunrise and didn't return until long after dark. I'd catch the school bus at 6:30 in the morning, go to school, head straight to band practice afterwards, and then to work, sometimes not getting home until 10:30 p.m.

I worked as much as I could because I was determined to buy a car. Most of my classmates already had one, and I didn't want to be a senior still riding the bus. I poured my weekends into work, too, unless there was a football game. My social life was nearly nonexistent, but I didn't mind. I was chasing freedom, and for me, at that time, freedom looked like four wheels and a set of keys. I didn't get my first car until a year after graduation, but that's a story for another day.

I graduated from high school on a Friday night in the summer of 1999. The following Monday, I enrolled in community college. I was only 17, but in my mind, I was already "grown". I took classes in the mornings and worked full-time after school. On the outside, I looked like I had it all together, but on the inside, I was miserable.

I needed to explore what I had been feeling. I needed to know if I was gay. The thoughts I'd tried to suppress had grown louder, stronger, more demanding. I couldn't ignore them anymore.

There were a few occasions when men approached me, usually while I was working or walking home. Some of them were bold and blunt about what they wanted. I was flattered, in a strange way, but I wasn't ready. I wasn't looking for something casual. What I wanted was something meaningful. I had always imagined love as a kind of fairy tale. Something like Kelly and Zack on *Saved by the Bell*, minus the fact that Zack dated Lisa and Jessie, too. I wanted a connection. Romance. Love.

That's not what those men were offering. One night, while walking home from work, a man pulled up beside me and asked if I could give him some "head." I stared at him, confused. I didn't even know what that meant. I was searching for something emotional, and they were searching for something physical.

Then one day, in my Intro to Computers class, I noticed the girl sitting next to me was clicking around online instead of doing her assignments. Anyone who knows me knows I can be a little nosy, so I asked what she was doing. She said she was chatting online. I had no idea what that meant. We didn't have a computer at home, so the internet wasn't on my radar.

After a million questions, she gave me a crash course, "Internet 1301," she called it. By the end of her mini-lesson, I had learned about email, chat rooms, and all the ways I could connect with people online. It was 1999, and I was utterly blown away.

From that moment on, I started arriving early just to use the computers. I stayed late after class, sometimes skipping altogether, to explore this new world. I'd sit in the computer lab for hours, not doing homework, but clicking around in search of something I couldn't name. Eventually, I started looking for gay chat rooms.

There's a saying: if you go looking for trouble, you'll find it, and I did.

I created an anonymous account and entered my first gay chat room. I was in awe. There I was, sitting in Houston, having conversations with people from all over the country. I even chatted with someone from Africa. Africa! It felt like I had unlocked a secret universe, one I never knew I needed.

The truth was, I had no idea what I was doing. I had no roadmap, no guidance. I had only seen stereotypes, openly flamboyant men on TV, often the punchline of a joke. I didn't know what it meant to be gay. I didn't understand the culture, the risks, or even the language.

If there had been a manual, I would've devoured it cover to cover, but there wasn't. Just me, a keyboard, and a growing hunger to understand who I was, walking blindfolded into a world I barely understood.

One morning, while scrolling through the chat rooms, I met someone who seemed different from the rest. He wasn't just fishing for attention or hiding behind quick, shallow conversations; he took the time to answer my questions. We spent hours typing back and forth, then talking on the phone, even mailing each other pictures like people used to do before everything went digital. We started calling ourselves boyfriends, though we'd never once stood in the same room. As a teenager, that was enough to make me feel chosen, but with time, I realized it was only an illusion. I craved something tangible, something that would silence the gnawing question of who I really was.

That hunger drove me back into the chat rooms. That's when I met him. On the surface, we were mirrors: both in college, both working at grocery stores, both trying to untangle the same questions about identity. The only difference was our skin color. He was White, and I was Black, but to me, none of that mattered as long as he reminded me of Zack Morris from *Saved by the Bell*. He had a slight slur in his voice, one of those cues people immediately clocked as "gay." Back then, I feared what others might see in him, and by extension, in me. I worried that his mannerisms might hold up a mirror to something I wasn't ready to face in myself.

When my parents went out of town one weekend, I decided to take the risk. We met at the go-kart track. It was lighthearted and easy. We raced, laughed, and played arcade games like two kids escaping responsibility. I remember thinking, *"This isn't so bad. Maybe this is what normal feels like,"* but later, parked in my sister's car, the air between us shifted. What began as small talk escalated, and in that moment, I discovered what "head" was. I didn't initiate it, but I didn't stop it either. Afterward, when he looked at me with expectation in his eyes, silently asking for reciprocity, I froze. I shook my head. The silence between us thickened. I drove home desperate, clinging to the idea that a hot shower might wash away not just the act, but the rising tide of truth inside me.

That night, I stood before the mirror, tears blurring my reflection. I asked myself questions no teenager should have to answer alone. Did I look gay now? Did I sound gay? I tested my own voice by repeating sentences out loud and listening for any trace of softness. I walked back and forth across the room, analyzing my movements, convinced that one wrong step might betray me. What I didn't know then, and what time has since taught me, is that I wasn't testing for "gayness." I was measuring myself against the narrow version of masculinity I had been handed. A version that told me love and desire between men stripped you of strength. A version that told me to be anything less than "masculine" was to lose my worth.

As a teenager, I thought I could prove my way out of myself, that if I spoke firmly enough, walked straight enough, hid carefully enough, I could silence what was stirring inside me. Looking back, I see the cruelty of that test. I wasn't searching for answers. I was searching for permission to exist.

The next morning, I went to church. As I walked into the sanctuary, my mind raced with thoughts I couldn't silence: *What's the point of being here? You're gay, and gay people aren't welcome in church.* I sat in the middle of the congregation, watching everyone clap and sing with abandon, joy lighting up their faces. On the outside, it looked like heaven. On the inside, I was convinced I was headed for hell. The self-condemnation pressed so heavily against me that halfway through the service, I slipped out the back, and I never called that guy again.

It took me days to admit to myself what had really happened, that I had crossed into a territory I had been taught to fear. The guilt was suffocating, but underneath it, I felt something else: the faint stirring of readiness. I had tasted a truth about myself that wouldn't disappear.

CHAPTER 3

When the year 2000, dubbed Y2K because of anticipated doom and destruction, rolled in without catastrophe, I felt relief, but I was also restless and lonely. I wanted connection, a relationship, a place where I didn't feel like I was performing for someone else's approval. By then, I had drifted from my high school friends and hadn't yet found a new circle in college. My days were full, classes in the morning, shifts at work from afternoon until midnight, but my heart was empty. Online acquaintances offered little more than surface-level advice. As Valentine's Day crept closer, the thought of being alone gnawed at me so much so that when a chat line friend told me someone had seen me at work and thought I was cute, my stomach flipped. He passed along my number, and when this new voice on the line started telling me all the things I wanted to hear, I was hooked. A few days later, on February 12, 2000, I had my first complete full-on sexual encounter with another man.

The body contact was electric, but the sex itself was clumsy, awkward, even disappointing. It wasn't the fireworks-and-soft-music version I had carried in my imagination. Instead, it felt like two amateurs fumbling their way through, both pretending to know what intimacy was supposed to be, and yet, strangely, I didn't count it as "real" sex. In my mind, I was still a virgin. Maybe that was denial. Perhaps it was the way years of church teaching had conditioned me only to recognize sex between a man and a woman. Either way, I was left feeling confused. I was frustrated when I heard other men in chat rooms describing sex between two men. It just didn't feel like sex to me, and I was disappointed that it didn't feel like what I had dreamed.

Looking back now, I see how much of that moment was about hunger, not just sexual, but emotional. I was searching for belonging, for proof that I wasn't alone, for the affirmation that who I was didn't make me unlovable. I thought sex would provide that answer.

What I didn't realize was that I was still carrying the script handed to me by church and life: that intimacy was supposed to look a certain way, and that anything outside of that mold was broken. I wasn't just fumbling with another body. I was fumbling with my own identity.

A few days later, the calls between him and I slowed, then stopped altogether. By then, I barely cared. I had already set my sights on someone new, and we had hit it off quickly.

A few weeks later I was giving a ride to a friend to meet his boyfriend so they could finally meet in person. I didn't know then how much of my social life revolved around cars: who had one, who didn't, who could provide the transportation. Having a car felt like a currency, and it often made me the chauffeur in other people's love stories, but my own social life was still lacking. The majority of the people I considered friends I had met either on the phone chat line or online, and I had never met them face-to-face.

When we arrived at his boyfriend's place, I offered to wait in the car, but he insisted I come inside. The second I stepped through the door and saw the boyfriend, my entire being was caught in suspended animation. He was magnetic in a way that drew my soul to his, and I knew instinctively he was who I wanted. As they cuddled and teased each other, I sat quietly, nursing my jealousy. I didn't say a word, but inside, a storm brewed: *Why not me? Why am I the one watching instead of being chosen?*

Looking back, that moment taught me something I didn't yet understand: I was confusing longing with love. I thought attraction meant destiny. That dangerous mix would follow me into relationship after relationship. My desire for belonging often blurred into envy, and envy into desperation. It was a cycle I didn't yet have the tools to break.

A few weeks went by, and as luck would have it, my parents were out of town again. One of my chat room friends suggested we go to a club, a *gay* club, to be exact. I had never stepped foot in a club. I'd heard whispers and rumors, wild stories of what went on behind those doors, but if you'd asked me then, I couldn't even have told you where a club was in Houston if my life depended on it.

Naturally, I was all in. My parents were gone, so I didn't have to worry about sneaking around. I was ready to experience the club scene.

The moment I walked into the club, I was utterly blown away. The room pulsed with flashing 3D lights, the laser lights danced around the room, fog poured out from the speakers, and the beat of the music thumped through my chest like a second heartbeat. I instantly fell in love with the energy and excitement of it all. The only thing that felt strange at first was seeing bodies swaying and pressed together, drag queens floating past in glitter and heels, transgender people walking around openly, and men dancing freely with each other, without shame, without apology. It was unlike anything I had ever witnessed. Everyone was just being themselves. No one was trying to hide who they were. There was no judgment, no condemnation, just a group of people enjoying themselves. It felt like I had stepped into another world. As I walked around the club, it felt like I was in a foreign land. I knew places like this existed, but I had no idea I would ever be inside one. For the first time, I saw men who looked like me, Black, gay, and alive in their skin. I hadn't realized how starved I was for that kind of visibility until it hit me all at once. The club became both sanctuary and spectacle: exhilarating, terrifying, liberating. If this world is real, maybe there's a place for me in it too.

In the middle of all that chaos, the lights, the fog, the music, I spotted a familiar face: my friend's boyfriend, the one I had met only briefly before. Something inside me stirred the moment I saw him. I don't know where I found the courage, maybe from the bass vibrating through my body or from the intoxicating sense of freedom in the room, but when he pulled me into a hug, (I had no idea gay people hugged so much!) I leaned close and whispered in his ear: "When you're done playing with him, give me a call."

Then, with a hand that trembled more than I wanted to admit, I slipped him a napkin with my pager number written on it. It was reckless, bold, and exhilarating all at once. I'd never approached another man face-to-face like that before. I had chatted online and on the phone, but this was live, in-person, and entirely new to me.

It felt thrilling, like I had crossed some invisible threshold into manhood. In truth, I was mistaking risk for confidence.

A few days later, my pager buzzed with his number. I could hardly believe he'd reached out. Somehow, we slipped into something that resembled a relationship, at least that's what I told myself. The truth is, it was less about romance and more about logistics. I became his chauffeur, not his boyfriend. Thursday through Monday, the routine never changed: pick him up, drive to the club, stay until closing, then drive him home. At first, I convinced myself it was enough. Being with him meant I belonged. I was now in the scene, finally living the life I had only heard about in whispers and chat rooms. I told myself I was lucky to have someone to call mine, even if I only "had him" in the flashing lights and heavy bass of the clubs.

In the quieter moments, disappointment gnawed at me. I craved intimacy outside of strobe lights and crowded dance floors. I wanted dinner dates, conversations, and laughter that wasn't drowned out by music. Instead, I settled for playing the role of driver and spectator, too scared to admit to myself that what we had wasn't real.

Looking back, I realize that I equated availability with affection. He had let me orbit his world; I mistook it for being welcomed into it. I had willingly shrunken my needs to ignore the ache for genuine connection, to avoid being alone.

One night at the club, as the music pulsed around me, someone leaned in close and whispered a warning in my ear: *"You need to leave him alone. He's not a good guy. He uses people to get what he wants"*. I brushed it off, convincing myself they were just jealous. I didn't want to hear it, especially not when I had already built a fragile identity around being his boyfriend. At that point in my life, I needed to believe in the fantasy more than I needed to protect myself from the truth, but the cracks showed anyway.

Another night, as we left the club, he spotted an "old friend." Without hesitation, he pulled my car beside his old friend's car, stepped out, and leaned through their window to kiss them. Looking back, I still can't believe I'd handed over my keys like some starry-eyed fool. I don't know what's worse: the kiss or the fact that I had actually let this man drive my car. I sat frozen in the passenger's seat of my own car, pretending I didn't see what was happening, pretending it didn't matter. When he slid back into the car, he was casual and unbothered. "I'm going to spend the night with him," he said, as if it were nothing. "You can go to my place or go home. I'll call you tomorrow." The casual cruelty stung, but I swallowed it down.

My late nights out eventually caught up with me. My parents began to worry, pressing me with questions I didn't want to answer. They had never met any of my friends, and my vague explanations only deepened their suspicion. Finally, they laid down the law: if I wasn't home by 1 a.m. I needed to stay wherever I was until morning. It was around 2:45 a.m., and I knew I couldn't go home. He knew it too. He also knew how much I hated going back to his house without him, especially because his older roommate had a habit of making unwanted advances toward me, but he didn't care. He left me with the choice: his house without him, or nowhere at all.

So I chose to leave.

The fog was thick that night, the kind of mist that clings to your windshield no matter how hard the wipers fight it. I drove aimlessly, the city blurred around me, my chest tight with loneliness. Every mile felt heavier than the last, so I turned up Whitney Houston as loud as my speakers could handle. Her voice filled the empty spaces in my car, in my chest, in the parts of me that longed for love but settled for fragments.I ended up at a 24-hour diner. I sat in a booth, staring at the menu without tasting the words, letting the hum of fluorescent lights and clatter of dishes surround me until I was sure my dad had left for work. Around six in the morning, I finally drove home.

Looking back, that night feels like a mirror of so many choices I made then: running from one pain only to sit with another, mistaking movement for progress. A few days passed in silence before he finally called. His voice was serious, almost rehearsed.

"I have something to tell you," he said. "But after I say it, I'm going to hang up."

I didn't know what he meant, but I played along and followed his instructions by hanging up the phone. A few seconds later, the phone rang again; it was him.

"Norman, I love you." Click. Dial tone.

That was all it took. The anger, confusion, and disappointment I had been carrying dissolved in an instant. Those three words drowned out the memory of him kissing another man right in front of me, of potentially being left alone at night with unwanted advances, and of sitting in a diner at 5 a.m. pretending I wasn't breaking inside. I chose to forget it all. Love, or at least what sounded like it, had the power to wipe the slate clean. It's amazing how well the lovelorn heart deceives itself for any perceived chance at love.

That evening, after work, he took me out to eat to "celebrate" our new beginning. I was swept up in the performance of it all: the dinner, the promise, the fantasy that maybe this time would be different. Afterward, we did what we always did: we went to the club, but on the way, we had to stop and pick up one of his friends.Even in that moment, riding shotgun in my own car, I didn't see the irony. He could disappear into the arms of others, but all it took was one declaration, one "I love you," to keep me coming back.

I was hungry for affirmation; I desperately wanted him to choose me. What I didn't understand then was that love isn't proven in grand gestures or whispered declarations; it's revealed in consistency, in care, and in showing up. He never truly did.

CHAPTER 4

One Saturday morning, my phone rang. It was my first "boyfriend," the first one I had met online. His voice carried a nervous excitement as he explained that he was meeting someone new, but he needed a ride. He asked if I could take him to the mall, where the guy would be waiting with his roommate.

I agreed, not thinking much of it, but when we arrived and the introductions were made, I barely noticed the guy my ex was there to meet. My eyes locked onto the roommate. He was magnetic, quiet, unassuming, yet impossible to ignore. I couldn't stop staring.

We exchanged numbers, and to my surprise, the roommate called me that same evening, and before I knew it, we had been talking for hours. Our similarities stacked up like proof we were meant to be: we both worked at banks, we both had cars, we both lived in the same area, and the cherry on top was that he lived directly across the street from me. It felt like destiny, like the universe had placed him within reach as if to say, *Here, this is yours*. Unlike my boyfriend, the roommate didn't go to gay clubs because he still considered himself straight. He was quiet, laid-back, and, of course, perfect.

Before long, we started sleeping together. He was only the third man I'd ever been with, but the pull toward him felt stronger than any sense of loyalty I should have had to the boyfriend I was ignoring. I split my time between them for a while, but eventually, it became obvious where my heart, or maybe just my body, wanted to be. My boyfriend faded into the background as I crossed the street again and again, chasing a connection that felt safe and intoxicating. He was the quiet alternative to the chaos of the clubs, the man who didn't broadcast his sexuality to the world.

While spending time across the street, I started forming a good friendship with my friend's roommate, Brodrick. Unfortunately his mall relationship didn't work out.He was often alone, the third wheel in every setting, so I decided to play matchmaker and introduce him to one of my friends. Even though his roommate and I weren't in a relationship, at least not in his mind, it felt good to spend time with someone outside of the club scene.

I was still enrolled in school, but I had stopped attending classes. It simply wasn't a priority anymore. My life was heading in a different direction, and at the time, I liked where it was going. I managed to keep my new routine hidden from my parents. They asked questions here and there, but since I wasn't getting into trouble, they didn't push too hard.

Through a friend, I met someone who would become my best friend, Daymond. At twenty-three, he was only four years older than me, but to my nineteen-year-old self, he seemed light-years ahead. We jokingly called him the "matriarch" of our group, even giving him the nickname "Mother Goose." Every Sunday, we gathered at Daymond's house. He cooked his famous meatloaf, and we'd spend the afternoon watching movies or listening to music. He always blended a pitcher of frozen drinks, which I politely declined. My mother had always told me alcohol would kill me, and those words were still enough to keep me away.

I loved being part of Daymond's circle, meeting his friends, and soaking in the easy comfort of our Sundays, but most of all, I enjoyed showing off my friend from across the street, as if having him by my side added weight to who I was becoming. In those days, life felt simple, full, and good. I couldn't imagine wanting anything more.

While my days were spent across the street, my nights at home grew heavier. I thought I was balancing two worlds: my gay family of friends where I could finally breathe, and my parents' house where I had to play the part of the dutiful son, but the act was cracking. My parents were noticing. My late nights, my evasive answers, the fact that they had never met a single one of my friends was raising alarms.

The confrontation came sooner than I expected. One Sunday, while I was at Daymond's house, my pager vibrated with urgency: my mother wanted me home immediately. I knew the tone of that message; it wasn't a request.

When I walked through the door, she wasted no time. "Bernard, who is Kevin?"

The name hung in the air like a trap. I tried to fumble together a story, but she was already a step ahead. She told me "Some boy just called here in a very high-pitched voice asking for you. Then, the question that had always been waiting in the shadows: *Are you gay?*

The truth was, Kevin was someone I'd met on a phone chat line. I wasn't interested in him, so when he paged me, I would usually ignore him. All of my friends knew the rule: don't call my house, page me, and I'll call you back. That afternoon, Kevin had been paging me repeatedly, but I was busy with my friends and didn't want to be bothered, so I ignored him. I figured he really wanted to talk to me when he called my home phone, which was against the rules.

I froze. My father sat in silence, disappointment etched across his face, while my mother pressed harder, each word a demand. I denied it, of course. I wasn't ready to hand them the truth, not when I was still wrestling with it myself.

My mother kept asking me if I was gay. Then she began to pray for me, anointing my head with oil and reading me every scripture she could find on homosexuality and sin. She quoted Romans: "The wages of sin are death." She preached to me for over three hours, even going as far as to say that the brown contacts I was wearing made my eyes look like a snake's, symbolizing deception. I was lying to her, she claimed.

I couldn't tell her the truth, so I sat there for hours, caught between guilt and defiance, until finally, I caved into a half-truth. "I'm not gay, but I have gay friends." It was the safest answer I could find, but even that gave her ammunition. If I wasn't gay, then why was I surrounding myself with people who were? The interrogation never truly ended that night. It only stretched into the weeks that followed, simmering in every look and unspoken question at home.

CHAPTER 5

I knew I couldn't keep hiding my truth while living under their roof. Outwardly, I was happy. I had a great circle of friends who had become my gay family. When I was with them, I could be myself: happy, free, and comfortable enough to "queen out" and live, but when the night ended and I had to go home, I had to put on another character and pretend to be straight.The problem with living a double life, though, is that eventually, both versions of you demand to be seen.

One Sunday, while we were having our weekly dinner at Daymond's, one of my friend's ex-boyfriends came over to visit. He had recently moved back to Houston and was trying to rekindle things with my friend. Immediately, he fit into our group, and he and I discovered that we had a lot in common. We were both living with our parents and wanted a way out. His mom knew he was gay, but she strongly opposed it. While we were all talking and enjoying the evening, Daymond suggested that, since our situations were so similar, we should consider being roommates. At first, I was taken aback because, while he was cool, I didn't know him. My pride got in the way, too. I felt like I had a job, so I didn't need a roommate. However, as reality set in and I began to contemplate true independence, my perspective shifted quickly. Within a week, he and I had signed a lease. I had no idea how my parents would react to me moving out, but thankfully, they were going out of town, which gave me time to pack up my things before they returned from vacation.

Now, I was on top of the world. I had friends, my car, my apartment, and, most importantly, my independence. I was living the life. I completely dropped out of school because I wasn't focused, and my bills took precedence. My roommate and I started hosting party after party, which made me and my gay family well-known in the gay scene. I also had several "friends with benefits." For the first time, I was living openly and unapologetically.

I was young, and my only priority was partying. I went to work to earn a check, so I could buy clothes to wear to the club. By Wednesday, I'd be planning my outfits for the weekend. On Fridays after work, someone would pick up a bottle, and we'd sit around, drinking, having fun, and preparing for the club. Over time, I realized that it was okay to drink. I had watched everyone around me drinking for months, and they were still alive, so I concluded that my mom had just been trying to scare me. Besides, Daymond was getting tired of stopping his fun to buy me wine coolers, so I had to graduate to the "big boys' club." Alcohol wasn't just a drink; it was an initiation of sorts. It made me feel like I belonged, even as it numbed the parts of me I didn't want to face.

I quickly learned the ins and outs of navigating the gay community, at least my version of it. I realized when it was okay to "prance around" and be flamboyant and when it was time to "man up" and act as straight as possible. I learned that some men liked feminine guys, and others didn't. I saw that most men defined a long-term relationship as being six months, and most relationships ended with someone cheating or hooking up with an ex. Casual sex was the norm, as long as you were strong enough not to get your feelings involved.

I started to see men as just a means to get sex. I had been the fool once, and I wasn't about to let it happen again. Someone's feelings were going to get hurt, and I made sure they wouldn't be mine, but mostly, I learned that there are many spectrums of gay.

My perception of it may be completely different from that of the next person. There isn't just one definition of being gay.

I had about 15 or 17 close friends. We were inseparable. We clubbed together, partied together, traveled together—we were a family. Once I moved out, I hardly saw my biological family. I can't blame my parents for the distance between us. The guilt and shame I felt for lying to them made it easier to distance myself from their lives. The sad part of it all was that my apartment was less than ten minutes away from theirs, and I rarely saw them. I wanted a relationship with my parents. I wanted to be honest with them, to share the truth of who I was, but deep down I knew they would never accept that I was gay. My dad is black and white when it comes to the Bible. There's no gray area, and I knew he would never accept me. Most men frown at the thought of gay men, but when it comes to a lesbian couple, they smile ear to ear. My dad didn't see the difference. Gay is gay, whether it's two men or two women; it's all a sin.

I thought I was doing a good job hiding who I was from my parents, but they already knew. They weren't dumb. The distance from my family wasn't just physical; it was spiritual and emotional as well. I thought if I stayed away, I could outrun their judgment, but the truth is, I carried it with me everywhere I went.

Several of my friends had parents who accepted them fully, even inviting our whole crew to family barbecues or game nights. Daymond's mom would host events just for us, treating us like her own. Deep down, I longed for that kind of family, one that would embrace my gay family and welcome them into the fold of my biological family, but that dream always felt out of reach. It was easier to keep the two worlds separate. On rare occasions, I'd see my parents at church, but Sundays were hard when I was staggering home at five or six in the morning.

That split between my two families haunted me. I wanted belonging in both places, but my fear of rejection kept me balancing in silence, pretending I could live in two worlds without being torn apart.

Somewhere in the middle of all the partying and the lies I told my parents, I met a guy—and we clicked. He was new to the scene, untouched by the jaded drama most of us carried. We grew close, and once again, I found myself calling it a relationship.

The year passed, and when our lease ended, my roommate planned to move back home with his family to save money. That wasn't an option for me. The apartment complex I lived in was hesitant about renewing my lease due to the complaints that had accumulated over the year. I had to convince the property manager that I'd changed and was slowing down, which is why I wanted a one-bedroom apartment, and they bought it. My relationship had fizzled out, and I was pretty much single, except for the occasional casual flings. Life became predictable: work during the week and parties on the weekends.I was generally happy.

When that relationship officially ended, it gave us room to reconnect. Life was so good we talked about living together, but I was still tied to my lease. Fortunately, I had a friend who needed a place to live, so I sublet my apartment to her, so I could play "husband and wife" with my boyfriend for a while. For a few months, everything seemed perfect: committed relationship, good friends, steady job. What more could I ask for?

That illusion shattered on my birthday in 2003. My boyfriend and I got into a huge argument right before my annual birthday dinner. We argued for about two hours until he finally said, "Go to your dinner, I'm staying home." My pride wouldn't let him have the last word, so I said, "Yeah, I'm going, but I'm moving out when I get home."

I arrived at the restaurant and announced to my friends that I wasn't celebrating my birthday anymore; it was now a divorce party. After the club, I needed someone to help me move out. Of course, they dismissed it as the alcohol talking, but I was dead serious. Late that night, or early the next morning, depending on your perspective, I stumbled into the house and started packing my things. The fight that followed ended with us swinging at each other over a gifted cell phone. That was the end. I thought I was reclaiming control, but really, I was acting out my hurt the only way I knew how, through anger, drama, and pride. Underneath it all, I was terrified of being left, so I chose to go first.

With my apartment still sublet, I was suddenly homeless. I'd been saving for a trip to Los Angeles, and I refused to touch that money. Priorities, right? I stayed with Daymond until we returned from the trip, then I found a tiny one-bedroom apartment. Since I had sold my furniture when I moved in with my ex, I ended up sleeping on the floor for nine months. The only things I owned were a computer desk, a fully stocked bar, and a closet full of designer clothes, because that was what mattered, right? My life was a contradiction: lavish on the outside, empty on the inside.

Over the course of two years, I had totaled two cars, lost a third one to repossession, and, at twenty-three years of age, I had nothing to show for my life except clothes, debt, and a barely maintained façade of grandiosity. I had nothing, and though I didn't think of myself as an alcoholic, every night I poured a straight glass of regifted whiskey from my sister until I got sleepy and passed out, only to repeat the ritual the next day.

CHAPTER 6

One night, broke and hungry, I called my parents for a loan. I prayed my mom would answer, but it was my dad who picked up. He agreed to help, but not before leaving me with words that burned: *"Son, the devil has stolen all your belongings and is trying to kill you, disguising it by making you feel like you're having fun."*

I brushed him off; I just wanted the money, but the words stayed with me

The club scene had become predictable. Seeing the same faces every weekend for two years made it boring. I started skipping weekends out, drinking alone in my empty apartment instead. I told myself I was fine, but the truth was sinking in: I was sliding into depression.I didn't want anyone to know, so I continued hosting parties in my empty apartment, making everyone laugh outwardly, while inside, I was miserable. I began to rationalize my life, and deep down, I knew there was so much more to life than just going to work, earning a paycheck, clubbing, and hosting parties.

I couldn't remember the last time I was in church, and my spirit needed a boost. Instead of drinking myself to sleep every night, I started drinking and pondering life. One night, I remembered the words my dad had spoken to me. Was he right? Could my position in life be blamed on sin? Was sin the reason I was sleeping on the floor, or was it my poor budgeting? I didn't know what to believe. I was torn. One part of me believed I was living in sin; the other part refused to accept that. I hadn't asked God to make me this way, so why was I gay? Everyone said I was born this way, but the Bible said God created me in His image, and in His eyes, homosexuality is a sin? How did those two truths fit together? What kind of God would create me this way, only to turn around and punish me for it? The mirror was turning on me, and ceaselessly asked: Was it sin, or was it me? Was God punishing me, or was I punishing myself? I was confused and didn't have the answers, so I drowned the questions in gin.

One evening, after getting home from work, I walked into my empty apartment and found the lights were off. Was this God trying to get my attention? I didn't know, so I sat in my beach chair, drinking a glass of tequila and watching the flicker of the scented candles. The only plausible cause that made sense to me was that my sexuality was to blame. So, in my mind, the solution was simple: deny that part of myself.

When the lease ended, I moved in with my sister, thinking a change of scenery would change my spirit and allow me to save money. I loved being around her kids, and for a while, life slowed down. On weekends, I spent time with my gay friends, mostly just sitting around, drinking, and reflecting on the fun we'd had over the years. Occasionally, we would go out. Even though I was spending less time in the streets, I still wasn't happy. Emptiness has a way of finding you, no matter where you live. I was looking for a change, and I thought that maybe the change I wanted was in my career, or perhaps it was time for me to move out of my sister's house. I felt that if I changed my social circle, it might take away the emptiness I felt. So, I started meeting my coworkers for happy hour after work and even tried going to clubs alone.

My gay family and I started growing apart. We were still close, but we began to divide into smaller groups. My friendship with Daymond stayed intact, and if anything, it grew stronger. Like me, he was going through his own challenges. They may not have been spiritual, but he had things in his life he was trying to work through. I developed a master plan. In late 2004, I quit my job and took a management position in the hotel industry. But I still wasn't done changing. I enrolled back in college and started searching for an apartment of my own.

The change in my physical surroundings was a much-needed breath of fresh air. Adjusting to the hotel industry and adapting to student life brought a sense of newness to the routine I had been living. But I still wasn't happy inside. I wrestled with accepting my identity and wondered if my unhappiness was simply because I was "living in sin."

My whole life had been immersed in the gay world: gay friends, gay clubs. Everything I did seemed related to the gay community. I had a friend once tell me that I could turn a fork gay, that's how much my world revolved around it. I didn't see a way out, but I wasn't sure if I wanted one. I just wanted to be happy again.

That was the heart of my struggle—not just with being gay, but with the fear that it defined me completely. I wanted to be happy, but I wasn't sure if I knew what happiness really was.

CHAPTER 7

Convinced that I couldn't pray it away, change it, or escape it, I figured I might as well try to be in a relationship. Eventually, I signed up for Adam4Adam, one of the early gay dating sites. I know that nowadays, social media is a standard way to network, make friends, hook up, or even meet a soulmate, but back in 2004, it wasn't as widely accepted, especially in the straight world. However, in the gay community, social media had already taken root, providing a safer and more anonymous space for gay men to meet each other. While browsing through profiles on Adam4Adam, I received a notification that I had a new message. I opened it, but I was disappointed to find that the sender hadn't included a picture. Usually, if someone doesn't have a picture, it's a sign they're hiding something, but this was a gay site, and some people withhold their pictures until they feel comfortable. I was bored at work, so I responded to his message.

Our conversation was dry, but it was a connection. We exchanged the basics: age, location, and preferences, but we didn't have much in common. Over the next few weeks, we continued chatting online. It was nothing serious, just small talk. He still hadn't sent a picture, so I didn't take him seriously, but I gave him my number. Some might ask why, and to be honest, there's no reason or justification for it. It's just part of chatting with someone online. We talked on the phone a few times, but again, there wasn't much to discuss. Sometimes, it wasn't about finding love; it was about not being alone, even if only through a screen.

On Christmas Eve 2004, my sister invited the family over for dinner. I was looking forward to spending time with them, but I had plans to attend a Christmas party hosted by a friend. It was still easier for me to spend time with my friends than with my family. I felt more comfortable around my friends, where I could be myself, rather than having to get into character and play a role with my family. Living with my sister had opened up some doors of communication between us about my sexuality, but she never pried; she didn't want to offend anyone. She knew bits and pieces about my life, but it was still the pink elephant in the room.

While she prepared dinner downstairs, I was upstairs preparing to go out. Gin in my cup, music setting the mood, my outfit ready. I was in full party mode. I got dressed and drove to the party. When I arrived, no one was there. The party had been canceled, and I hadn't received the memo. Besides being frustrated, I was highly disappointed because I was already in party mode. I called Daymond to vent, hoping to drag him out to go clubbing. It was Friday night—Christmas Eve! Let's party, I begged him. Daymond wasn't having it. No matter how much I begged, he wasn't budging.

With no other options, I drove back home. My plan was to regroup, maybe make some calls, and find something else to do. Instead, I walked into my family already laughing and enjoying each other. I planned to drop in, say hello, and disappear. But something unexpected happened: I stayed. I laughed. I forgot, for a moment, about running. And for the first time in a long time, it actually felt good.

Later that night, though, temptation came knocking. Literally. Around midnight, my phone buzzed. It was the pictureless guy from Adam4Adam with the kind of late-night call that, in my world, only meant one thing. Bored. Curious. Horny. He invited me to come over.

My mom begged me not to go. She wanted me to stay with the family, to hold on to that rare good night, but my curiosity was louder. I left anyway. As I drove through the quiet streets, something felt off. It wasn't the lateness, or even the risk of meeting someone from online; I'd done that before. No, this was something deeper, though I ignored it. For the first time in years, it began to snow. At the time, I brushed it off. Looking back, it feels like a warning I refused to see.

When I arrived, he told me just to walk in because the door would be open. That didn't sit right with me, so I knocked. He answered the door, naked, in a pitch-black house. Shock turned quickly into sex, and before long, to the surprise of both of us, the front door swung open!

His house had a simple floor plan, and standing in the front door, you could see directly into his room. There was no time to dress or cover up; we were busted. His mom and younger sister were standing there, staring at us. His mom slowly walked over, her face mirroring the same panic we felt. She stood in the doorway, blocking my exit, and demanded that his sister get a knife and the phone.

My friends later asked why I didn't run or why I didn't push her out of the way and leave. For starters, my clothes and car keys were in the living room. I should have known better than to leave my belongings in another room. When you're meeting someone for the first time, you never really know who else lives there, or if their roommate has sticky fingers. I learned that lesson the hard way once, with a guy whose pictureless profile claimed he looked like Ginuwine. I naively thought parking in his garage meant it was safe to leave my car windows cracked, but his roommate ended up stealing cash from my armrest and taking my CDs. Plus, sometimes the vibe shifts and you need a quick exit.

Everything about this night was off. First, my clothes and car keys were in the living room, which was a mistake. When meeting someone online for the first time, keep your personal items within easy reach. Second, I didn't think it was that big of a deal. My only thought was, "Okay, I hope his mom knows he's gay." She shouldn't have to find out like this.

She held me at knife point and told me that if I moved, she would kill me. That's when I started to freak out. She asked her son, "How could you do this in my house, in my bed?" Then she looked at me and repeated, "In my bed." Probably not the best answer, but all I could say was, "I'm a guest in your house. I don't know whose room is whose."

She asked her son how he knew me, and he lied, saying we knew each other from school. Trying to defuse the situation, I interrupted, "Tell the truth," but by then, she was already on the phone with the police. I stood there, wondering what the police would do. I didn't force myself on her son; I didn't break into her home. I was a guest, and if anything, she was going to get in trouble for pulling a knife on me.

CHAPTER 8

My initial reaction wasn't fear but compassion. I tried to imagine how my own mother might have felt if she had walked in on me like this, especially with another man. It was a shocking moment for everyone, including her. Trying to ease the moment, I innocently asked if I could give her a hug, but she immediately jerked away, shouting, "Stay away from me!" I couldn't blame her. She had just witnessed something that changed everything she believed about her son, and I genuinely felt sorry for her; she had to witness her son having sex with another man, and I was ashamed that his younger sisters had witnessed something so private. She stood there wide-eyed, caught between confusion and shock. At that moment, I couldn't help but think how overwhelming it must have been for her, walking in and seeing her brother in such a vulnerable and un-expected situation.

When the 911 operator answered the line, and I heard her say the words, "a grown man in bed with my 16-year-old son," the ground dropped out from under me.

Once I heard that, I immediately explained that her son had told me he was 18, and the website I met him on strictly required all users to be 18 to join. I begged her to listen to me, but it was to no avail. Her mind was already made up.

It's funny, I never considered myself "grown" until that moment. Of course, when I was at the club or partying, I'd say, "Boy, please, I'm grown," or, "I'm getting my grown folks partying on," but it was more of a sassy remark. That night, for the first time in my life, I felt the weight of being "grown." Not the playful, club-night kind of grown I used to brag about. This was the kind where choices echo, where every decision carries consequences bigger than your-self.

The officers arrived, along with the EMTs, and the officer hand-cuffed me and took me outside to sit in his patrol car. This was serious. I watched the EMTs walk in with their medical bags, and I assumed they were performing a rape kit on him, which made me angry. Why was everyone focusing on him? He was the one who had lied. I was out here in the cold while everyone treated him like the victim.

The police came back to the car after taking statements from him and his mother. Then, they took mine. After making a few phone calls, the officer came back and told me I was being arrested and charged with Sexual Assault of a Child (14-17). I sat there in the back of the patrol car, not fully understanding what that meant. Sexual assault is rape, and I didn't rape anyone, I thought.

CHAPTER 9

From the back of the police car, I watched the EMTs drive off. Moments later, we pulled away, too. It was Christmas Day, and I was going to jail. The roads were slippery, and the officer was speeding. I asked him if he wouldn't mind slowing down a little, to which he replied, "This isn't a taxi."

I arrived at the city jail around 3 a.m. It was so cold and lonely. I remember sitting in the processing tank, thinking, "If only someone would listen to me, everything would be alright." Early Christmas morning, the guards took me and the others arrested that night upstairs and assigned us housing. I spent the entire day in my cell, hoping that I could sleep through this, thinking that at any moment a guard would come and tell me I was free to go. The call never came. Around 8 p.m. on Christmas Day, the guard opened my door and told me to get ready. Finally, I thought, I'm going home. It was then I learned I wasn't being released, but instead I was being transferred to the county jail. I felt my heart drop.

Up until that point, I hadn't called my parents. I had been holding on to the hope that once someone listened to my side, I'd be free to go. One of the officers behind a desk jokingly told me I wouldn't be going home anytime soon. He said it was a holiday weekend, and it would take at least two weeks before a court date could even be set. That's when it hit me that this was more serious than I had imagined, and I needed my parents' help. I couldn't face this alone.

CHAPTER 10

Sitting in the holding cell, I debated whether to make the call. Then, another inmate started talking to me. He explained why he was in jail and asked what someone like me could have done to end up locked up. I started telling him what had happened, and for the first time that night, someone was finally listening, and it felt good to tell my side of the story. Then it dawned on me that this was just another inmate, and he couldn't do anything to help me. Still, I couldn't keep it in any longer.

After hearing me out, he advised me not to share my story with anyone else while I was locked up. He warned that some people could take it the wrong way and that I might end up in danger. He also told me I needed to call my parents because I would need all the help I could get from the outside world. Reluctantly, I picked up the phone and made the collect call.

When I heard my mom's voice on the other end of the line, I immediately told her, "Mom, I'm in jail." Before she could ask what had happened, she began reassuring me, telling me how much she and my father loved me and how they would do everything they could to help me. As tears fell from my eyes, I told her everything. There were no more lies. For the first time, the truth was out.

I remember thinking, "Wow, after all these years of hiding my truth from my parents, it all came out in one phone call."

A guard was yelling that it was time for me to be transferred, so I ended the call with my mom and got in line. I had no idea where the county jail was, only that I was somewhere downtown. The booking process at the county jail took hours, and I spent the day moving between holding cells. The final step was being interviewed by a classification officer, who asked me a series of questions: Was I involved in a gang? Did I have any enemies locked up? Did I have any family members who worked at or were currently in the county jail? The final question caught me off guard: "Are you gay or straight?"

I had heard stories mostly rumors about how gay people were housed separately from the general population. I was too embarrassed to be housed with the gay population, worried someone might recognize me from the club, but the thought of being placed with straight men was even more intimidating. So, I reluctantly told the guard I was gay.

The officer, knowing my charge was considered "high profile," said that I would usually be placed with other inmates who had committed sexual crimes, but because I was gay, there was a conflict, and he decided to house me in isolation. I was assigned to a one-person cell and placed on a 23-hour lockdown. I was allowed out of my cell for 30 minutes in the morning and 30 minutes in the afternoon.

For the first few days, I slept as much as I could. I didn't want to be awake because I didn't want to face the harsh reality of being locked up. Nothing prepares you for the feeling of steel closing behind you. The sound of the lock echoed through me in a way I can still hear. It wasn't just the cell shutting; it was the shutting of everything I thought I knew. I couldn't get comfortable in the tiny cell, and I refused to walk on the cold concrete floor without my slippers. I spent most of my time dehydrated, avoiding the sink because it was attached to the toilet. In my mind, the water was contaminated, so I refused to drink it. My depression settled quickly. The kind of heavy where breathing feels optional. The kind where silence becomes so loud it presses against your ears. The humiliation was complete. Every part of me was exposed and judged.

Sleeping became my escape, but as the saying goes, "Nothing comes to a sleeper but a dream," and my dreams only made things worse. In my dreams, I was at home, at work, or hanging out with my friends. The imagery felt so real that for a brief moment, I thought I was free, until I woke up and realized I was still in that cell. I cried every time I woke up, feeling more hopeless and isolated than ever. I kept that routine for the entire first week. I wanted everything to end.

Tormented by fear and depression, I found myself contemplating suicide. I didn't know how I would do it, and I knew my mom would be devastated. I thought about what my funeral would be like, imagining my family's grief. Would they understand why I felt so trapped, or would they see me as a coward?

Deep down, I knew that suicide wasn't the answer. I had to find a way to cope with the pain and keep my mind occupied. I was able to get a Stephen King novel slid under my door from another inmate who was out of his cell for his 30-minute recreation period. I got lost in that book and found a mental escape from being in jail. The problem was, I read it in one day, and the despair quickly returned. Every day around 6 p.m., my mom would come to see me after work. Since I was housed in isolation, I had to be handcuffed around my wrists and ankles whenever I was moved, and an officer had to escort me. It was surreal because when other inmates were in the hall, the guard would yell, "Clear the hall!" and, just like I was some VIP or celebrity, the inmates would clear a path for me to walk through.

It was hard for my mom to see me shackled, but she always fought back her tears, trying to stay strong for me. Looking back, I can laugh because she would bring disinfecting wipes to clean the intercom. She swore she could smell the breath of the last person who used the booth. Because I was in isolation, my visits were private, just my parents and me, no other inmates. I felt exclusive in that sense. My parents would spend the entire 15-minute visits encouraging me and assuring me that things would get better, but I still felt hopeless, embarrassed, and full of guilt.

On my first commissary order, along with bottled water, sodas, and junk food, I bought a Bible, which was a priority on my list. That King James Bible became my best friend. I spent day and night reading, and it was funny because, even though I had heard most of what I was reading before, either preached in church or by my parents, it felt like I was reading it for the first time. All the stories and Bible heroes I learned about growing up seemed new again. I read stories about people facing impossible situations but emerging victorious with God's help. Stories like Daniel's, Jehoshaphat's, and many others really renewed my faith. For the first time, I began to feel a little hope.

However, not everything I read encouraged me. Some of the verses made me question my identity. I had heard my parents preach against homosexuality, but as I read those scriptures for myself, it felt like my eyes were starting to open. I sat in my cell, pondering day and night about my life, and it just didn't make sense to me that being gay could be such a major sin or abomination. Who was I hurting by being gay? It's not like I was breaking the law. What was so wrong with me wanting affection from a man? If God wanted me to be straight, why didn't He put a desire in me to be attracted to women?

I never once prayed, "Lord, make me gay," but I wondered, how could I have been born this way if it was so wrong? Why would God allow me to be born gay and then say I was going to hell? How could God give us free will and then punish us if our choices don't align with His word? I spent two days contemplating those questions, and the only scripture that made sense to me was Isaiah 55:8: "My thoughts are not like your thoughts. And your ways are not like my ways." I took that verse as God's answer to all of my questions, and it brought an end to my two-day deliberation.

Finally, I accepted the fact that I had hit rock bottom and needed help that no person could give. One night, while reading my Bible, I prayed a simple prayer: "God, I know it's time for me to repent. If you show me how, I'll change my life and serve you." I spent the next few days rebuilding my relationship with God and strengthening my faith.

CHAPTER 11

My trial date was set for January 5, 2005. Early that morning, around 3:45 a.m., I was escorted to court. I moved from one cold holding cell to another, reciting faith-based scriptures, rebuking the devil, and standing firm in the belief that God would help me win this case. I was convinced that God was on my side, that the battle wasn't mine, but the Lord's, and I would be going home soon. It took us four hours to travel through the underground maze from the jail to the courthouse. I still can't understand how the jail is directly across the street from the courthouse, yet it took so long to get there.

I sat and waited outside the courtroom in another holding cell, praying, but still feeling a little afraid of the unknown. Some of the other inmates paced back and forth, while others discussed their cases, complained about being cold or hungry, or lamented their exhaustion. I had expected the process to be more private, like on television, where my lawyer and the prosecutors would meet to discuss the options available to me, but that's not how it works in real life. In real life, I was in the same holding cell as everyone else. When my lawyer came, he called me to a window and discussed my case in front of everyone.

"Mr. Harris," a slow, gravelly voice called. I turned toward a man whose cadence carried the hoarseness of a throat ruined by cheap cigarettes. He introduced himself as my court-appointed lawyer. He wasn't anything like the sharp-suited attorneys I'd seen on TV. He slid consent papers allowing him to represent me through the partition, asked me to sign before bluntly informing me I was facing *two to twenty years in prison.*

My chest tightened and my eyes widened in fear as I shouted back at him, "2 to 20 years?! That boy lied to me! Get the charges dropped!" I demanded.

"Give me a second," he muttered, disappearing for what felt like an eternity. In those twenty minutes, my mind ricocheted between panic and denial. Surely, I wasn't going to prison for something I hadn't done. When he returned, he shoved another paper toward me. No explanation. He said, "Sign here," and left. That was my introduction to "justice."

The document informed me that my trial had been reset for one week. Surely, this couldn't be it. I was supposed to go home today. The judge was supposed to review the facts of my case, issue a warning, and let me go. I sat in that holding cell, confused and disappointed, until the bailiff escorted me back to the elevator to begin the long, 4-hour journey back to my cell. Once I was back in my cell, all I could do was cry as disappointment overwhelmed me.

"God, what happened?" I cried out in despair. Isn't it funny how we live the way we want for so many years and then expect God to step in and instantly fix everything? I cried myself to sleep, consumed with frustration, until I heard the guard calling me for a visit. Of course, it was my mother. As always, she was steady, her encouragement unwavering. Looking back, I marvel at how much strength my parents carried on my behalf when I had none of my own.

During our visit, my mother explained that she attended court had had the opportunity to speak with my lawyer. During their conversation, he informed her that he was going to push for me to get probation. Even though the "victim" had lied about his age, the court wasn't willing to drop the charges. The burden of proof, my lawyer explained, lay with me. As the adult in the situation, it was my responsibility to verify the other person's age before beginning a relationship with them.

So, here's my public service announcement: *before becoming intimate with anyone, verify everything. Don't assume. Protect yourself.* It's one of those truths you wish you could tattoo onto your younger self's forehead.

My lawyer assured her that probation was likely. The logic behind the trial delay was spending a few more days in jail would make it appear as though I wasn't getting off too easily. During the week of waiting, I spent my time reading books that I obtained from other inmates, and I also studied my Bible. I fought off anxiety, but I found myself becoming impatient. I reflected on all the things I had missed while in jail. I didn't get to celebrate Christmas, nor could I attend any New Year's parties. New Year's had always been my favorite holiday, a chance for a fresh start. I've looked at it as an opportunity to leave behind any shortcomings or failures from the past year and try again. Spending New Year's in jail felt like I had lost out on my fresh start.

Even after rededicating myself to the Lord, I couldn't deny that part of me still planned to go out and get drunk at least one weekend after my release. I thought about my friends, most of them gay, and the promise I'd made to God to change my life. That tension between what I'd vowed and what I wanted was already setting in. I wondered how my friends would react when I told them I was going to try to live according to my renewed faith. I had always heard that when you're trying to change, you can't keep hanging out with the same crowd. It's like a recovering addict trying to hang around the same environment. I could accept that, but I had good friends. No, I had great friends, and I was confident that I could still hang out with them and stay on track with my new walk with the Lord. I didn't want to lose my friends, but I was determined to change my life.

All this thinking and planning made those seven days pass quickly, and before I knew it, I was called to court. This time, I was prepared. I knew what to expect, so the four-hour journey across the street wasn't as bad. I spent the entire time praying and thanking God for giving me the victory. Even though I was a little nervous, I still felt at peace. My lawyer had convinced me that I would be going home; all I had to do was plead guilty, accept the court's offer of probation, and move on with my life. He presented the process in a way that made it sound like he had fought for me, and that probation was the best option I could hope for.

I'd had a few friends who were on probation, and according to them, it seemed pretty simple: take a drug test once a month and pay a monthly fee. I figured I could handle that. When I met with my lawyer again, he told me he was 99% sure that I would be granted probation, and all I had to do was plead guilty, which meant waiving my right to a trial. Of course, I didn't care about the trial. All I cared about was going home. That's all that mattered.

My lawyer went on to explain that as part of the plea, I would be placed on deferred adjudication probation. This meant the offense wouldn't appear on my criminal record, and once I completed probation, it would be as if I had never committed the offense. Everything sounded perfect. I felt like I was getting a great deal, and my heart soared until he dropped the bomb on me that shattered everything.

As part of the plea, I would have to register as a sex offender for the rest of my life.

Those words stunned me, and I blacked out for a few seconds. I sat frozen, trying to process what I had just heard. A moment ago, I had been on cloud nine, thinking I was finally going home. Now, it felt like I had just been hit by a truck. Me, a sex offender? That didn't make sense. Sex offenders were people I had always pictured as older men with thick glasses, wearing suspenders, and luring children with candy. It wasn't me. I hadn't "sexually offended" anyone. I was lied to. He invited me to his house. He had a fake profile. He had preyed on me. There was no way I was going to agree to those terms.

I argued with my court-appointed lawyer, trying to convince him that I wasn't a sex offender. I'll never forget the look on his face, that nonchalant expression, as he looked back at me through the glass partition and basically said, "I don't care about all that. Do you want to go home or not?"

His indifference was chilling, and it was in that moment that I realized precisely what a court-appointed attorney does. Nothing. He baited me into thinking this was the best option for me. He convinced me that this was the only choice I had, leaving out all the essential details, just hoping I would sign the plea. I wasn't his client. I was his case file. He'd get his check. I'd get the label.

I asked him, "Why can't I talk to the district attorney myself? Why won't the judge see me?" I questioned how I could trust that he was arguing my case when I was locked away in a holding cell, while he and the district attorney made decisions about my fate. It didn't feel fair. Lady Justice wasn't blind; she was selective. Her scales weren't balanced; they were tilted toward whomever held the most power in the room, and in that moment, it definitely wasn't me.

My court-appointed lawyer was growing increasingly impatient with me. "Mr. Harris, I need you to make a decision. You have an opportunity to go home. Take it."

I sat there, contemplating his last comment. He was right. I had a free pass to leave jail; all I had to do was sign on the dotted line and agree to be a registered sex offender. Alternatively, I could take my chances, plead not guilty, and try to convince a jury of my innocence. My lawyer informed me that the judge and the law didn't care that I was lied to. I had broken the law by having sex with someone underage, regardless of the circumstances. I could take my chances, but if I lost, I faced 2 to 20 years in state prison.

Reluctantly, I asked for his pen, and I signed the plea agreement. He anxiously leaned into the partition, watching me as I signed. I felt like an aggressive used car salesman was trying to take advantage of me. Before I had even finished signing the documents, my lawyer beckoned for me to slide them through the security glass. Once he had them, he excused himself to speak with the district attorney. While he probably celebrated closing another case, I sat there, thinking about how my life would be different as a registered sex offender.

I thought about the shame I would bring to my family. How would my Christian parents feel, knowing their son would be labeled a sex offender for the rest of his life? Would I show up on the "predator check" segment of the local news? In my mind, being labeled a sex offender felt like wearing a scarlet letter. I tried to rationalize my decision: On one hand, I was going home, and that was all that mattered. On the other hand, I realized we live in the information age. In seconds, anyone could search the sex offender registry online. Simply enter your zip code, and it will display a list of all registered offenders in your area, including their name, picture, and address.

Even I had been guilty of browsing the website in the past, out of boredom and curiosity. I would filter by age and even joked about meeting those who seemed attractive, naively assuming that their actions were purely driven by sexual desire. That was no longer a joke. I was about to be on that list.

The bailiff came in to escort me out of the holding cell. It was a short walk, but for some reason, I counted the steps. FIFTEEN. Fifteen steps that would change my life forever. Fifteen. With every step, I knew I wasn't walking toward grace; I was walking deeper into a system where mercy was conditional. Mercy didn't meet me at the end of those steps. Judgment did.

I was amazed at how contemporary the courtroom appeared. I had never stepped inside a courtroom before, except for traffic court, which was located in a much older building a few blocks away. The polished wooden desks shined under the fluorescent lights, and the dark brown pews reflected the light perfectly. The Texas flag stood proudly next to the United States flag, with Lady Justice firmly positioned between them, symbolizing the fairness and steadfastness of justice that were meant to be upheld within these walls.

I couldn't help but notice the sharp contrast. Inside this side of the door, everything was clean, modern, and orderly. On the other side, there were just concrete and stainless-steel cages, holding cells, a far cry from the polished courtroom.

The court clerks moved with practiced efficiency, signing and stamping documents, translating for non-English speaking defendants, and at times, rolling their eyes in a way that made it clear some of them would rather have been anywhere else. The documents moved from one clerk to the next like an assembly line, passing through different hands. One clerk would get my signature and thumbprints; the next would explain what I had just signed; another would discuss the fees involved, and so on.

Surprisingly, most of the shiny wooden pews were empty. My parents sat on the right side, in the first pew. My mother smiled, wearing her best Sunday church suit. Her smile was wide, full of relief. It was the smile of someone who knew I would be coming home soon. It was the strength and support I needed, and I knew that if she was smiling, everything would somehow work out. But even in her smile, I could see the weight my father carried. His smile couldn't hide the hurt, shame, and disappointment in his eyes.

Seeing my friends Tonya and Monique in the courtroom boosted my ego. Their presence confirmed that I had genuine, loyal friends.

It's easy to be friends with someone when things are fun and simple, but when things get real, when life gets tough, who's really there?

The plan seemed simple enough: accept the plea deal, plead guilty to Sexual Assault of a Child (14-17), and avoid a lengthy prison sentence if convicted by a jury. My court-appointed lawyer explained that by pleading guilty, I would be saving taxpayers the expense of a trial, showing responsibility for my actions by not burdening society with the costs of my poor choices. But the deal didn't just benefit me; it worked in the District Attorney's favor too. A guilty plea meant another easy conviction, one more statistic to pad their record and bolster their "tough on crime" image. It was good optics, especially during election season. My court-appointed lawyer also stood to gain. A quick plea deal meant one less case to prepare, one less trial to fight, one more file off their overflowing desk. Efficiency, not advocacy, seemed to be the name of the game.

In the end, what was a win for the District Attorney's record and a convenience for my lawyer came at the highest cost to me; my guilty plea would change the course of my life forever. In exchange, I'd be granted probation, a second chance, a "slap on the wrist," as my lawyer put it. On paper, everything seemed to be in place. But inside, I couldn't shake the feeling that I was losing.

CHAPTER 12

My parents, friends, and I all thought that once I pleaded guilty, it would be over and I'd be free to go home. What we didn't know, what we couldn't imagine, was how drastically and deeply our lives were about to change. I use the word "our" because this plea deal affected not just me but everyone I loved, in ways that were harsh and bitter.

The bailiff called the court into session. Unlike what you see on television, the judge didn't walk into the room. He was already seated behind his bench, his throne of justice. He was a middle-aged Caucasian man, clean-shaven, with a short, flat-top haircut that was likely his style since his younger days. He was a heavyset man, with stiff, conservative, and stern mannerisms. He made no effort to smile or greet me, other than to call me to the bench.

As I stood before him, I made sure to keep my gaze fixed on his eyes. My freedom was in the hands of a man who couldn't even offer me a simple "good morning." In his mind, I was already guilty. He barely glanced through the pages of my file. It felt like an injustice. The last 23 years of my life, my family, my struggles, my hopes, meant nothing to him. His decision on whether I would be released was based on just a few pages in a manila folder.

Looking down at the folder, he read my charges aloud and explained the potential punishment under Texas law: 5 to 99 years. My knees buckled slightly as the reality of serving five years in prison sunk in. I couldn't even imagine 99 years. Fighting back tears, I kept my eyes fixed on him, determined that he would remember my face. I wasn't going to be just another name in a manila folder.

Finally, after flipping through all the pages, he lifted his head, his eyes meeting mine. We stared at each other, both of us holding our ground, neither of us willing to break the gaze. He explained that the District Attorney recommended a plea of deferred adjudication, but the final decision was his: whether to accept the plea or go to trial.

I could feel his disdain, his disgust toward me. It was clear from his body language and tone that he was offended by my presence. Was it because I was Black? Gay? Or because I was charged with a crime against a minor? Maybe it was a combination of all three, but whatever it was, he made it personal. There was no empathy in his voice, no mercy in his demeanor. It made me question why he was being so harsh. Was it possible he was projecting something from his own life onto me?

As a heavyset Caucasian man, he naturally reminded me of the stereotypical "bear," so I briefly wondered if he might be gay, but even a closeted gay person would show some subtle signs of compassion. I quickly dismissed that thought. I know some of you may be judging me, ignoring my intuition as a way to deflect, but I couldn't shake the feeling that he was either someone who had been abused as a child or he was capable of abusing others. He had that look. I intend to give him the courtesy he didn't extend to me and assume he was simply a law-abiding, impartial judge, tough on crime. Still, there was no justification for his approach.

The facts were right in front of him. The profile of the young man clearly stated that I was talking to an 18-year-old. His confession admitted he had lied about his age. This case should have been dismissed.

"Are you in your right mind?" the judge asked. "Have you ever been declared mentally unstable? Did anyone promise you anything in exchange for your plea?"

I hesitated before I answered. My lawyer had assured me that I was going home. Was that the promise the judge was referring to? I glanced at my lawyer for guidance, and he mouthed, "Answer no." So, I said no, no one promised me anything.

The judge rolled his eyes, sighed, and reluctantly agreed to accept my plea of guilt and the prosecutor's recommendation for seven years of deferred adjudication. He pointed out that this didn't mean the case was resolved. He was simply delaying his decision for seven years.

Then, with a chilling finality, he delivered the kill shot—the reminder that I would have to register as a sex offender for the rest of my life. I still cringe at the thought of hearing those words, "sex offender for the rest of my life." My pride wouldn't let me cry. I couldn't give him the satisfaction of seeing his victory. He had won, and I had lost.

I had no way of understanding what "the rest of your life" truly meant. My mind couldn't grasp that far. I was thinking in hours, days, how soon I could leave this place, how quickly I could get back to breathing air without bars around me. Freedom was the only horizon I could see.

Looking back now, I ache for that younger version of myself. He couldn't know that those three words, Registered Sex Offender, would echo through decades. He couldn't know the friendships it would cost, the jobs, the peace of simply existing without stigma. He couldn't imagine how many times he'd replay that day, wishing someone had stopped him, explained, cared.

The gavel came down anyway.

And just like that, I was sentenced not only by the court but also by a system that labels people and rarely, if ever, allows them to escape.

Once he finished his final instructions, he explained that a representative from adult supervision, also known as probation, would outline the conditions of my probation. After reading, signing, and stamping my thumbprint on a few documents, I turned to look at my parents. It was clear they were relieved that it was finally over. My mom smiled at me, mouthing "we love you," and my dad nodded in agreement. Their support gave me the strength to endure.

All those years I spent hiding, trying to keep one secret from them, were for nothing. They were there, with open arms and open hearts. I learned that no matter how bad a decision or mistake someone makes, showing love and offering support during their hard times can make all the difference. My parents carried me from the very beginning; they were my backbone. In addition to their love, I am truly blessed to have so many people go out of their way to support me, and I will always be forever grateful. Galatians 6:10 reads,

"Whenever you can, do good to everyone." Every gesture, big or small, makes a huge difference.

CHAPTER 13

The bailiff led me back to the holding cells behind the court-room, where I would wait to speak with the Probation Officer. As I sat there, all I could think about was freedom. It may have only been 18 days, but those 18 days felt like the longest of my life, so far.

As I waited, I couldn't help but reflect on the value of freedom. As a child, I submitted to my parents, teachers, and elders. As an employee, I followed my employer's rules and expectations, but it was always my choice to submit. I understood the consequences of disobeying my parents, disrupting class, or breaking work rules, and it was always up to me whether I obeyed or rebelled. In jail, howev-er, submission was forced upon you. You couldn't rebel, and you didn't have the right to choose. Losing your freedom can deeply un-dermine your sense of self-worth. It's the greatest loss.

Holding onto my newfound appreciation for freedom, I started planning a late New Year's party. I had missed both Christmas and New Year's, and I was excited to celebrate my "fresh start." I imag-ined myself drinking and laughing, telling all my friends about my time in jail. Life was about to begin anew, fresh and clean.

I couldn't start my new life without a fresh haircut, so I planned to call my barber first and then let my manager know I'd be at work the next day. Business as usual. I had learned my lessons, and I was ready to put the past behind me and move on.

Foolish. Foolish. Foolish child. Life had different arrangements.

Those plans came to a complete stop the moment the representa-tive entered the room. He was a middle-aged gay man, White, with unkempt hair, one hoop earring, and thick silver rings on his fingers. His clothes looked hastily thrown together, and his appearance was odd, out of place.

He started by reviewing my charges and explaining what a plea deal involved, reiterating the judge's earlier words. His first instruc-tions were that I had 24 hours to report to the probation office, or my probation would be immediately revoked. Then came the worst part: He handed me the conditions of my probation, calling it a contract between me and the state. I always thought of probation as just paying a few fees, doing a couple of hours of community service, and undergoing random drug tests now and then, but the contract listed thirty conditions, far more than I had expected.

Some conditions were basic and standard, like providing proof of my high school education, staying within the county, and abstaining from drugs and alcohol. I didn't fully understand the alcohol restriction, since it was legal. There were also specific conditions that caught my attention. I couldn't have contact with the victim or his family, but that didn't bother me. I was required to pay a $25 monthly fee and make a one-time $50 contribution to Crime Stoppers. The judge credited the 18 days I spent in jail toward court costs, and he didn't believe in assigning community service to sex offenders, believing it was safer for the community.

Then came the heavier stipulations. In addition to registering as a sex offender for life, I could no longer live, reside, or go within 1,000 feet of places where children commonly gathered: parks, schools, public swimming pools, and any public organizations that served children. I could no longer have any contact with anyone under the age of 17. I would also be required to submit to yearly polygraph tests and participate in a court-approved sexual treatment program. I wasn't allowed to have access to a computer. The judge amended this condition to say, "Defendant may have access to a computer, but the computer cannot have internet access." What could I do? I had already agreed to probation. I sat there, speechless, unable to breathe or think. The rest of the conversation with the probation representative felt like a blur. I could see his mouth moving, but I couldn't process what he was saying. I nodded along, pretending to be unshaken by the unbearable restrictions he was explaining, but inside, tears began to flow. Heavy tears ran down my face.

I was no longer interested in hearing what he had to say. My thoughts were centered on my life. How could this judge be so merciless? These conditions seemed designed for a serial pedophile, someone who preys on innocent children. I had been deceived. I had no idea that the "victim" wasn't 18 years old. My big party plans faded, and I couldn't see any path to success anymore. I felt hopeless. Was it that serious?

The representative handed me copies of all the documents he discussed, emphasizing that I needed to report to the probation office within 24 hours of my release. After inquiring if I had any questions, he excused himself and told me to wait for the bailiff, who would escort me back to my cell.

After a brief wait, the bailiff arrived and escorted me to the elevator. "Basement," he announced through the intercom, and the doors closed. The trip back to my cell wasn't as long as the journey to the court. I overheard other defendants trading stories about their cases. Some celebrated dismissals, others sighed with relief at being granted time served. A few complained about yet another reset, while others fought back tears, trying to act brave even as they faced years behind bars. Same story, different lives, each one caught in the shadow of Lady Justice, their voices blending into a blur of lives swallowed by the same machine.

I found myself in the last holding cell where we changed from our "free world" court clothes back into the orange jumpsuits. I hadn't bothered to change before court because I knew I was going home, so there was no need to impress the judge. As I sat there, waiting for everyone to change, I quietly started to cry. Watching the clothes and garment bags move around the carousel, I couldn't help but think of the revolving door to jail. A person leaves, tastes freedom, and for whatever reason, ends up back behind bars. I began counting the seconds it took for a piece of clothing to make a full rotation. When I had the cycle down to a 30-second count, I heard a voice say, "Lil brother, you gonna get dizzy following those clothes like that."

For a moment, I took my eyes off the rack, barely missing the blue-and-white pen-striped suit that flew past. It looked like a designer brand, and I tried to catch the name. The voice belonged to a tall Black man with the shiniest, most polished shaved head I've ever seen. He proudly wore his county orange jumpsuit. He started to bend over to loosen his shoes. It wasn't uncommon for inmates to borrow a pair of tennis shoes to wear to court, making the underground journey to the courthouse a little easier than wearing county-issued rubber slippers, most of which were held together by homemade string.

His Jordans were stylish, but I could see the relief in his eyes when he took them off and let his feet breathe. "Looks like you borrowed a size too small," I joked.

"Well, they're better than those cheap, torn-up shower shoes you're wearing," he laughed. "I don't see how you walked to the courthouse in those."

He pointed to my torn sandals, and I instinctively tucked my toes in, hoping he wouldn't notice. Too late. "I already saw them," he chuckled. "Trust me, they're way better than mine," he added.

Refocusing on the clothes rack, I managed a small smile. I guess he could tell I was deep in thought, so he asked, "Did you just sign for time?"

"No, I'm going home. I got probation."

"Well, you should be in better spirits, little brother. You're about to be in the streets."

"Yeah, I know. It's just…"

"Just what?" he cut me off. "Lil brother, you're going home. Do you know how much I would pay to be going home, probation or no probation? Probation's still better than being locked up. Man, if you knew how many times I've been in that white man's face, begging for probation. That's why I borrowed these shoes," he said with a chuckle. "I'm tired of making that trip flip-flopping in sandals."

"Yeah, you're right," I responded. "But man, that judge put some tough restrictions on me." And suddenly, the floodgates broke. Tears streamed down my face, and I couldn't stop them. I opened up to him, sharing everything about my case, my court appearance, and how I felt about everything. When I finished recounting everything, he put a hand on my shoulder and said, "Look, I'm not going to lie, you've got yourself in a jacked-up situation, but you can't let these people bring you down like that."

"Yeah, you're right, but I don't have anywhere to live, I can't use computers, I can't work, I can't go to school. It's so much I can't do,"

I whined, my voice thick with frustration. He looked at me then laughed, shaking his head. "Probation ain't no punk," he said, before adding, "Oh, my bad. No pun intended. However, all probation does is ensure you stay on track in life. Don't let yourself feel like your life is over. Man, you can walk out of here, hit the lottery, or someone could die and leave you a bunch of money. You could write a book or something. Whatever you decide to do, DON'T LET THEM STOP YOU. LIVE YOUR LIFE!"

After his words of encouragement, my entire outlook shifted. I was filled with optimism, picturing how I'd spend my lottery winnings. Just as the blue-and-white pinstriped suit swung by the rack, the guard called my name, telling me it was time to move. The guard cussed at me, saying if I wasn't changing clothes, I shouldn't have been in that area. I didn't respond, just nodded along, too focused on my thoughts to care.

Shortly before 2 p.m., I finally got back to my cell. Home sweet home. Believe it or not, it felt good to be back in my cell, like coming back from a long road trip. I was relieved to sit on my concrete slab of a bed, kicking off the rubber slippers to let my feet rest. I immediately started packing up my belongings. My ankles ached from walking so long in those slippers, but the pain didn't stop me. I was on my way home.

I wasn't sure what I could take, so I stuffed everything I bought from the commissary into a brown paper bag. I reread some of my notes and Bible verses before carefully placing them and my Bible in the bag. The last thing I packed were the pages of this memoir, promising myself I would finish it someday. After packing all my belongings, I lay on the mattress for the last time, thinking about how different my life was about to be. I looked forward to going back to work and doing my best not to let probation or the charge defeat me.

The guard brought our dinner trays, but I didn't bother to get up. I left the tray in the food slot and told the trustee helping the guard that he could have it or give it away. I was too focused on anticipating freedom. Then, the intercom buzzed in my cell. "Harris, pack your shit. ATW."

Confused about what "ATW" meant,I pressed the intercom button with my right hand, holding my belongings in my left hand to let them know I was already packed. I might not have known what "ATW" stood for, but I knew "pack your shit" meant one thing: FREEDOM.

CHAPTER 14

This was the first time I was allowed to leave the tank without being shackled or escorted by a guard. Before letting me out, the guard handed me my Inmate Identification Card, which looked like a postcard with my name, SPN number, and classification details. He pointed toward the elevator, and I headed out.

For 18 days, I lived in cell 6EJ at Harris County Jail. The other inmates wished me luck, shouting "Don't forget us!" and "Don't come back!" from their cells. I was too excited and anxious to leave, to turn around and wave goodbye. In the Bible, Lot's wife turned into a pillar of salt for looking back at the city she was fleeing. I wasn't about to make the same mistake.

I handed my inmate card to the gate officer, who examined it, asked to see my wristband, before opening the doors.There I was, standing in front of the elevators.

When I entered the elevator, a female guard shouted through the intercom, "Where you going!?"

"Basement!" I yelled back, adding some bass to my voice. I was overwhelmed with emotions, bold and confident, and I didn't bother to face the back wall of the elevator. I was in full rebel mode until the guard yelled back, "Face the wall or you won't be going anywhere." Like a child being told to put his nose in the corner, I turned and faced the wall as the elevator started to move.

After reaching the basement, I handed my card to the picket officer (who is in charge of central control). He examined it, matched it to my wristband, and then directed me to another holding cell. I waited there for about an hour and a half, but it didn't matter. I was going home. By then, I was used to hard cement benches, so I had no problem lying down, using my brown paper bag as a makeshift pillow, until I heard footsteps.

Immediately, I jumped up, thinking it was time to leave. To my disappointment, it was another inmate. I tucked my arms back into my shirt and laid back down.

I really couldn't relax, so I started rummaging through my bag looking for something to eat. The sound of the rustling drew the attention of the man next to me, who kept watching to see what I would pull out. I went ahead and offered him a candy bar and a soda. I didn't mind sharing. I was going home. These jail snacks could stay here as far as I was concerned. As we munched on the junk food, we started making small talk until the guard called my name. He gave me some instructions and directed me to another holding cell.

Walking into this new cell, I couldn't help but wonder how many more of these cells there might be. It seemed like some storage for overflow, just more space for people to wait. This cell was quite small and already crowded. As the door slammed shut behind me, I found a spot on the floor and kept playing the waiting game. Everyone in the cell was planning the first thing they would do once they were free. I sat there listening to the conversations, patiently waiting for my name to be called. With nothing else to do, I settled into my little spot and eavesdropped on everything.

The sound of keys fumbling in the lock made my heart race. The room went quiet as we all waited for the door to open. After a moment of cussing, the guard finally found the right key and slid the door open.

"Shut up," the guard said. "I'm only going to say this once. Listen for your name. When you hear your name, step out of the cell, strip down, and we'll give you your clothes." Before handing us our street clothes, the guard instructed us to lay our county-issued uniforms on the floor in front of us. I thought to myself, "Who would want to take an orange jumpsuit home?" The guard counted the heads. "Okay, 10," he muttered. "I should have 10 complete uniforms." One by one, we filed out of the room when our names were called. In the next holding area, we all stood, cold and naked, waiting for the guard to take inventory of the orange jumpsuits. Once he had counted all 10 sets, he started handing out brown bags containing our clothes. It felt so good to have my clothes back. I could practically taste freedom.

Once we were all dressed, it was back to another holding cell. Before walking into the cell, I turned to glance at the counter. Something told me that was the check-out counter. The guard hurried us into the cell, which was already crowded, despite its size. All the benches were taken, so without hesitation, I found a spot on the floor, hoping to claim one before the better spots were taken. There were so many conversations going on that I had a hard time finding one to listen to. A guard came into the cell, called out a few names, paused, and then walked out without taking any inmates. The sound of him slamming the door got everyone's attention.

"What did he say? Did anybody hear what he wanted?" someone asked.

After about 20 minutes, the guard unlocked the door and returned to the cell. This time, we all fell silent, waiting for him to make his announcement. "You can talk all night if you want," he said with frustration. "I'm leaving at 10 p.m. Now, for those who want to get out of here, listen up. I'm going to call you ten at a time. When I call your name, grab your stuff and come to the door. If you don't hear your name or aren't here by the time I shut the door, too bad. You'll keep waiting." He left, and once the door slammed shut, some inmates cussed back at him. The noise level quickly grew as everyone became anxious, waiting for their names to be called. It took another hour, but the guard finally returned and called out the first ten names. One heavyset guy didn't make it through the crowded cell before the door shut in his face. Learning from his disappointment, I moved closer to the door to make sure I wouldn't miss my opportunity when my name was called.

Time slowly passed, and before I knew it, it was 10 p.m. shift change. The guard had processed just enough people to end his shift. The cell was still crowded, but I could tell there was no way we'd all be processed out before the second shift ended. I counted seven guards working the counter. When the third-shift officers settled in, one of them entered the cell and made the same announcement as earlier.

"I've got until 6 a.m. and nowhere to go. The quieter you guys are, the faster we work."

To my surprise, he called out the first 10 names. The conversation in the room eventually quieted as we grew tired, worn down by the constant transfers from one holding cell to another. The third-shift officers processed us faster than the second shift, so I sat there patiently waiting for my name to be called.

"Harris," the guard finally said. I jumped up. Finally! My name was being called. I'm not sure how many names were called before mine, but I do know I was the first one at the door. When I got to the counter, I was fingerprinted, signed for the rest of my property, and given a check for the balance of my inmate trust fund account. "If you don't have a ride or don't feel comfortable being released this late, you can stay until 6 a.m. when the sun comes up," the guard explained as she processed me out.

Did she ask me to extend my stay? I didn't care how late it was or how far I had to walk. Open this door and let me out. I had given the county the last 18 days of my life. They weren't getting any more of my time. She pointed to a door. "You can cash your check down those stairs on your way out." I entered the stairwell, where a big red arrow pointed down and read "FREEDOM." I followed the arrow down, to a small booth where a barely awake cashier was. I slid the check through the partition, and she handed me $21.76 before pointing to a door behind me.

I opened the door, expecting it to lead to more stairs, but instead, I was greeted with a blast of fresh air. Downtown had never smelled this good. For a few seconds, I just stood there, breathing it in. Even though I'd only been locked up for 18 days, I felt an overwhelming sense of freedom. Once the initial shock wore off, my feelings shifted from relief to confusion. I'd never been on this side of downtown before, so I wasn't sure where to go.

"Cigarette, lighter, ride home, what about a phone call, you need to make a call, little brother?" a voice interrupted my thoughts. I turned to see who was speaking. It was a short, heavyset Nigerian man with a thick accent. "Excuse me, you need a ride home?" he asked again. "Anywhere you need to go for $20," he persisted. "I've got Newports for a dollar, or you can use my cell phone to call home —five dollars for five minutes."

I couldn't believe what I was seeing. Here I was, fresh out of jail, and there he was, hustling phone calls and cigarettes. Sadly, he wasn't alone. There was an older Hispanic couple selling tacos and cold drinks. Everyone seemed to be trying to get a piece of the pie. I politely tried to ignore their pitches, but they were so aggressive. You name it, they had it, and they were doing their best to sell it. I thought about asking for directions to Travis Street, but I figured there might be a fee for that, so I decided to rely on my instincts. I licked my finger and felt the wind. I wasn't sure if it would work, but I had seen it in movies before, and it seemed cheaper than asking for directions.

I looked around: left, right, in front, and behind me. To my right, tall buildings rose above, while to my left, the structures were short-er and looked more run-down. So, I decided to head right, toward the skyscrapers. I started walking, and part of me wanted to grab a drink. I noticed a few bars were still open, though almost empty as expected for a Wednesday night. I wasn't sure what I'd do on Travis Street; I only knew it headed north out of downtown, and that's where I needed to go.

My phone had been disconnected—naturally, I'd missed the payment—so I had to walk a few extra blocks to find a payphone. I laughed at myself as I looked for one, wishing I had accepted the Nigerian man's offer to use his phone. I finally found a payphone, and as I dialed the number, I couldn't help but laugh again. It had been years since I used one. When my mother answered, hearing her voice made me feel a thousand times better. "Hello?" she asked.

"It's me, I'm out," I replied. She started preparing to come pick me up, but then I remembered two things. First, my mom was al-ways slow. I knew I could call her thirty minutes from now, and she would still be "on her way." Her usual lines were always, "I was at the door, and had to go back to use the restroom," or "I'm looking for my purse." Then I remembered the last thing I heard the guard say: "If you don't have a ride, you can try Metro or stay the night if you don't feel safe on the streets."

So, while I could hear my mom getting ready, I asked, "What time does the last bus run?"

The last bus was just minutes away. I had just enough time to hang up the phone and sprint a few blocks to the bus stop. As I caught my breath, the 56 Greenspoint bus pulled up! Entering the bus, I struggled for a moment trying to feed my dollar into the fare feeder. The bus driver, seeing my frustration and probably a little annoyed with me for holding him up, waved me on and said, "Don't worry about it."

Feeling like I had just won the lottery, I took the first seat behind the driver. The bus was nearly empty. A teenage couple sat in the back, laughing and teasing each other, while a few other passengers either slept or struggled to stay awake. There was a middle-aged woman, judging by her expression, she was tired and just wanted to get home from work. I caught her glancing at me a few times, and I could tell she knew I had just been released from jail. Her half-smile and nod confirmed she recognized the look. I'm sure she had seen other Black men, fresh out of jail, with their belongings stuffed in a wrinkled brown paper bag, catching the last bus home. As we made our way onto the freeway, the driver took full advantage of the empty lanes. He was ready to get off work.

Since my phone was disconnected, I couldn't call anyone, so I decided to call my provider's customer service line to get my phone reactivated. I knew how to manipulate the system. I had told every sad story imaginable to customer service before, lying my way into temporary credits. Whether it was pretending to cry about losing a loved one or cursing at the representative if they didn't buy my story. I did whatever it took to get my phone back on. I once got an agent to slip up by reading aloud the notes on my account: "Irate customer and no more credits."

I stopped bothering with the automated prompts. I quickly pressed zero, zero, zero, zero, until I heard a human voice. When the agent greeted me, I let her access my account, knowing she had already reviewed the notes. Her friendly tone quickly turned defensive as she prepared for my call, but this time, my sad story wasn't a lie. I didn't have to pretend I was stranded on a dark road with a flat tire or make false promises to pay off my past due balance. This time, I told the truth. I had just gotten out of jail, and I needed my phone turned back on so I could call a ride. I'm downtown and need to call my mom, I explained. (Okay, I lied a little.) She listened quietly, and once I finished, she sympathized with my situation. Just when I thought my phone would be turned on, she apologized, telling me there was nothing she could do for my account. Refusing to accept no for an answer, I demanded to speak to a supervisor. I had to argue, pretend to cry, and curse the rest of the trip home, but finally, my services were restored!

CHAPTER 15

The bus dropped me off just a short walk from my parents' apartment. As I strolled down the familiar sidewalk, I couldn't help but feel nervous about what awaited me behind their door. It was as if I were the prodigal son returning home, unsure of how I'd be received after so many years of avoiding the reality of my situation.

For five years, I stayed away, running from the Christian values I thought I had left behind when I moved into my first apartment. Don't get me wrong; I knew my parents loved me, but I also knew they would never accept that I was gay. Still, I couldn't stand on their porch all night, so I gathered my courage and knocked on the door. When my mother opened it, her arms went wide, and we hugged as if I had been gone for 18 years instead of just 18 days. My dad was already asleep, having to leave at 4 AM for work, so there was no need to wake him, but I couldn't resist running upstairs to let him know I was home. I wasn't sure who was more relieved to have me back, me or my mom.

She followed me around their townhome, asking if I was hungry, if I wanted to take a shower, or if I needed fresh sheets for the bed. She apologized for the spare room not being ready. I reassured her, "Mom, this room is a palace compared to that cell." The last 18 days had been spent in a cage no bigger than a closet. I would have been grateful for anything. A pallet on the floor would've been luxury compared to jail. I was just glad to be out and back in familiar surroundings. We didn't want to disturb my dad any more than I already had, so we went back downstairs, where I recounted the whole experience of the last few days. She asked question after question, and I joked, "Look, am I on trial again?"

We sat and talked like long-lost friends until we both admitted we were exhausted. She had to get up early for work, and I had to report to the probation office first thing in the morning, so we called it a night. The next morning, we arrived at the probation office at

7:45 AM. As we walked in, my mom pointed to a building across the street and asked if I recognized it. I turned to look, and I was struck by how different downtown looked in the daylight, lit up by the sun instead of the moonlight from the night before.

"That's the jail," she said, almost like a child who couldn't keep a secret anymore. "Yep, that's where you were the last 18 days," she teased. I couldn't believe it. I had seen that building countless times and never realized that the county jail was right in front of me all these years. She then pointed to the building where I had been released. It didn't seem as far away now that it wasn't shrouded in the mystery of underground tunnels.

There was a sign prohibiting family, friends, or anyone under 17 from entering the probation building, so my mom and I exchanged goodbyes as she headed off to work. She reassured me, boosting my confidence for what lay ahead. "The worst is over," she said as she left. Inside, the probation building was old, musty, and depressing. The lights were dim, and the ceiling had brown water stains. At the entrance, a check-in booth was located, protected by thick plexiglass. If I didn't know any better, I'd think I was at a check-cashing store in a rundown neighborhood.

I approached the window and spoke through the thick glass to the clerk, who asked for my court documents. After reviewing them, he stamped them with the time and date, then pointed to some plastic chairs for me to sit and wait. "Someone will be with you shortly." After what felt like an eternity sitting in the cold plastic chair, a short man came out from behind a door and called my name in a thick accent. I was the only person in the lobby, but he pretended not to see me until I stood up and walked toward him.

"Are you Hah-ris?" he asked.

"Yes, sir, I am," I answered, trying to hide my amusement at his pronunciation of my name.

His demeanor was cold and uninviting. "Follow me," he instructed. I had to move quickly to catch the door before it closed. On the other side was a small room with a blue backdrop hanging between two clips attached to a ceiling that had seen better days. The man pointed to a worn taped "X" on the floor and gestured for me to stand on it. My pride wanted to rebel. I didn't want to be treated like a dog, but I complied, standing on the mark.

As I stood there, I realized my hair was messy, and I was still wearing the same clothes I had on last night. I tried to straighten my shirt and run my fingers through my hair, but he wasn't impressed. "Why do you smile?" he asked. "Do not smile. Just look straight ahead," he instructed. The picture came out of the camera, and without saying a word, he stapled it into a folder. I caught a glimpse of it, and it wasn't my best shot, but I didn't dare ask for a retake.

"Follow me," he said again, and led me to his cramped office filled with clutter and legal folders.

After a few moments, he pulled out a box of latex gloves and muttered a curse when he found it was empty. He angrily slammed a drawer shut, searching for a new box before finally opening one. He quickly slid the gloves onto his dry, ashy hands and signaled for me to follow him to a bathroom.

I expected at least a small sense of privacy, but as he handed me the specimen cup, his eyes never left me. He didn't leave the room; instead, he leaned against the wall and folded his arms, watching me carefully. I unzipped my pants and glared at him out of the corner of my eye. After a moment, I stopped mid-stream to show him the cup. "Keep going?" I asked. He nodded and took the cup from me once I was finished, sealing and labeling it. He pointed me toward a sink to wash my hands, and after I did, he handed me a pen to initial the label on the cup.

We walked to a refrigerator, and I naively thought he was grabbing a quick snack or drink. Instead, I was met with a fridge full of urine samples. I quickly placed mine in an empty spot and looked away, disturbed by the sight of the different-colored samples.

"Now, you can't say I tampered with your urine," he said, and I followed him back to his office. There, he handed me more legal forms to sign, which required my thumbprints and initials. Finally, he told me, "You're done. Go to the lobby."

I sat back down in the lobby, playing Ms. Pac-Man on my phone, before realizing I hadn't checked any of my voicemails. My mother and I had stayed up most of the night before, and I was glad to be home, so checking my voicemails hadn't even crossed my mind. I had several missed calls and voicemails from the last 18 days, but I figured I'd listen to them after my visit. I kept myself busy playing games, and as Ms. Pac-Man ate dots and dodged ghosts on my screen, I heard my name being called.

CHAPTER 16

"Harris, Norman," a short, wide-hipped Black woman called out from the elevator. She didn't step out but repeatedly pressed the open button on the elevator button when the doors began to close. I was the only one waiting in the lobby, but she called my name again, even though I was already walking toward her. Her attitude was frustrating; she muttered under her breath and rolled her eyes, clearly annoyed. I'll never understand why some public employees are so miserable in their work. If it's that tough, they should find something else to do!

Once in her office, she reviewed more rules and regulations. I tried to listen, but it was hard to show her the respect she seemed to expect. The whole process was excessive. I wasn't a criminal mastermind or a predator. I had met someone online who misrepresented their age. The entire situation felt overwhelming for someone who had made a mistake but was trying to move on.

Her tone was condescending, and she asked questions that didn't feel genuine. Instead of asking if I had a high school diploma, she bluntly asked, "Did you finish school?" When asking about drugs, she assumed I used them, saying, "So, along with weed, what other drugs do you use?" I corrected her, but her response was dismissive, telling me not to get offensive. It felt like I was being painted with a broad, unfair brush.

As we went through the risk assessment, which felt like a pointless exercise, she told me I was considered a high risk because of the nature of my case. Despite having no criminal history, no drug use, and a steady work history, she insisted my case was higher risk because the "victim" was the same sex as me. She explained that automatically scores higher on the risk scale. I asked for an explanation, but she remained firm, breaking me down in the process. My shoulders slumped as I fought back tears; my pride wouldn't let her gloat.

After reviewing the thirty-two conditions of my probation, she gave me a list of instructions, including the requirement to register as a sex offender. I was told I needed to visit the driver's license office to get a "sex offender" license, which surprised me. When I reacted, she quickly explained that the only difference was a code on the back of the license, visible only to law enforcement.

At that moment, I was drained physically, mentally, and emotionally. I just wanted to go home, get into bed, and wake up from what felt like a nightmare. However, she gave me my next instructions: to visit the fifth floor to get my probation ID and she would take me to meet my probation officer.

• • •

My probation officer was a large Caucasian woman with a long braid down her back. When we entered her office, she was on the phone, talking with someone. We waited silently until she hung up. She sighed, and apologized. Still, her attention wasn't entirely on me as she handed me her business card and dismissed her colleague.

Back in the elevator, she muttered something about how people don't understand the difficulty of being a probation officer, but I barely listened. As the elevator door closed, I couldn't shake the feeling that I was just a number to these people. The elevator ride was shaky, and when I stepped out, I was reminded of how far I had come from the sterile, polished environment I had worked in for years.

I had spent four years working in a prestigious tower, proud of its height and reputation, but now I was in a place that felt completely different from anything I had known. The floors trembled beneath me, and I couldn't help but think about how much my life had changed in just a short time. The staff at the probation office, who issued ID cards, were much friendlier than the officers. They even made small talk with me while my card was being printed. One clerk joked, or at least I hoped she was joking, about how bad my picture was. She passed the card around for her coworkers to see. "You could have at least smiled or made an expression," one said. "Why do you look dead?" another asked as she handed me the card to review. They were all right; it was a bad picture.

Walking back to the elevator, I reviewed the requirements again to see if there was anything else I could complete before heading home. The next requirement was an education assessment, which could be done on the same floor. Since I was already there, I decided to take the test. Thankfully, no appointment was needed, and walk-ins were accepted.

"They're on lunch," I heard from the waiting area. I could hear the sounds of shadows moving behind the closed partition and smell food, so I sat down and waited. After a short while, I could hear a lady's voice struggling with the partition, muttering curses under her breath as she tried to slide it open.

"If you're here for the assessment, have a seat in the room over there," she instructed, pointing to a makeshift classroom. Once inside, she passed out the exam, pencils, and began to give instructions. She quickly grew frustrated as people kept asking questions. I, too, hoped they would just be quiet so we could get started. "Are there any more questions?" she asked, both of us secretly crossing our fingers. She set a timer and left the room.

Like the nerd I was, I quickly ripped the seal off the test booklet and flipped to the first page. I didn't know whether to laugh or cry at how simple the questions were. The math section was basic addition and subtraction. The grammar section felt like elementary school, focusing on period and comma placement. Any third grader could have aced this test in their sleep. It took her longer to get my Scantron to feed through the reader than it took me to finish the test. She entered my results into the computer, and I was ready to go home. I had had my fill of nasty attitudes for the day and was in desperate need of a drink, oops, I meant nap. As I started to walk out of the room, I heard, "Uh-uh, Harris, you ain't done yet. There's one more section. You gotta write a paper."

The paper was a short essay. We had 60 minutes to finish it. The essay needed to be one page, and it took me just ten minutes to write. I can't remember the topic anymore. I handed in my paper and asked, "Any more tests I need to take before I can leave?"

"You've been free to leave," she said, not missing a beat. "No one made you stay." I couldn't tell if she was being serious or trying to joke, so I stood there with a blank look on my face, long enough for her to roll her eyes and tell me, "Uh, that's it. BYE!"

As I looked over the conditions and walked toward the elevator, I realized there was another assessment—a psychoanalysis test filled with tricky questions. I knew I couldn't rush through this one, so I decided to take my time. No matter what the instructions say, you should never answer those questions honestly; they're a trap. "How many times have you 'borrowed' something without permission?" Or, "After an argument with a family member, it takes ____ drinks to calm you down: A) 1-3, B) 4-7, C) I drink until I can't remember, or D) I never drink." If you answer honestly, like admitting you drink or that it's frustrating when things don't go your way, you're stereotyped and sent to AA or anger management. It's funny how, before you're convicted of a crime, your leisure activities and coping mechanisms seem normal.

This test was designed to compare turning a drink at happy hour into a drunk's behavior, or to liken taking a pen from work to breaking into the Federal Reserve. The next question continued: "A person who calls into work sick when they are not is A) Irresponsible, B) Liar, C) Undependable, D) None of the above."

In my mind, I thought, E) a person who calls in sick might be an overworked employee who's tired or maybe stayed out a little too late the night before, but of course, that wasn't an option.

I finally finished all the assessments. No bragging, but I had 60-120 days to complete them, and I did it all on my first day. I passed the education test, proved I wasn't a sociopath, and convinced the county that I didn't need any drug or alcohol classes. The only thing on my mind now was getting out of that building. Every time I thought I was heading for the elevator, I found another assessment to take, so this time I decided to take the stairs.

CHAPTER 17

The evening at my parents' house was a bit awkward. They were welcoming, sympathetic, and genuinely concerned, but it was clear there was an elephant in the room. Over dinner, I gave them a day-by-day recap of my experience in jail. We laughed and enjoyed each other's company. I couldn't remember the last time we sat at the dinner table together, and it felt good. It took me back to a simpler time.

Later that night, I lay in bed, reflecting on the situation and trying to make sense of it all. The weight of everything was overwhelming, so many requirements and even more restrictions. It felt like the only thing I was allowed to do was breathe. Everything else seemed forbidden.

My mother, with her natural sensitivity, must have sensed my despair. She called me into her room, and before she could ask anything, I started crying. "It's too much, Momma. It's too much," I sobbed, clutching the court papers in my hand. "I can't do all of this."

My father woke up, and together, they started encouraging me. They reassured me that everything would be okay and promised we'd face this together. The conversation lasted about 30 minutes, and for every reason I gave for why I couldn't handle it, they provided a reason why I could. For every "I can't," they responded with "You will, and you can."

They wouldn't let me give in to despair or self-pity. My mom didn't want to keep my dad up any longer, so she motioned for me to follow her to my room. We sat on the bed, and one by one, she went over each requirement, restriction, and condition with me, just like she had when I was a child and she helped me with my homework. Together, we made a plan to handle each item on the list. We laughed, talked, and prayed, and by the end, I felt ready for the challenge. It was going to be tough, but I knew I could do it.

The next morning, as my mom got ready for work, she reminded me not to worry and to take it one day at a time. I sat on the couch, flipping through channels, and then remembered I hadn't checked my voicemails. I listened to them, laughing and temporarily forgetting about probation.

The best message was from my dear friend Stephanie, left on New Year's Eve: "Hey, it's Steph. Wishing you a Happy New Year! However you celebrate, be safe, and don't go to jail." A little too late, I smirked and moved on to the next message.

It was from the "victim."

I froze. I had no plans of ever hearing from him again. Why was he calling me? My heart pounded. Was this considered contact with the "victim"? Had I already broken a condition of probation? I didn't know what to do. I pressed the phone to my ear, repeatedly pressing the delete button until that message disappeared, and so did the weight of it in my mind.

Realizing I couldn't stay on my parents' couch forever, I got up to make breakfast, just a bowl of cereal and a glass of orange juice. The juice was sweet and refreshing, completely different from what it would be when mixed with gin. After washing the dishes, I sat down and reviewed the probation papers to determine which appointments I could schedule. Just holding the papers made me cry. Who knew a few sheets of paper could weigh so much? I threw them down and went to the restroom to run cold water over my face.

Standing in front of the mirror, I noticed how rough and unkempt my reflection was. The ID card lady wasn't lying; I needed a makeover, an extreme makeover. I was still wearing the same clothes I was released in from two days ago. I tried adjusting my shirt, but by then, the wrinkles had already set in. All my clothes were at my sister's house, so for now, I had to make do with what I had. Looking at myself in the mirror, I couldn't help but laugh and make fun of my appearance. My hair had grown, and the wave pattern was turning into naps. I was used to weekly haircuts, and I was long overdue.

My mom had left me a few bucks for lunch or in case something came up, and I was glad there was a barbershop nearby. After returning home from the barber shop, I started calling my friends to tell them about my time behind bars. By the time I finished exaggerating the details, I had them all convinced I'd done hardcore time, like something out of a movie. It may have only been 18 days, but to me, it felt like a life sentence.

As I checked my contacts list, the only call I needed to make was to my job. While I was in jail, my mom contacted my manager, informing her of what had happened and promising to keep her updated on the outcome of my trial. My boss had told my mom that I still had my job, assuring her she would cover for me and that everything would be fine. Ha!

After making sure I was okay and expressing her relief that I was home, she offered a few words of encouraging advice. I was holding the phone, smiling from ear to ear, thinking things were going to get better, until I asked when I should come back to work. I even suggested I could be there the next morning.

"Here's the thing," she began quickly, and my smile faded. "Corporate found out what happened, and they made the decision to let you go."

I couldn't believe what I was hearing. How did Corporate find out? I felt hurt and confused. She had promised my mom that everything would be fine and that she would cover for me. What a big lie. Angry and eager to end the conversation, I told her I would drop off my keys in the morning and hung up.

Losing that job hit me harder than I expected. Back then, I thought work was just work, but what I really lost was stability and, with it, my dignity. At twenty-three, stability meant a paycheck, an apartment, and a future I could depend on. Without those, every step feels like sinking in quicksand. Looking back, I see now how quickly systems fall apart when you're branded. Corporate didn't need to hear my side of the story; the label alone was enough. That was my first real lesson in how fragile opportunity becomes when your name is tied to a record. You stop being an employee, a student, a neighbor, and you start being a liability. Probation only made that feeling worse.

I couldn't help but cry. I was so disappointed. There I was, planning to move on with my life, ready to put the last 18 days behind me, thinking things would go back to normal, as if a "boom" would make it all happen, but the boom wasn't what I expected. Little did I know, my life was about to be shattered into tiny pieces, pieces that would take years to put back together. Like a baby, I cried myself to sleep.

Later that evening, I told my parents the news. Once again, they tried to reassure me that everything would be okay, reaffirming their love and support. But at that moment, I couldn't see past the disappointment and despair to fully appreciate their words of encouragement. I had plans for the new year. Before the holidays, I paid a deposit on my apartment, getting ready to move out of my sister's place at the beginning of the year. Not only did I lose my job, which meant I couldn't move, but I also couldn't live with my sister because her children were all under 17. According to my probation conditions, I couldn't have contact with minors.

I was clueless and helpless, thinking everything would go back to normal once I was released from jail.

CHAPTER 18

By the end of my first week out, I had made all the necessary appointments, submitted the required paperwork to various county departments, and was slowly working my way through the requirements. My parents were right: "Day by day," I thought, looking over the conditions and checking off the terms I had already met. It was comforting to realize that, in one week, I was nearly done.

My victory celebration was brief. Seven days went by, and it was time to see my probation officer again. My mom dropped me off in front of the probation building, and just like a mom dropping her kid off on the first day of school, she was hesitant to leave. I told her I could handle myself and that she didn't need to worry about me. In my mind, I had already prepared for this meeting.

The first time I was in this building, I felt nervous, scared, and confused. My appearance was just as bad as my demeanor. I had collected all my belongings from my sister's house, worried about being followed by undercover officers to make sure I didn't have any contact with children. To meet my probation requirements, I moved everything out while my niece and nephews were at school.

This time at the probation office, I was prepared. I dressed sharply, telling myself I could control the impression I made. My hair was freshly cut, and from top to bottom, I walked in confidently wearing a Kenneth Cole shirt, pants, belt, boots, and cologne. Even my messenger bag was Kenneth Cole. I thought I'd walk in and prove that I was different. Better. Not like the others in the waiting room. All those underdressed county employees, with their last-season sweaters and messy outfits, were about to see exactly who they were dealing with.

Walking into the building, no one seemed to care or even notice me or my Kenneth Cole. The intake clerk even deliberately ignored me, flipping through paperwork for a solid five minutes before finally acknowledging my presence. When he finally looked up from his work, he asked for my appointment sheet, stamped it, and buzzed my officer to inform her that she "had one." He slid my stamped appointment sheet through the glass and returned to his work without a word. I made a mental note to complain about his poor customer service (though I doubted it would matter). No matter how polished I looked, I was still just another file folder on someone's desk. The county employee didn't see Kenneth Cole; he saw case number X. Maybe that was the most humbling part, realizing that my self-presentation couldn't save me from a system designed not to notice.

I took the elevator up to the 5th floor, checked in with the clerk, and took a seat in the cold, sterile lobby. A few other men were also waiting for their officers. I sat next to a heavyset white man with large, thick glasses that made his eyes look cartoonish. His suspenders stretched against his faded jeans, and a walking cane rested between his knees. He fumbled through a worn-out file folder, preparing his paperwork for his meeting.

I caught myself thinking he looked like a pedophile. The thought came quickly and harshly, and almost as fast, I regretted it. Still, the stereotype stayed in my head like gum on a shoe. That was the kind of judgment I had picked up from the world around me, snap assumptions about who fit into certain categories. What I didn't realize then was how much those same stereotypes were being directed at me, too.

Across the room, a young Black man in his early twenties paced back and forth, constantly checking his phone. His frustration with the wait annoyed the clerk, who snapped at him to sit down, flicking her blue-streaked bangs across her face in what resembled a cheap Jennifer Aniston impression. I smirked. Even in that tense, sterile space, I managed to distract myself with petty observations.

Here's the thing: as I share these moments, you might notice my blunt critiques of the people working within the system. Some may sound harsh, maybe even unfair, but when you've been processed through the machine of probation, you begin to see how little humanity there is in the way people are treated. I'm sure many government employees genuinely care about their jobs and the people they serve, but it amazes me how many of those behind the desks didn't seem to see us as people at all; we were just names on files and cases to move across their desks before lunch. I don't think they realize or care how much damage that kind of treatment causes. When you strip someone of their dignity, you don't just hurt them; you weaken the entire system. It's a disservice to the community, the victims, and the individuals in their caseloads.

Of course, I'm not expecting five-star service, since this process isn't meant to be enjoyable, but their job is to ensure compliance, not to belittle, disrespect, or waste a person's time.

Back to my story.

I glanced at the clock behind the clerk's desk and realized how much time had gone by. "No respect for my time," I thought. In any other job, someone working this slowly would have been fired. In this office, power flowed in the opposite direction. We had no choice but to sit and wait, so they treated us however they saw fit.

Patience was never my strong suit. Waiting, especially without explanation, always gnawed at me. Restless, I stood to pace the room until the clerk pointed to a poster on the wall. "Patience is finding something to do while you wait," she said. I mouthed the words, smirking as I watched her reapply her lipstick. She rubbed her lips together, ensuring the color was even, then kissed the air before closing her compact and putting it away. I noticed the red-stained straw in her kiwi strawberry juice can. That's where all her lipstick went, onto the straw. For some reason, that detail stuck with me.

Taking the sign's advice, I pulled out my phone and started texting. The lobby seemed to buzz with anticipation as one by one, men heard their names being called. When a woman called for Mr. Grant, the young guy jumped from his seat, slipped his grill back into his mouth, and strutted toward the door.

"About damn time," he muttered as he passed the clerk.

"Watch your language in here, boy," she snapped.

Hope seemed to ripple through the lobby as each man waited for his turn. I made small talk with another man who told me this office was specifically for people with sex-crime convictions. I laughed at first, assuming he must be wrong. In my head, sex offenders had a "look," but as I sat there, I began to realize the truth:

there is no face of a sex offender. Young or old, White or Black, rich or poor, anyone could be one. The truth is, you can't see someone's choices on their face. It's unsettling to admit, but the same stereotypes I had thrown at that man in suspenders were being thrown at me. I wanted to be seen for my whole self, not just for my mistakes. Yet here I was, judging others in the exact way I didn't want to be judged.

Finally, my officer called my name. I walked into her office, which looked just as chaotic as the first time: papers piled high, files spilling across the desk, an organized mess that somehow reflected the way my life felt at that moment.

Thick green file folders were scattered across her desk, with stacks of papers beneath the hole punchers and staplers. The desk had just enough space for a can of Diet Coke and a bowl of fruit. For some reason, I expected her to offer me a handshake, like you would in any professional setting. Naively, I reached out my hand. She sat down, shuffled a few folders around to clear space, and completely ignored my gesture. I quickly withdrew my hand, feeling foolish.

She reintroduced herself, almost as if it was my fault we hadn't met last week. She looked over the desk for my folder but couldn't find it. After a few moments of searching, she saw it on the floor behind her desk, tucked under a grocery store bag, likely her lunch, as evidenced by the visible foil paper. She sighed loudly, realizing she would have to get up.

The folder was slimmer than the others in her office, divided into three sections. She flipped through it quickly, scanning the summary of my offense and clearly familiarizing herself with my case. I sat there, squinting, trying to read the details over her shoulder. When she finished with the summary, she moved on to the conditions of my probation.

She stopped reading and asked me to explain why I was on probation.

Finally, I thought. Someone was going to give me a chance to speak, to tell my side. I took a deep breath and laid out the facts.

"I met someone online on an adult dating site. He told me he was 18. We chatted for a few months, and eventually, he invited me to his house. I went, and we were having sex when his mother walked in, pulled a knife on me, and called the police." I paused. "That's when I found out he was sixteen. He lied to me, and now I'm here."

She rolled her eyes. "All you're doing is blaming your victim," she scolded. "You need to take responsibility for your actions."

"I'm just stating the facts," I replied, trying to stand my ground. I rolled my eyes and wagged my finger in frustration. I wasn't going to sit there and let her blame me. "You read the police report. He admitted to lying about his age."

"Well, he's not in my office," she snapped back.

The tension in the room increased. The longer I sat in that office, in that hard chair, the more I realized there was no point in trying to convince her I was a victim of his lie. Her mind was made up, and I was the guilty one. I tried to keep my composure, but it was becoming harder as she kept being condescending and patronizing. Gradually, I felt the fight drain out of me. I was desperate for someone, anyone, to believe me, but probation isn't about truth; it's about compliance. My case officer didn't see a confused young man caught in a nightmare. She saw a file. A box to check. Maybe I was naive to expect compassion in a system built for punishment, not understanding.

She started reading aloud the conditions of my probation, one at a time, asking if I understood each one. I nodded along, feeling defeated.

"Good," she said. "So, you won't have any excuse for not complying."

I accepted my defeat and decided to try impressing her by showing that I had already completed most of the required assessments, but she remained unmoved.

She read from the file, "You have 90 days to provide proof of your high school diploma or GED."

Proudly, I pulled my diploma out of my bag. "What is this?" she asked, clearly annoyed that I interrupted her. "I'll need a copy of that," she snapped.

Since we were discussing education, I decided to let her know I was in college, hoping it would show her that I wasn't the monster she was making me out to be.

"You know you have to register with campus police, right?" she asked.

"No, I wasn't aware of that condition," I replied.

"Before you set foot on any school campus or grounds, you must get approval from campus police, or you'll be in violation of sex offender laws," she said, almost shrieking.

"But this is college!" I protested.

"Mr. Harris, the purpose of sex offender registration is to make the community aware of your presence, including on educational campuses, to protect the safety of your neighbors, students, and professors. Be sure to provide me with proof that you've notified your campus police department."

I was overwhelmed with disbelief and confusion, trying to understand why I was being called a threat to my community. This was my first run-in with the law, and suddenly, I was being treated like a dangerous criminal, like a predator.

"Under no circumstances are you allowed to have contact with anyone under the age of 17," she continued, emphasizing the number "17."

Seeking clarity, I asked, "What if I'm in a store and there are kids around?"

"You will need to leave immediately. It's your responsibility to remove yourself from all potential contact with minors under 17 years of age," she emphasized.

"What if I'm on the city bus and children get on?"

"Mr. Harris, you need to remove yourself from any environment where someone under the age of 17 will be or is present."

"So, I'm supposed to get off the bus?" I asked, incredulously. "That doesn't make any sense. I'll never get anywhere."

"Well, you do what you have to do to avoid all contact with children," she said.

She couldn't be serious. Where was I supposed to go? Children were everywhere. Was I supposed to stay home all the time? This was impossible. I couldn't understand how anyone could reasonably follow these conditions. Frustrated with my confusion, she moved down the list, continuing her lecture, while I sat there, stunned and overwhelmed by how impossible the situation was.

"By your next visit, you need to complete the psychological and sociological testing," she said.

"I already did that last week," I replied, hoping to ease the tension.

"There's no way you could have taken the test. You don't even know where the testing office is," she shot back.

"I found it when I was leaving last week," I countered, sitting up straighter and feeling a little more confident. I pulled the completed documents from my bag, hoping she'd take me seriously this time.

She flipped through my files, eyes narrowing as she examined the papers. "There's no way you could have taken the assessment," she muttered. "I would have your results."

"I don't have to lie about taking the test," I said, sarcasm slipping into my tone. "How would I have the dated receipt from the testing office?"

"Well, until I have your scores, you aren't in compliance," she replied coldly.

Our power struggle was interrupted by a knock at the door. Both of us sighed in relief as we turned to see who it was. The clerk entered, holding a stack of papers.

"Excuse me, these came in a few days ago. They were buried on my desk. Sorry for not having them in your mailbox," the clerk explained.

"Oh, no, it's fine. I understand," my officer replied, her tone sweet as sugar, trying to wipe the nervous smile off the clerk's face.

I couldn't help but think, "Had you been doing your job instead of applying lipstick, this would've been done." I exchanged a quick look with the officer, our silent understanding clear.

The officer shuffled through the stack of papers. As she sorted them, she reached for her hole puncher and started punching holes in the documents without making eye contact with me. She reluctantly muttered, "Your results are in."

Score one for me! However, she refused to acknowledge my effort to be proactive. Instead, she kept going down the list of conditions I needed to meet.

"You still need to call and make an appointment with the police department to register. You need to submit a DNA sample to the state, which can only be done by appointment. You also need to enroll in sex offender treatment program and schedule your first polygraph," she continued, her voice firm.

"First polygraph test?" I asked. "How many do I have to take?"

"You're required to take yearly polygraph tests, and you're responsible for the $300 cost," she stated, without a hint of sympathy.

I bowed my head in defeat, feeling the weight of it all. She won.

I had hoped for some encouragement, maybe even just a "Good job" or "It's good to see you being proactive," something to give me hope that I could succeed, but she didn't acknowledge my efforts. She kept reviewing the list and stressing everything I still needed to do. Before scheduling my next appointment, she noticed I'd marked "unemployed" on my check-in sheet.

"On your first visit, you told us you had a job. Now you don't?" she questioned, her impatience growing. "Which is it? Are you working or not?"

I explained that I spoke with my employer last week and had been fired. She didn't show any sympathy.

"You need to submit a job search log," she said, handing me a blank form. "You're required to make 10 employment contacts per week until you find a job. As a condition of your probation, you must maintain suitable employment."

I could feel the weight of her words pressing down on me. With a dismissive wave, she scheduled my next appointment for two weeks from then and told me I was free to leave.

Without hesitation, I jumped out of the chair and headed for the elevator. Physically, emotionally, and mentally, I was exhausted. My pride was hurt, and a pounding tension headache began at the back of my neck. I couldn't get out of that building fast enough.

I walked to the bus stop, head down, trying to hide the tears welling up. Over the next few years, I would leave that building feeling the same way, like a failure.

I used to think survival was about appearances: clothes, cars, and image, but probation removed that illusion. In that sterile lobby, surrounded by other men waiting for their turn, I started to understand: survival in this new life wasn't about how I looked; it was about how much I could endure. On the bus ride home, I sat in the back, praying that no children would board. When I finally got home, I went straight to bed, too exhausted to think.

CHAPTER 19

I woke up later, feeling hopeless. Not suicidal, but wishing I were dead. The pressure of everything was too much for me to bear. I allowed myself a moment to sulk, then realized that giving up wasn't an option. I didn't yet have the language for trauma. I only knew that lying in bed could swallow me whole, and that I had to keep moving to stay alive. I needed to move forward.

The first thing I did was call campus police. The spring semester was about to start, and I didn't have any time to waste. The conversation with the police chief lasted an hour. He asked me about every detail of my case, big and small, wanting to know everything. He told me he would pass the information along to the department heads for approval, and they would vote on my admission. I wasn't expecting a vote. I thought I only needed to notify campus police about my enrollment. Once again, I felt confused and in disbelief.

Next, I called the Texas Workforce Commission to apply for unemployment benefits since I had been fired. The interview forced me to relive everything, from Christmas Eve to the 18 days I spent in jail, the court appearances, and of course, my probation meeting. Every time I retold the story, I lost energy, drained by the effort to convince people I wasn't a monster. There was no easy way to explain that I was a registered sex offender. The agent told me I needed to contact my former employer to find out the reason for my termination. I was also told that my employer would have seven business days to dispute my claim, more waiting. Just what I needed, I thought, sighing as I ended the call.

I kept working through my to-do list, calling the city police to schedule my registration appointment, then the agency to arrange for my DNA sample. My last call was to set up my appointment for sex offender treatment. The condition required me to enroll within 90 days, but I figured I might as well do it now. Maybe, just maybe, my probation officer would recognize my effort and give me some lee-way.

After everything was scheduled and the paperwork organized, I felt a sense of relief. The only thing left to do was wait. I tucked everything away in my bag; I didn't want to see it anymore. For the first time, I could exhale.

Needing a break, I called Daymond. We hadn't had much time to talk since I got home, and I was craving a little normalcy. It took hours to fill him in on everything that had happened, and by the time I finished, he was crying too. When he asked if I wanted to come over, I jumped at the chance. I needed a taste of life before this nightmare, but I was careful not to let my parents know. They had become more protective of me since my release, and though they meant well, their understanding of my life didn't quite match my truth. I didn't want to disrespect them, but I also needed some space just to be myself. I suggested meeting the next day for lunch, trying to avoid any conflict.

Daymond hesitated. He'd just been laid off a few weeks before and wasn't broke, just in that awkward in-between where every dollar suddenly had a job. "You know I don't have the money for lunch, right?"

"I've got it covered," I reassured him.

"How do you have money, Piglet?" he asked, genuinely curious.

I explained that I had received a check while I was in jail and hadn't had the chance to cash it.

"Hold on to your money, Piglet," he warned, always the voice of reason.

Despite his reluctance, we made plans. I promised him I wouldn't whine when my money ran out—though we both knew I probably would.

Finally, I asked, "What time are you coming?"

"11 AM," he said with a sigh. "But you better not come to me complaining when your money's gone."

I agreed, and we made plans to meet, both secretly looking for-ward to some time away from our usual struggles. I needed a laugh, and with Daymond, I knew I'd get one.

Once my parents got home from work, we went over everything: my visit to the office, the conversation I had with campus police, and all the appointments I'd scheduled. I told them about what I still needed to do. They reminded me, as they always did, "One day at a time."

I was excitedly looking forward to lunch with Daymond. It had been almost a month since I'd seen my best friend. I'd planned it carefully, while my parents were at work, so I wouldn't have to explain anything to them, but as the clock crept toward 1 PM, my excitement gave way to nerves.

"Calm down, I'm pulling in now," he said, and just like that, my heart skipped a beat. I ran downstairs to peek out the window, and there he was. Finally. "Oh my God, you look so skinny!" he exclaimed as we hugged. Daymond and I had been through a lot together, and in many ways, he was the only one who truly understood me. It's funny that we're total opposites. I'm loud, outgoing, and maybe a bit obnoxious, while he's quiet, reserved, and shy. I thrive on being the center of attention, but he's perfectly content staying in the background.

I remember carpooling to work with him early in the mornings. I'd be wide awake, cracking jokes, and he'd be struggling to stay awake, looking over at me from the passenger seat, half asleep. "It's too early to be this happy," he'd mumble, turning toward the window, trying to catch a few more minutes of sleep. I'd keep talking, making him laugh and annoy him at the same time. "Norman, do you always have to be so gay? Pay attention to the road!" he'd tease.

As we sat down at the table, I automatically flipped through the drink menu. Just as I was about to order an apple martini (gin instead of vodka), I heard Daymond clear his throat.

"Uh-huh, excuse me," he said, drawing my attention. "Aren't you forgetting something?"

Confused, I looked at him. "You can get one too, I told you I have money."

"Norman, you're on probation. Dr. Pepper for you!" he said, shaking his head.

He was right, of course. As we ate, we caught up with each other. Even though he'd heard my jail stories before, hearing them in person, with me acting out the emotions and reactions, made it feel fresh to him. Daymond always listened so intently, especially when I was animated. We laughed, but then he shifted the conversation.

"People have been asking about you. Wondering why you haven't been out," he said, clearly noticing the absence of my usual social presence.

"Well, it's nice to be missed," I joked. "But they might as well get used to missing me."

"What do you mean?" he asked, his confusion evident.

"I'm through," I said, my voice steady. "I'm not gay anymore."

Daymond choked on his food. "What do you mean you're not gay anymore? It's in you, Norman. You are gay."

"No, I'm not," I insisted. "When I was in jail, I spent a lot of time reading the Bible. Long story short, I'm not gay anymore. I'm saved," I said, trying to explain.

"You're not making sense," he replied, looking at me with disbelief.

"Look, Daymond, everything that happened to me was a sign. I needed to repent and be straight. You should think about it too."

"I have nothing to think about, Norman. I am gay, and so are you. Look at you, carrying a Coach purse. Oops, I mean *boy bag*. Straight men don't carry purses."

"Yes, I'm still a little feminine, but I'm not gay. I'm saved," I replied firmly.

We went back and forth, but it was clear to him that my mind was made up. Finally, he sighed. "Well, if you want to be straight, go ahead and be straight, but you'll always be a queen in my eyes."

I chuckled. "Look, there you go. She's pretty," he said, pointing to a waitress.

"Uhm, I'm not that straight...at least, not yet." I laughed, pretending to vomit.

When the waitress brought the check, Daymond grabbed it and handed it to me, saying, "Here, since you want to be the man."

When he dropped me off at home, I felt a warmth in my chest. It had only been a few hours, but for the first time in what felt like forever, I felt normal again. Even though I hadn't convinced Daymond I was straight, I was able to laugh and just be.

Even now, I can still feel the relief from that day, how a friend's teasing and a shared meal broke down the wall of shame. I was Norman again, not "Harris, sex offender case number 1053681." I didn't want the moment to end, so I decided to enjoy the rest of the day. Sitting on the couch, I looked down at my bag and saw some court papers sticking out. Not today, I thought, stuffing them back inside and zipping the bag shut.

CHAPTER 20

The next day, I returned to my usual routine. The first item on my to-do list was to call the sex offender treatment provider. As I waited for the phone to ring, I reflected on the absurdity of it all, making an appointment to see a shrink. Someone finally answered with a simple "Hello." I was expecting something more formal, like "Thank you for calling" or "Dr. So-and-so's office," so I hesitated before replying, "I think I have the wrong number."

She asked who I was trying to reach, and I explained I wanted to enroll in the sex offender treatment program.

"This is the right number," she replied, introducing herself. After I confirmed my identity, she explained the program to me. The sessions were held in group settings with 10-15 participants, meeting weekly for an hour each time. She told me the sessions cost $35 each, and before I could start, I'd need to complete a $200 assessment to evaluate my sexual history and any issues that might need addressing.

I was taken aback. She's sitting on a gold mine, I thought, doing the math. Six sessions a day, seven days a week, each with 10 participants, added up to more than $14,000 a week. I wasn't sure if she was being kind or simply motivated by profit.

She asked if Sunday at noon worked for me. "Sure," I said, agreeing to the time.

As I hung up, I was just about to close my phone when an incoming call interrupted me.

The call was from Dr. Gordon, the chief of police at my college. He was calling to update me on the college's decision about my enrollment.

"Unfortunately, you won't be able to attend classes, Mr. Harris," he said. "We think your case is a little too fresh for us to determine your risk level to other students and faculty. However, you can appeal our decision by writing a letter explaining why you should be allowed to continue your education with us."

He provided me with his contact details and said he would be in touch.

My heart sank. Another door had closed. My day had only just begun, but in those first two hours, I learned that I needed to come up with $200 before Sunday, plus $140 a month for treatment. On top of that, I had just been kicked out of college, no less, a community college.

Once again, the tears started to form in my eyes. This wasn't fair. My life was being torn apart and ruined for what? Because a 16-year-old was old enough to create a fake profile on an adult social site, lie about his age, and then get treated like a victim?

How can he still go on with his life, still online, lying about his age? What laws exist to prevent him and other minors from falsely presenting themselves to adults? Shouldn't he be made to wear a sign that says, "I lied about my age, and in doing so, I've ruined an innocent person's life. Beware! By lying, I'm a threat to your freedoms and society."

I want to make this clear: I am not a cruel or heartless person. Sexual abuse is a terrible thing, and no one, especially an innocent child, should ever be subjected to it. His sexual history wasn't relevant, nor should it ever justify abuse. But I couldn't ignore the fact that his mother told mine this wasn't the first time he'd been caught in such a situation. So why are minors allowed to falsely present themselves as of legal age, without consequence?

I understand that critics and experts might say I'm blaming the victim and not accepting responsibility for my actions, but I call bullshit on that. The truth is, if he had told me he was 16 when I met him online, our conversation would have ended right then and there.

Eventually, I developed some empathy for him, but at this point in my story, my life was being torn apart. I can see the mess of contradictions I was holding. I wanted someone to blame, anyone but myself. Anger was easier than grief, but deep down, I knew: both could be true. I had made a choice, and yet, I had also been deceived.

That tension would sit in me for years. Once the tears dried, survival mode kicked back in.

My sister picked me up to take me to the Texas Workforce Commission so I could start my job search. I was surprised by the diversity in the office; it seemed that hard times didn't discriminate against anyone. I signed in to meet with an employment counselor and was told the wait would be about an hour. "In the meantime, we have computers, fax machines, copy machines, and a phone for employment-related calls," the receptionist emphasized.

My sister and I searched the crowded room for an available computer, but all the stations were taken. "Y'all can sit over here," someone called out. My sister and I looked around to find where the invitation was coming from. "Right here!" she waved, and we headed toward her. Unfortunately, there were still no open computers.

"Get y'all's asses up so these people can use the computer," she instructed her children. Like a pop tart, they scrambled out of their seats, grabbed their coloring books, and made room for us. As my sister sat down in one chair, I whispered to her, "I have to leave."

She turned, confused, and stared at me. "What?"

I have to leave," I repeated.

I explained that my probation officer had warned me it was my responsibility to leave any establishment where children were present, especially since the computers had internet access. I wasn't allowed to use it.

"That doesn't make any sense," my sister said. "Grab that empty chair and bring it over here. This is a business office. You don't have to leave. Children are everywhere you go. What does she expect? You're supposed to stay locked up in the house all day? If that's the case, they should have just left you in jail."

I couldn't help but chuckle at her frustration. "Don't say that," I replied. "That place was horrible."

"Those conditions are standard rules for pedophiles", she assured me, they didn't apply to my situation. "You're with me and plenty of other adults, so I promise you, nothing will happen to you."

"Okay, but what about the internet? I'm not supposed to be on it either," I hesitated, still uneasy.

"Look, Bernard, you have to do what you have to do. Children and the internet are part of our world. There's no way you're going to find a job without using it in this day and age. If it makes you feel comfortable, I'll do all the searching while you watch. Just let me know what jobs you're interested in."

As the older sibling, my sister had always protected my brother and me, so even though I felt hesitant, thinking that the court might have undercover officers watching my every move, I trusted her plan. Together, we started applying for jobs and submitting my resume.

My sister, who was also unemployed at the time, quickly grew frustrated with the job search. She stopped typing long enough to point to the computer next to her. "This is stupid. You're not a sex offender," she said. "I have to look for a job, too, so get online and do your job searches."

As the young mother and her kids were leaving, my sister urged me to hurry before someone else noticed the open computer.

I leaned over to whisper to her, "What if they're watching me?"

She laughed, "Boy, you aren't that important. They don't have the time or resources to watch you or everybody else on probation that closely. Isn't one of your conditions to be employed?" she asked. "It's 2005! Companies post jobs online now!"

I hesitated, sitting at the computer for a few minutes before opening the browser, anxiously waiting for SWAT to burst through the door and arrest me. My hands shook as I finally opened the browser, feeling like I had just violated my probation.

Fear makes ordinary things seem dangerous. Every click of a mouse felt like a crime. Every look from a stranger felt like suspicion. That's what living under a label does; it distorts reality until you can't tell danger from paranoia.

Once I realized SWAT wasn't coming, I started checking my emails. It had been a month, and just like my voicemail, my inbox was full of messages from friends wondering why I'd fallen off the radar, praying that I was okay. Responding to those emails made me feel good, knowing people were genuinely concerned about me.

I was getting too caught up in my inbox, though, because my sister glanced over at me and said, "That doesn't look like an employment site. I'm going to tell your PO."

"Norman Harris, last call for Norman Harris," a voice called out, making my heart race. My eyes widened in panic.

"I told you they were watching me!" I whispered to my sister, fear all over my face.

She just smiled, "Relax, that's the employment counselor calling you."

Relieved, I walked over to the lady and followed her to her cubicle.

She asked me for my Social Security number so she could access my unemployment claim. While we waited for the information to load on her screen, we made small talk.

"How long have you been unemployed?" she asked.

"Almost a week," I replied.

"Well, that's too bad, but something will open up for you," she said, tapping on the monitor. "I hate when this thing acts funny."

I didn't understand why she was tapping on the monitor, but I sat there, watching and hoping it would work. When my claim loaded, she started verifying the information. She explained that the fax machines were near the printers, and all the computers had internet access.

"Do you have any questions about the resources available to help you with your job search?" she asked, looking at me as if she'd just delivered an impressive PowerPoint presentation. Before I could even respond, she said, "Well, that concludes your required orientation."

"That's it?" I asked, my confusion evident.

"Yes, the orientation is really simple," she replied. "It's just required so people can come in and familiarize themselves with the available resources to help them find employment before their unemployment benefits can be paid." She smiled, "The state doesn't like to hand out free money," she joked.

"Your resume looks fine, so I don't see you having any problems bouncing back," she added.

I thanked her for her time, feeling a little disappointed, then made my way back to my sister.

"Did she tell you about emergency food stamps?" my sister asked.

"Nope, she didn't tell me anything."

"Well, since you were just released from jail and are recently unemployed, you should qualify for emergency food stamps," she explained. "I wonder why she didn't mention that."

"Don't blame her," I said. "I didn't tell her I was locked up... too embarrassed."

"You should have," she scorned. "I've heard there are resources to help people once they've been released from jail. I'll go talk to her since you were too embarrassed."

Just like she always did, my sister jumped out of her chair and walked toward the counselor. I sat in my chair, watching her conversation, and I could tell my sister was fighting for me, just like she always had. I don't know what she said, but she came back with the instructions and directions to the "food stamp office." Two and a half hours later, we left the unemployment office and headed back to my parents' house.

"If you need anything, call me," my sister instructed as I got out of the car.

As soon as I entered the apartment, I collapsed onto the couch and drifted off to sleep. My nap wasn't as long as I had hoped. Just as I was getting comfortable, my phone started ringing. I reached for the coffee table, but my phone wasn't there. I felt around in my pockets and still couldn't find it. My Beyoncé ringtone was blaring, but I couldn't locate the phone. I didn't want to get up, but I couldn't risk missing a call, so I reluctantly got off the couch. Of course, the phone had fallen between the cushions. Not bothering to check the caller ID, I flipped open the phone to answer.

"Hello?" I said, my voice thick with frustration.

"Hi, I'm calling for Norman Harris," a perky, high-pitched voice said.

"Speaking," I replied suspiciously.

"Hi Norman, this is Becky from ABC Job Agency. I ran across your resume and would love the opportunity to discuss your experience for a possible position I'm trying to fill."

Wow, I thought to myself, finding a job is pretty easy. I had just left the unemployment office a few hours ago, and I was already getting calls. Surely the counselor was right. I'd be back on my feet in no time.

"Great," I answered, changing my tone to a more professional one. "I have time to discuss my resume with you right now."

"Wonderful," she replied. She began asking me questions about my previous experience, the type of position I was interested in, and other general questions.

"I have all the information I need, and based on our conversation, I believe you'd be a good candidate for our client."

The job was a temp-to-hire position within walking distance of my parents' apartment. I had to chuckle to myself. My car was sitting at a storage lot, but with those daily fees, it felt like it was already repossessed. I was so excited. My mom was right: "One day at a time."

"All we have to do now, Norman, is bring you in and let you complete the new hire paperwork," she said. "We do perform a drug and background check. Will you have a problem with either of those?" she asked shyly.

"No ma'am," I confidently answered.

"Good, good. Can you come in tomorrow morning?"

"I sure can!"

I hung up the phone and immediately started thanking God. Words couldn't express how grateful I was; the past few weeks had been overwhelmingly tough physically, mentally, and spiritually. This new position felt like a major victory, restoring my hope and faith. I couldn't wait for my parents to get home from work. Just as I expected, they were just as excited about this new opportunity as I was.

The year 2005 started hectically for my family. My parents, siblings, and I faced intense stress and pressure. Our lives were turned upside down, but thanks to our faith in God and our love for each other, we managed to get through each day. My mom summed up the beginning of the year simply: "We didn't know how we were going to make it." Our family had never experienced anything so devastating. Sex offender registration had completely upended our world.

My parents were forced to swallow their pride and carry the shame every time they shared our experience with relatives or close family friends. On top of all the restrictions and the negative stigma linked to being a sex offender, my parents had to admit that their son had been caught in a situation with another man. My sister and her kids' lives were also thrown into chaos. I could no longer help her take care of my niece and nephews or be a part of their young lives. Despite everything, what was supposed to tear my family apart actually brought us closer, and this new job opportunity turned out to be a much-needed win for all of us.

The next morning, I walked with a little extra bounce in my step as I dressed for my interview with Rebecca. I entered the office smiling, eager to close the deal. I hurried through the paperwork and confidently finished the data entry and entry-level accounting tests. According to Rebecca, my scores would have employers flooding me with job offers.

The drug test was conducted on-site, and I waited for the instant results, thinking about how I would spend my first paycheck. After finishing with Rebecca, she explained that the shift was from 4 p.m. to midnight, which wasn't ideal, but I needed a job and wasn't in a position to be picky. She asked if I could start as soon as tomorrow, and I immediately agreed. I left that office feeling like I'd signed a million-dollar movie contract.

The whole bus ride home, I sat in the back, gazing out the window like a tourist, trying to distract myself from the excitement of the new job. When I got home, I felt like I could finally relax. A weight had been lifted off my shoulders, and things were finally beginning to shift in my favor.

Scratching "find a job" off my mental to-do list felt monumental. For the first time since everything happened, I had momentum, something that looked like progress instead of punishment. I told myself I'd devote my full attention to being 100% compliant with probation and moving forward with my life.

For the first time, the probation contract felt less like a sentence and more like a structure, something I could manage. I sat at the kitchen table that evening, flipping through each page. My mother's neat check marks trailed alongside my completed tasks, small affirmations in ink that I was reclaiming order. All that remained was registering with the Houston Police, just a few days away.

When I looked at that almost-finished list, I felt something I hadn't felt in months: peace.

That night, my parents and I sat down to dinner together. The air was lighter. The food tasted like relief. They didn't have to say it; I knew they were proud, even if the pride came mixed with worry. For a few hours, we were just a family again. No probation, no case numbers, no shame. Just laughter and food and the soft rhythm of forks against plates.

Later that night, lying in bed, I realized I wasn't thinking about officers, restrictions, or courtrooms. My mind was still for once. That kind of stillness can be frightening because it feels unfamiliar, but I gave in to it anyway.

That night, I slept deeply, peacefully, and uninterruptedly, the kind of sleep that comes only when the noise inside you finally quiets.

CHAPTER 21

The Perfect First Day - Sometimes a pause can mask itself as peace, just a small breath before the next demand, but in the moment, we melt into the pause and let go, because those small pockets of time are untouched by fear. Our nervous systems breathe sweet relief, even if only temporarily.

The alarm on my phone went off early the next morning, its shrill ring becoming the soundtrack to my excitement. Even though I didn't have to be at work until four in the afternoon, I was already awake, too giddy to sleep in. There were small tasks I needed to attend to around the house, but nothing too significant.

Honestly, I was just thrilled to be starting work again.

When I was in my late teens, I had applied to this company several times and never heard back. Now, a few years and a lifetime of lessons later, I was walking through the same door that once refused me. It felt poetic, like God was giving me a full-circle moment. Proof that maybe, just maybe, redemption wasn't out of reach. Oh, sweet redemption.

Still, the nerves buzzed under my skin. I knew too well that good things could disappear overnight. Hope had a habit of evaporating as quickly as it appeared, but for now, I let myself have this small joy.

When you've been through enough loss, even simple things, like a first day at work, can carry a weight that others can't see. I wasn't just clocking in; I was reclaiming something. Dignity. Purpose. Maybe even a piece of myself.

The night before, I had dreamt about the outfit I would wear. I wanted the mirror to reflect something new back at me. Something better, even if deep down, I knew I was still rebuilding from the inside out.

I needed the perfect first day. New job. New coworkers. New year.

It was a challenge navigating the guest room closet, where my clothes and a few boxes were crammed into a small space, but I eventually found the pants, shirt, shoes, and belt I was looking for. Lying my chosen outfit neatly across the bed felt symbolic, as if I were piecing together fragments of the man I used to be.

I was the first person at the barbershop, but the shop wasn't open yet. According to the sign, it would be another 30 minutes before they'd start cutting. I instantly began to miss my car. If I had it, I could sit in it and listen to music, but with no other choice, I found a spot in front of the shop's door and tried to make myself comfortable. Sitting there on the hard concrete made me even more thankful for my new job. It was only a matter of time before I saved enough money to buy another car. As I waited, I mentally focused on numbers; I created a budget, set financial goals, and visualized the life I was trying to create. According to my calculations, it wouldn't take long to get back on my feet, especially since I was living at home with my parents and didn't have to worry about rent or utilities.

By the time the barber arrived, my nerves had settled into something that almost felt like hope. I was so caught up in my mind that I didn't notice my barber walk up to open the shop's doors.

"Come on in, youngsta! Out here looking like a stray dog," he teased as I took a seat.

I laughed, but my thoughts drifted. How would my coworkers treat me? How would my coworkers be? Would I have an office or a cubicle? If we worked in cubicles, would they be the short ones with no privacy? All kinds of thoughts flooded my mind. I was just as anxious as a transfer student starting at a new school.

About 20 minutes later, my barber finished cutting my hair. He handed me a mirror so I could check his work. His following comment made me feel as though he could read my thoughts. "Yeah, youngsta, I got you ready for your first day. I know I earned a big tip."

I laughed and thought about how people expect tips. Waitpersons and bartenders? Sure, I get it. But people like barbers, beauticians, or the nail shop ladies—what makes them tip-worthy? Why not just include the tip in their price? Have you ever gone to your boss and asked for a tip at the end of your shift? It doesn't make sense, right?

Anyway, back to my story. I'd have to contemplate the history of tipping another time. I handed him the money, watching as he patted his pockets as if looking for his stash to give me change. Seeing through his tactic, I rolled my eyes and told him not to worry about it—that it was all for him.

"Good looking out," he said, shaking my hand.

As I walked out, a woman pushed a stroller toward the door, her belly round with another child, and a small boy, no older than five or six, trailed behind her. Being courteous, I held the door open for her while she struggled to lift the stroller over the entrance's hump. "Thank you," she said as she walked through.

When her trailing son saw that his mom was already inside, he started running to catch up, but he tripped, and his juice box and toy car fell to the ground. He hit the ground pretty hard, and I could see his knees were scraped. Naturally, he began crying loudly, letting the whole world know he had fallen. My hands twitched to help him up, but then, my mind snapped back: *No contact with minors.* The rule echoed like a warning siren. I froze. Every possible consequence flashed before me: the probation officer's voice, the judge's signature, my parents' disappointment.

The right thing to do, the human thing, was to help, but the law said otherwise, so I stood there watching him cry. His toy car slid toward my foot. What was I supposed to do? I felt horrible and awkward standing there, watching him cry. I looked inside the shop for his mom, who was struggling to turn the stroller around. Finally, she picked him up and comforted his scraped knee. As they entered the shop, the little boy cried, "My car, my car!" His mom looked down at the toy car, which was still at my feet.

The least I could do was pick up the car and hand it to her. I bent to pick it up. The boy reached for it too, and instinct made me pull back just in time. I handed it to her instead, careful not to brush against his small fingers. Her confused glance said everything. How strange it must've looked, a grown man refusing to hand a toy to a child.

Walking home from the barbershop, I felt awkward, almost like I didn't belong in society anymore. I had obeyed the law, but it didn't feel like righteousness; it felt like a small kind of death. Every time I passed someone, I had this strange feeling, as if they knew I was a sex offender. Would the rest of my life be filled with uncomfortable situations like what had just happened at the barbershop?

How could I be part of society while constantly fearing that I'd be "outed" as a sex offender? Lost in my thoughts, I almost didn't hear my phone ringing. The hard vibrations against my belt jolted me, and I was nearly too late to answer.

"Norman, this is Rebecca Pearson from ABC Job Agency." The brightness in her voice from the day before was gone. Flat. Tight. Controlled. Something was wrong.

"There's an issue with your application I need to discuss before sending you on assignment today." The minute she said issue, my stomach clenched. Her tone told me whatever was coming wasn't small.

"Norman," she continued, "the results of your criminal background check came back, and there's a very disturbing conviction that you failed to mention on your application."

My heart stopped.

"Uhm, what conviction?" I asked, genuinely confused.

She must've thought I was lying because, without hesitation, she asked, "So you were not convicted of a sex crime against a child?"

I froze. Speechless. My legs refused to move. I could barely hear her voice through the rising panic. The world fell away—the street noise, the wind, everything. For a moment, all I heard was the pounding of my own heartbeat.

"Norman, are you there?" she snapped, irritation blooming in her voice.

A gust of wind suddenly blew dirt into my eyes. I blinked rapidly, vision blurring as a bus roared past me. The timing felt cruel, almost symbolic.

"Norman, I'm sorry, I can barely hear you."

" I-I'm here," I finally managed, voice tight. "A bus just passed. I'm walking home from the barbershop, getting ready for my first day."

I wanted to keep talking, but the shame lodged in my throat like a stone.

I forced myself to explain, reliving everything I'd been trying so hard to rebuild over.

"Deferred adjudication isn't a conviction," I said, quoting the judge word for word. "I've been *charged*, but the conviction is pending successful completion of seven years of probation. That's why I didn't check the convicted felon box."

I hoped—*begged*—she'd hear the truth in what I was saying.

I wasn't dishonest.

I wasn't dangerous.

I wasn't what that paperwork made me look like.

But then came the crushing blow.

"Norman, the thing is," she said, her voice had cooled to ice, "I won't be able to present you to my client on this assignment with your criminal background."

My heart dropped.

"Do you have any other assignments I can fill?" I asked, my voice barely a whisper.

She sighed, long and disappointed, as if she couldn't believe what I was asking. "Norman, the bottom line is I won't be able to work with you on this assignment, or any others going forward. I'm sorry."

Just like that, she hung up.

No compassion.

No pause.

No breath to let me respond.

I stood in the middle of the sidewalk, cemented in place as the reality sank in. My legs went numb. The rejection, the failure, the overwhelming disappointment, they all hit me at once, as if a weight had settled in my chest. It burned, and I could barely inhale.

Then the tears came. Not the soft kind. They were the heaving kind. The type that scraped their way out of your body like they were trying to take your soul with them. They didn't help. They couldn't extinguish the fire of shame and despair I was feeling.

I could see traffic passing by on the street and watched as cars sped by. The drivers seemed so certain, so confident in their destination, while I was standing still, lost in the weight of my own failure. I felt detached from it all, like I was watching life through glass. The rejection from losing the job still burned in my chest, a cruel reminder of my new normal. As I stood there, a dark thought whispered, "Just step in the flow of traffic and end it all," but something, maybe instinct, maybe God, perhaps the memory of my mother's face behind the visitation glass, pulled me back. My feet finally moved, slow and heavy, carrying the heavy burden of hopelessness with every step, dragging me toward the only place left where I could collapse without being seen by strangers.

Home.

The two-minute walk felt like twenty. When I reached the door and saw my reflection in the hallway mirror, I caught myself whispering, "Damn, he really did a good job cutting my hair... all for nothing."

Just like that, the tears started to flow before I could stop them.

I must have cried myself to sleep because when I woke up, my dad had come home from work. I didn't have the courage or the heart to tell him that I had lost the job. What kind of failure gets fired from a job before their first day? We made small talk as he relaxed after a long day at work. This was the first time he and I had been alone together since I was released from the county jail. I knew he had questions, but I didn't want to answer them. I had moved out to avoid facing him about my sexuality. This was all new for my parents. They knew things. I'm sure they knew I was gay, but I had always vowed I'd never confirm it. Now here I was, no more hiding. Mothers are typically more understanding, but fathers are different. I could handle Mama, but facing Daddy was another thing entirely. Daddy lived by his Christian values, and I knew I violated them. When I had my own apartment, I could keep my visits short and straightforward, avoiding the tough conversations. Now I was on his turf, and there was no escaping.

"See, son," he began, "this is what living in sin does for you, but I'm not going to condemn you. You've been through enough. Too much, if you ask me. Just think about what I said."

"Yes, sir," I whispered. It was all I could say.

He got up to head to the kitchen, where he would start preparing dinner for my mom. Yes, I said my dad was going to cook for my mom. Daddy always cooked dinner because he got off work before she did. And before you think how thoughtful he is, you should know his favorite line: "If I don't cook, we'll both starve." He'd say it with a laugh, but it was his truth. He claimed that Mama stopped cooking once all her children moved out.

I felt sick to my stomach. I had to tell him about the job. He'd expect me to leave at four, and I couldn't fake it. But I didn't know how to say it. How do you tell your father you couldn't even keep a job for a full twenty-four hours?

I tried to distract myself with the only thing that might bring good news—the mail. My unemployment decision should've arrived. I got off the couch to get a better view of the mailbox. I was waiting for an answer from the Texas Workforce Commission regarding my eligibility for unemployment benefits. Now that I was back to being unemployed, I needed a cash flow. Sprint wanted its money, and I had run out of reasons to ask for credit extensions. I also needed $200 for the initial treatment assessment and some pocket money. Just as I peeked out the living room window, I saw the mail carrier heading back to her truck. The mail crates in her arms swung easily and weightlessly, the kind of sway that told me her route was finished and her day was winding down. Meanwhile, I carried the opposite: everything in me felt heavy and unfinished, as if I were dragging the whole day behind me.

"Hey, let me see your mailbox keys," I called out.

"They're somewhere on the dining table."

"No, they're not. I already looked. I need your keys."

"Boy, calm down. That mail is still gonna be there, I promise you," he said, reaching into his pockets and tossing me the keys.

Sure enough, the letter I had been anxiously waiting for was waiting for me inside the mailbox. I pulled out the rest of the envelopes and advertisements, stuffing them under my arms. Right now, they weren't my concern. As I read over the letter from TWC, all the excitement drained out of me. "At this time, your unemployment claim is being denied."

I stared at the words, numb. Fired before my first day. Rejected by unemployment.

Still needing $200 for the treatment assessment. Still needing money for Sprint.

Still needing to breathe.

Inside, I called the unemployment office immediately. I was so flustered that I pressed the wrong button, and the automated system switched to Spanish. I felt like the universe was mocking me. "When all else fails, press and hold zero," I muttered.

How could my employer deny my claim? They fired me—they have to pay me! A representative finally answered. "¿Cómo puedo ayudarte?"

"No, no, no—I speak English."

"Okay, sir, no problem, I can still help you. What may I do for you?"

I explained the letter I received and how I didn't understand why my claim was being denied. He asked for my Social Security number so he could look up my claim. Once he accessed it, the following sentence out of his mouth was, "Okay, sir, I see your claim is being denied."

"I already know that," I shot back, my voice strained with anger, barely able to contain the frustration. A curse word slipped out before I could catch it, sharp and reflexive rooted in pure frustration and disappointment. I felt the rejection hit me again, like a weight pressing on my chest. It was hard to keep it together, but I managed to do so, sort of.

To which he replied, "Sir, using that language, I won't be able to help you."

"I'm sorry," I apologized, realizing how frustrated I had become. "It's just that I really needed this money."

"No problem, sir, I understand your frustration. I'm sensitive to your situation."

"Oh, really? You have a job, so how do you understand my situation?" I wanted to ask, but I reminded myself I wasn't speaking to a Sprint representative, so I held back my rudeness. He explained that my claim was denied because of the amount of time I had worked for my previous employer. I had started a new job at the hotel a month before I was arrested. "Okay, that makes sense," I agreed.

He went on to tell me that my former employer had denied my claim because I was fired for failing to report to work as scheduled. According to them, I had abandoned my position.

"That's not true!" I shouted into the phone, interrupting him. "I was in jail. How could I come to work? Plus, my mother notified my manager and kept her updated on when I was going to be released."

He took a breath before continuing, "Okay, sir, you have two options. Your first option is to appeal their decision. If you choose to appeal, we'll set up an arbitration between you, your former employer, and one of our mediators. The mediator will hear both sides and use that testimony to either approve your claim or side with your company and uphold the denial. Your second option is to work a total of 240 hours, and then your claim will automatically be approved."

That didn't make sense to me. "Why would I need benefits if I already had a job?" I asked in disbelief.

"Well, sir, those are your two options. Would you like to set up an appeal?"

"Sure, go ahead," I replied.

He provided me with a time and date for my appeal and informed me that the mediator assigned to my case would contact me then. He also urged me to continue my job searches and keep an accurate record of all the job leads and contacts I made. He thanked me for calling and asked if I had any other questions. I didn't bother to answer. I just hung up on him. I wasn't trying to hear anything he had to say.

"God, it's getting worse and worse," I told my dad. "They denied my unemployment."

"Well, son, it's not the end of the world."

"Easy for you to say," I pouted, my frustration boiling over.

"Son, please!" he replied, his voice calm but firm. "I wanted you to get that unemployment check, too. Do you think I like going into my pocket and giving my money to them folks? If you don't have any money coming in, that means it's up to your momma and me, and we have no problem helping you out, but you have to do your part and keep a good attitude. Anger will tie the hands of God."

His words stung, but they rooted me again, just enough to breathe.

"Yes, sir, you're right," I mumbled, my pride bruised. "But it's too much, Daddy. Plus, the agency called."

By this time, I couldn't hold back the tears. Everything hit me at once—the disappointments, the numerous rejections in one week, the constant battle to prove I wasn't a lie, a monster, a mistake. I broke, unequivocally.

The charge showed up on the background check, I explained, and they rescinded the job offer.

My dad didn't flinch. "N.B., God is still in control. All that crying isn't going to change anything." His voice was steady, like he had already made peace with something I hadn't caught up to yet. "The Bible says, 'Where sin abounds, God's grace does much more abound.' That means grace outweighs that lifestyle you were living."

He wasn't whispering comfort. He was preaching. "Son, that very grace is going to get us through this. You're just reaping the reward of your sin. But God is good; He loves you. Your momma and I love you, and you're going to be alright. If you want, I'll tell your momma about the job and the unemployment when she comes home."

I didn't respond. I didn't have to. I let the tears do the talking, releasing, and cleansing. I had lost the unemployment appeal, but somewhere in the middle of drowning, I told myself I'd survive. Daddy was right; God was seeing me through.

CHAPTER 22

Before I knew it, January was gone. February 2005 had arrived, and I was unemployed, exhausted, and fighting to hold on to the little hope I had left, wrestling with the overwhelming urge to give up. Eighty-three more months of probation stretched out in front of me like a sentence with no finish line. I knew I wasn't going to make it if things didn't turn around soon. All I could think was: *I can't do this.* I even thought about writing to the judge, asking him if I could exchange the probation for a short prison sentence.

Two years behind bars felt easier than seven years of living outside, like I was already locked up. Then all of this would be behind me.

Why did I let my court-appointed attorney convince me that probation was easy? Why did I believe it was a gift from the court? I didn't understand how I could continue to live life with all the restrictions. The rejections were unbearable. Freedom didn't feel like freedom when every breath came with restrictions.

Registering with staffing agencies was exhaustive. Four-hour tests. Personality quizzes. Software assessments. Smiles that turned cold after background checks. They never told me *no* to my face. They whispered it with polite emails and sudden silence. I relived that experience numerous times with various staffing agencies.

I didn't know how I was going to make it, but I knew I had no choice but to keep pushing through. I refused to give the judge, the judgmental probation office workers, or the world what they expected: a guilty, broken, and soulless monster. I was not the pedophile they wanted me to be. I had been lied to. The "victim" had presented himself on an adult dating site as an eighteen-year-old. I refused to let the system paint me with a broad brush. In my mind, I was innocent.

Thankfully, my college refunded the money I had paid for the semester after they denied my admission due to the sexual offense charge. Although I was disappointed, I decided to use that refund to pay for the $200 initial assessment required for the sex offender treatment program. The assessment itself was unlike anything I had ever experienced. It was uncomfortable on a level I couldn't have imagined. The questions dug into my sexual history, both past and present, and I cringed at the ones about bestiality, fetishes, and fantasies. They asked about women's bodies like I should know my way around them. I was a closeted gay man who had never even pretended I liked women. I had to ask the counselor for clarification on the female anatomy. I had no shame in admitting I knew little about the female body.

There were questions about cross-dressing, and according to the assessment, cross-dressing was labeled as "sexual deviance." I couldn't understand what was so deviant about my friends and I dressing up in drag on Halloween. I couldn't help but laugh to myself, recalling the fun I had in those Halloween drag adventures, which, now, were categorized as deviant behavior.

The entire assessment lasted two hours, and afterward, the counselor explained that she would review my answers to create a treatment plan based on my sexual history. She scheduled my first session for the following Sunday from 1:00 p.m. to 2:00 p.m. As I left her office, I felt filthy, overwhelmed by the nature of the questions. I thought to myself, "Is this what the Bible means by abomination? The thought stuck with me as I walked to the bus stop.

When I arrived home, I was relieved to see my sister's car parked outside. I was excited to see her, especially because her visit would shift my parents' attention away from me. A distraction and a break from being the problem in the room. Sweet joyous relief. When I walked in and saw my dad playing with my niece and nephews, my body froze, as if the doorway was a border I couldn't cross.

"What are they doing here?" I demanded, pointing at the kids. Their presence made me too anxious to walk in.

"What do you mean, 'what are they doing here?'" My sister responded defensively. "Get in the house and close the door."

"I can't! I can't come in as long as they're in there!" I shouted, pointing at my niece and nephews like they were strangers. "You all know I can't have any contact with anyone under the age of 17! Why are you trying to set me up?" I was shaking. My heart was sprinting. I genuinely thought the police would show up and drag me away. This was a violation. They knew better than to put me in this situation.

"You're not going to prison, and no one's trying to set you up," my sister said, trying to reassure me.

"Y'all don't understand," I replied, "the judge said no contact with anyone under 17."

"They aren't minors, Bernard, they're your family," my mom cut me off, her voice firm. "I'm not going to let the judge or anyone else keep you from seeing your own family. In fact, I'm going to the courthouse tomorrow and tell him so."

"No, you can't do that!" I panicked. "You'll get me in more trouble!"

"Bernard, we're about to eat. We aren't leaving, so you might as well calm down," my sister told me, her voice softer now.

I didn't want to, because fear doesn't listen to reason; fear hears handcuffs, but I eventually went inside. I made a conscious decision to stay as far away from my niece and nephews as possible, watching as they continued to play with my dad without a care in the world. The situation felt like a constant reminder that my life and my interactions with my own family had changed forever.

My niece noticed I was crying as I remained in the doorway. "Never mind," I told my sister, wiping my face quickly as I made my way to the unoccupied couch. I didn't want to explain myself, but as I walked away with my back turned, my nephews saw an opportunity to attack. They loved to wrestle and climb on me.

Before I could even think about escaping, one of them was climbing up my neck, his small hands gripping my shoulders while the other hung off my back, testing gravity and my patience at the same time. Usually, I would've welcomed their playful antics, laughing and engaging with them, but not this time. Not today. I felt a sharp wave of panic as their innocent energy surrounded me. My nieces and nephews, full of love and playfulness, reminded me of the distance I had to keep. I couldn't be around minors, not with my situation, and the fear of what could happen if I let my guard down kept me frozen. Their affection tugged at me, but the weight of the situation forced me to hold back, unable to fully embrace them. If I did, I might end up in a place where their love and playfulness couldn't reach me. Their small arms around my neck felt like ropes leading me to a prison cell, and I panicked.

"Y'all get off me, NOW!" I raised my voice, frustrated.

"What's wrong, you don't want to play?" my oldest nephew innocently asked.

"I can't," I told him, my voice breaking. "I want to, but I can't. So y'all have to get down off me and leave me alone."

The disappointment in their eyes cut deep. It made me feel guilty, as if I was failing them. All I ever wanted was to be the best uncle, but now I couldn't even play with them. How do you make that make sense to a six-year-old and a three-year-old?
They didn't ask for any of this. They didn't ask for their uncle to suddenly become off-limits, or for the grown-up chaos swirling around them. All they saw was that they were being scolded for the simple act of loving me out loud. They had no idea what was happening behind the scenes. All they knew was that playing with their uncle somehow became a reason to get in trouble—and that broke something in me.

"I'm going to go upstairs until y'all leave," I said to my sister.

Upstairs, lying in bed alone, I couldn't shake the overwhelming sense of desolation. How was I supposed to make it through this? I was drowning in emotions: fear, anger, and self-pity. Why me? I kept asking myself. Why my life? Was my father right? Am I reaping the benefits of "sin?" Does God hate me this much? Then, I got angry… angry at God, my parents, the judge for refusing to listen, furious at the world. All I could do was cry myself to sleep, but even when I woke up, the anger still lingered.

I told myself the anger would fade once I slept it off, but I couldn't shake the thought of how everything had turned upside down. I woke up with it burning behind my ribs, tight and heavy like a fist I couldn't unclench.My mind replayed the same moment over and over, the same decision, the same night that flipped my life upside down. I was trapped, trying to understand how one choice could strip me of everything: my freedom, my safety, my closeness to the people I loved most. The "victim" was out there breathing normal air, living a regular life, while mine was boxed in by rules, court orders, and constant fear. His freedom came at the cost of mine.

CHAPTER 23

The day I dreaded more than jail itself finally came: registration. Nothing about it felt normal. I wasn't ready to deal with the rude municipal employees, the blank stares, the disgust they didn't bother to hide. To make matters worse, registration took place at the city jail, the same place I'd been processed like livestock a month earlier. I never wanted to set foot in a jail again. The memory still haunted me. There's something about being inside those walls that drains you. You can't help but feel small, helpless, and paranoid. The guards parade around like they're gods, withholding all information. You're not allowed to feel like a person; you're just a number.

Walking through those doors again made my stomach twist. I expected cold bars, overcrowded cells, and the smell of sweat and disinfectant. Instead, I stepped into a lobby with a vending machine and a receptionist's desk. It felt wrong.

"May I help you, sir?" A voice asking, bringing me back to reality.

I was caught off guard. The voice sounded too polite. I was used to hearing "Next!" or "Listen up, inmates." I stammered like a child caught in a lie. "I—I have an appointment to reg… regis… register."

"You're here to register?" the officer asked, looking at me.

My head dropped, and I nodded in submission.

"It's alright, little brother," he said kindly, noticing my embarrassment. "Pick your head up." He directed me to the fourth floor. "The elevators are right there, or you can take the stairs," he added.

I couldn't even look him in the eyes to thank him. My shame was too much. If he'd barked at me, I could've handled it, but kindness? That was worse. Kindness meant seeing me as human. I didn't know how to hold that, and my shame at the same time. I took the stairs, running from his politeness like it was punishment.

Out of breath, I finally made it to the fourth floor, where humiliation had a waiting room. I followed the signs down the narrow hallway to the sex crimes office and rang the bell, my heart pounding as I waited for someone to come to the window.

A middle-aged white man who was sitting in the lobby looked up at the sound of the bell. He wore jeans held up by camouflage suspenders, and his thick glasses magnified his eyes, giving him a look that made my stomach churn. He scratched his bald head and then shifted his gaze to me, studying me in a way that made the air feel heavier.

I thought to myself, He's undoubtedly an old pervert. I noticed the other people waiting around. There was another white man in a pinstriped suit, and I couldn't help but think that he didn't look like a sex offender. He had a tailored suit, and his posture was confident, nothing like the image I had of someone who had committed a crime. Next to him sat a Black man, probably in his early 30s, dressed in khakis and a long-sleeve shirt. There was also a young Hispanic man fidgeting with his flip phone, but the most surprising of all was the woman sitting there, waiting.

What was she doing here? Surely, she must have been driving someone to their appointment, and was just waiting in the lobby for them to finish. "Ms. Johnson, you can come on back," the male clerk called from the partition. I couldn't imagine her as a sex offender, and in that moment, I realized something important: there is no particular look or type for a sex offender. Hollywood and the evening news have painted a specific picture, but the reality is different. Including myself, there were seven people in the lobby, and other than the man in camouflage suspenders, we all looked like regular people. I thought to myself, I guess anyone can be a sex offender, even me.

"Sir, have you signed in?" The clerk's voice broke my thoughts.

"No, I haven't," I said, reaching for the clipboard. I realized that my mental assessment of the lobby had taken too much of my attention. As I signed my name, I glanced through the partition and noticed the officers walking around. They didn't resemble the uniformed police officers I was accustomed to; they were dressed in plainclothes. If it weren't for the guns resting on their hips, I would have thought I was in an ordinary office.

After signing in, the man in suspenders, who had been holding a walking stick, kindly moved it from an empty chair and motioned for me to sit next to him. I was taken aback. Why would I want to sit next to him? He had committed an offense against a child. In my mind, he belonged in jail. I couldn't understand why he would think I'd want to sit with him.

Pretending not to notice him, I sat in the chair that Ms. Johnson had vacated.

"First time registering?" the man in the suit asked, his voice casual, as if we were sitting at a bar having drinks.

"Yes," I said, "how could you tell?"

He smiled, maybe out of politeness, but I felt like I could let my guard down around him. After all, he didn't seem as intimidating as the suspenders man.

"You're on lifetime registration?" the suspenders man asked.

I looked at him, annoyed. Why was he talking to me? I'm 23, not 13. I wasn't his type. I chose to ignore him and responded to the man in the suit.

"You asked if it was my first time. How could you tell?"

"You look uncomfortable," he said. "Like you don't belong here, or at least you think you don't."

I thought for a moment before responding. "I don't belong here. I didn't touch a child like some people," I said, glancing towards the suspenders man.

During my little rant, the Hispanic man in the corner started laughing.

"I don't know who invited you to join this conversation," I barked at him.

He raised his hands in defense. "Yeah, you're right. I should mind my own business."

The man in the suit apologized, but his words felt too late. I had already put him in the same mental category as suspenders man, while I simultaneously became what I despised the most: someone who judged before knowing.

The room fell into a heavy silence as we all sat there, waiting for our names to be called. The tension in the air seemed to grow with each passing minute, and I could feel my frustration building. Just as I was starting to spiral into my thoughts, the door opened. Ms. Johnson walked out. Was she done with her appointment? She'd only been gone ten to fifteen minutes. A small sense of relief washed over me. Maybe this wouldn't take much longer.

My relief quickly turned to shock when a young white man also emerged from the open door and walked over to the older fellow in suspenders. He helped the older man out of his chair, adjusting his walking stick before turning to him with a smile. "Ready to go, Dad? Hope it wasn't too long of a wait," he said.

Dad? Wait, what? I thought to myself. Suspender man wasn't the monster I had made him out to be. I felt horrible for judging him. As he and his son walked to the elevator, the old man looked back at me and said, "Jesus loves you, son. God bless you."

I was frozen in place. Talk about putting my foot in my mouth. I was too embarrassed to make eye contact with anyone else in the lobby. Here I was, worried about being judged, mad at the world for not understanding me, and yet, I judged "suspenders," and the only thing he was guilty of was loving his son unconditionally. I felt smaller than any cell I had ever been in. I learned a vital lesson that day about casting premature judgments.

Just then, a short, stocky officer came to the door and called for "Mr. Harris." I felt a wave of relief at the sound of my name. It was finally my turn, and I could get this process over with, but the officer waiting for me wasn't a stranger.

When I entered the office, the officer locked eyes with me and shook his head. "I can't believe it's you," he said.

Confused, I asked, "What's wrong? Did you not call for me?"

"No, I called for Harris, but I wasn't expecting to see you," he said. "Man, didn't you used to work at Kroger?"

I couldn't believe it. I hadn't worked there in years. I left when I was 20, three years ago. "Yes, I worked there a long time ago," I said, trying to understand why he recognized me.He chuckled and said, "What happened to you? What kind of trouble have you gotten yourself into?"

I couldn't explain it all in one sentence. "It's a long story," was all I could say.

He led me to a small area by the wall, marked with an "X" on the floor. I was surprised at how casual this whole process felt. There was no interrogation or harsh treatment, just simple questions about my address and a request to see my current driver's license.

He informed me that I would have to come in once a year on my birthday for the rest of my life to update my registration. He explained to me that every time I change jobs or enroll in any school, I would have to update my registration, but there's good news, he added. You don't have to come in to change your employment or education information; you can do that over the phone.

I stood on the "X" as he took my photo and thumbprints. Jokingly he told me that this picture was the one going on the internet and anyone would be able to see it so be sure to pose right.

Just like that, I walked out. Registered. Branded. Public.Confined. Not by bars. Not by chains. By permanence. I imagined registration would feel like punishment, but it felt like exposure. Prison takes away your freedom. The registry takes away your identity. I wasn't just paying for what I'd done; I was paying for what people imagined when they read my name printed under that label. That day taught me something probation never mentioned in the paperwork: Once the world believes you're a monster, proving you're not becomes a full-time job.

• • •

One afternoon, after leaving a job interview, I decided to visit my old co-workers at Kroger. Walking through those automatic doors felt like stepping into a version of myself that still had hope. A version untouched by courtrooms, probation officers, and labels. Even though it had been five years since I had left the store, I still had a good relationship with many of them. They were more like friends than merely colleagues. Walking down the store's aisles brought back so many memories.

I remembered my 16th birthday while home on summer vacation, when my mom walked in with a bag of groceries and told me, "Get ready, you have an interview at 3 PM."

Stunned, I asked, "Interview? Where? I haven't applied anywhere."

My mom replied, "While I was shopping at Kroger, I spoke with the hiring manager, filled out an application for you, and set up an interview. Happy Birthday!"

I worked at Kroger for nearly four years, during which I learned a great deal about work ethics and had a great time doing so. As I walked through the store, I ran into one of my old co-workers, and we immediately started catching up. I told them about my Christmas holiday spent in jail, and naturally, they thought I was joking or playing around, until I started crying. It was then that they realized I was serious. Being the good friends that they were, they comforted me. We laughed and cried together in the floral department.

After shopping a little, I stood in line flipping through a magazine, waiting for the cashier to stop struggling with her acrylic nails long enough to scan the items. Lost in my magazine and amused by the delay, I didn't notice that someone had parked a grocery cart behind me. As I turned to leave and head to the following line, I bumped into the cart, startling the woman who was leaning on it.

"Oh, excuse me," I began.

"No problem," she replied as she looked up at me.

Then, there was silence. I stood frozen in my tracks, eyes locked with hers. We stared at each other, just like that night. It was her, the "victim's" mother. There she was, right in front of me, and I couldn't move. We stared at each other, both caught in the same shock, the same silent horror. She looked… uncomfortable. Scared? Confused? I couldn't tell. I felt so uncomfortable. It was apparent she was just as uneasy as I was, and neither of us wanted to be in this situation.

I didn't say a word, and neither did she, and without breaking eye contact, she simply moved her cart to the right, giving me the space I needed to leave the aisle. I passed her quickly. At the next register, waiting to check out, I kept replaying her face. Her silence.

Her eyes, and the strangest thing rose inside me: *I hope she sees I'm not a bad person.*

I drove home thinking I'd left the moment behind... until I looked in the rear-view mirror.

Was that her car behind me?

I turned left; she turned left. I slowed down; she stayed behind me. Maybe I was paranoid. Perhaps she was going somewhere nearby, or maybe she was following me home. Before I could decide, I was already pulling into the median to enter my parents' apartment complex. I hurried into a parking spot, grabbed the bags, and rushed toward the door without looking back. By the time I got inside, I was shaking, fear, anger, humiliation all blurring together.

With no more interviews or appointments planned for the day, I changed clothes and began preparing lunch.

I'd always wanted to be a personal assistant; something about it just seemed like the perfect job, especially for someone rich and famous. Well, my parents weren't rich or famous, but they had taken me in, and since I wasn't working, the least I could do was help out around the house.

Once my meal was finished and the apartment cleaned, I had nothing left to do but watch TV. My dad always got off work before my mom, so I wasn't surprised when he walked in. What surprised me was his demeanor. He walked in slower than usual. Quieter. His face heavy.

He placed his empty lunch box on the table, and instead of speaking, he pulled out a folded sheet of paper, not a bill, not a note, but something official. Something that made his hands tremble.

He sat there, staring at it, studying each word with disbelief. I stood there, not knowing what to do or say, waiting for him to speak. On the back of the paper, I saw #901 written in black permanent marker. I assumed it was a note from the leasing office. Without saying a word, he passed the paper to me.

I unfolded it, and the words punched straight through me:

7-DAY NOTICE TO VACATE

Reasons:

• Unknown tenant not on lease

• Unknown tenant has a felony conviction, specifically Sexual Assault of a Child (14-17)

I stared at the letter in disbelief. What could I possibly say in response to that? I folded the paper back in half and tried handing it to my dad. He shook his head, dismissing it, so I laid it back on the table. The silence was suffocating, so I spoke, trying to lighten the mood.

"To say I'm unknown, they sure do know a lot about me." I joked.

Daddy didn't laugh. Not even a smirk. He just sat there, motionless, then finally placed his hands on his head and whispered, "Lord… where are we supposed to go?"

The guilt swallowed me whole. I couldn't fix it. I couldn't offer them anything except tears and empty apologies. I was overcome with shame. The day I moved out of my parents' home, I made sure that my life was 100% independent from them. I kept my family and personal life separate, determined not to answer to them or subject myself to their version of how my life should be lived, and now, they were facing homelessness because of me.

My parents lived a quiet, simple life. They're hard workers, good Christian people. They don't drink, smoke, use drugs, or engage in heavy partying. My mom's idea of a good time is watching reruns of In the Heat of the Night. They're not perfect, but this eviction was completely unwarranted. My dad works, comes home, and reads his Bible. That's his idea of a fulfilling day. It's not like they were behind on their rent or throwing wild parties. They were being evicted for doing what any good parent would do: taking in their child.

I was briefly reminded of the man in the suspenders who had waited patiently for his son to update his registration. It struck me how far good parents will go for their children, how they show up quietly, without questions or conditions, even in places no parent

140

ever imagines standing. He didn't look ashamed or angry. He looked steady. Like a man who understood that loving your child sometimes means sitting beside them in uncomfortable rooms, carrying burdens that were never supposed to be yours.

I felt the need to defend myself. I couldn't take the full blame for all of this. "You know, I bet that lady had something to do with this," I snarled. "Yeah, she did. I know she did."

"What are you talking about, son? What lady?"

"That boy's mom. I saw her today at the grocery store. After I left, I noticed she was following me home. I bet she called the office and told them something."

My dad, ever the voice of reason, spoke calmly, "Son, did she follow you to the door? How would she know where you were going? For all she knows, you could be visiting a friend or someone else."

In protest, I threw back, "Well, how else would the office know I'm here? I'm telling you; it was her."

My dad, unshaken, said, "I don't see why she'd do that. She had nothing to do with this."

I didn't understand why he was so convinced it wasn't her. I wanted to argue, but his following words stopped me: "I'm going to shower. We'll talk more when your mom gets home."

When my mom finally arrived, I couldn't hide my feelings. I just looked at her, and something in my stare must've given me away. Immediately, she knew something was wrong.

"What's wrong, huh? What's going on?"

"Uhm…nothing's wrong," I muttered, trying to shake off the tension.

"Where's Dad?"

"He's upstairs."

Trying to change the subject, I added, "I made some spaghetti."

Just then, my dad made his way downstairs. As he greeted my mom, he handed her the eviction notice. She took it from him, her expression changing as she read the paper. The weight of it all settled in. What had once been a simple life for them was now unraveling, all because of me.

"That's a shame," my mom said at first, before she re-read the eviction notice. After a moment, she sighed. "Well, we weren't planning on living here forever. We'll do what we have to do."

"I'm sorry," I blurted out, feeling the weight of it all, knowing it was my fault.

"Boy, now ain't the time to be sorry," my mom said firmly. "It's time to seek the Lord."

"Amen to that," my dad added, his voice heavy with emotion as he prayed aloud, "God, I need some direction."

I couldn't let it go. "You know, all this is that lady's fault," I said, trying to make my case. I had to prove my point to my parents.

"N.B.," my dad said, using the nickname he often called me, "not now, let it go." He said it with such authority, as if he knew something I didn't.

At that moment, my mom's curiosity took over. "What's going on? What are y'all keeping from me?"

I took a deep breath and explained everything, how I saw the victim's mother at the store, and how she followed me home. Just when I thought I had her on my side, my dad interrupted me.

"This has nothing to do with that," he said, his voice calm but firm. "Saturday, you were in the newspaper."

"Huh?" I said, confused. "What paper?"

"The Houston Chronicle," he answered. "They print the list of newly registered sex offenders every Saturday. I saw it over the weekend, but I didn't want to show you. I wanted to protect you."

I couldn't believe my ears. For one, it was my fault we were being evicted, and running into his mom at the store had nothing to do with the eviction. Secondly, hearing my dad say that he wanted to protect me hit me harder than anything else. For years, I had felt like a disappointment to him, especially for being gay. I never had the courage to tell him, but here he was, trying to shield me in his own way from the consequences I couldn't escape myself.

It humbled me. All those secrets and all that silence were for naught. I didn't have words. Only understanding. Only humility.

As we sat down to dinner, my dad said, "Well, I'll call Mother Randolph," my paternal grandmother. "I sure don't want to, but Lord knows I don't have any other choices."

Later that night, my mom came to my room. "Just checking on you," she said softly.

"I should be the one checking on y'all," I replied, guilt sitting on my chest like a boulder. "Y'all are being evicted all because of me."

"Bernard," she said, her voice gentle but firm, "this isn't about you. This is spiritual. The devil comes to steal, kill, and destroy, and that's what he's trying to do to you and this family, but God is greater." She paused, her face softening. "Anyway, Maw-Maw said we could move in with her."

I looked at her, my heart racing. "Wait a minute," I interrupted. "What did y'all tell her?"

"The truth," she said plainly.

"What truth? All of it?" I asked, trying to wrap my mind around it.

"Boy, you know your daddy can't hold water," she said with a laugh. "He's already told the family what happened." Just as my dad walked into the room.

"Tomorrow I'm going to get a U-Haul," he said, his voice low, almost resigned. "We'll move our stuff to storage. The rest is coming with us to Maw-Maw's."

He and my mom left my room for the night, but not before encouraging me and assuring me that, as a family, we'd get through this together. They bid me good night, and my dad turned off the light as he closed the door behind them.

I lay there in the dark, almost childlike, trying to remember the last time my parents had tucked me in. I had once longed for the day I could move out on my own, to feel free, to live my life the way I thought it should be. I remembered the first night in my apartment, feeling liberated: "Finally, I can be me!"

Fast forward a few years, and here I was, back at home in the extra room, interrupting their lives because I wanted freedom. I didn't just interrupt their lives; I had caused them to be evicted. At 23, I had to swallow my pride and admit I had messed up, so much so that I had to move back in with my parents. I couldn't help but think about how my dad must have felt. Here he was, in his late 40s, having to move back in with his mom because of me. Not only he, but my mom and me, their adult son.

I tried to imagine how my mom felt about moving into my grandmother's house. Even though my mom and grandma had a good relationship, according to my mom "no woman wants to share her kitchen with another woman". She didn't say anything else, but the way she said that let me know she understood exactly what this move meant, and she was doing it anyway.I never asked my dad how he felt about moving back in with his mother, but I didn't need to. The disappointment was written all over his face. My mom, on the other hand, let me know exactly how she felt.

The next day, my dad, my mom, my dad's co-worker, and I packed up the townhome. No one said much, just worked silently, like busy ants carrying out their tasks. Breaking the silence, I asked my dad why we were moving so fast. I thought the leasing office had given us seven days.

"No sense in putting it off," he replied. "We can't stay here, and I'm not living anywhere I'm not wanted." Without another word, he grabbed a box in his arms and headed out the door. By mid-afternoon, the U-Haul was packed, everything my parents owned loaded in the back. My mom was inside the leasing office, returning the keys. I stood on the front porch, looking around at the place where my family had spent so many years of our lives. We'd called 501 Greens Road home for sixteen years. Even after moving to a different complex nearby for a while, my parents eventually returned to 501. I have so many memories here: playing in the courtyard with my brother and our friends, swimming in the pool on hot summer days, picking wild berries from the bushes in the field behind the property, and catching crawfish after a good rain. It felt surreal, knowing this chapter of our lives was coming to an end, but those childhood moments would always be with me, as if they'd just happened yesterday.

I thought back to the days when the drug raids were a constant, when the Houston Police Department Drug/Gang Task Force would kick in doors, and the constant fear of the Greenspoint Rapist haunted us all. As a child, I didn't pay much attention to the news, but I knew the situation was serious. I'll never forget walking in one afternoon to find my dad showing my mom how to aim his .357 Magnum, just in case the Greenspoint Rapist decided to visit our home while my dad was away. It was a strange and unsettling thing to witness, watching my father, who was usually calm and composed, teach my mom how to protect herself with a gun.

Come to think of it, my niece spent her first years in 501 Greens. Second-generation Harrises had lived in that complex. My family could have been the picture-perfect family on the brochure advertising the property.

I was so caught up in the past that I barely noticed my dad standing in the threshold of the door. Unlike on television, when the series finale ends, and the TV family takes that final walk through the home, sighing or humming a farewell tune, my dad simply closed the door, shook his head in disbelief, and loaded the last small box into the U-Haul. He didn't want to face the ladies in the leasing office, so he leaned against the truck and prayed quietly under his breath.

Unloading my parents' belongings at the storage unit didn't take long. My mom made the task a little more difficult, though. It was hard for her to part ways with some of her things.

"Woman, we can always come back for things as we need them," my dad said.

"Yeah, but Tony, who wants to go through all that? Let me at least take the rest of my sheets and linens." They went back and forth for a few minutes before my dad finally conceded, letting my mom take the things she wanted. He knew this move was hard on them both, but he didn't want to make it harder.

Before closing and locking the storage unit, my dad paused, his hands raised to pull down the roll-up door as he surveyed the stack of boxes and furniture. He stood there for a moment, the quiet of the afternoon surrounding him. With a deep sigh, he lowered his head and prayed, his voice soft but steady, asking God to watch over and protect our things from theft, fire, flood, and destruction. As he finished, he took a final look at everything inside the unit, his eyes lingering on each item as if trying to hold on to the memories they represented.

"I worked hard every day for years, and now my whole life fits inside this small storage unit," he muttered, his voice barely above a whisper. There was no denying the truth in his words. All that hard work, all that sacrifice, now reduced to these boxes. Then, without another word, he reached up to pull the storage door down, the metal scraping against the tracks with a sound that felt too final.

He stopped for a moment before the door fully closed, his face a mixture of disbelief and sorrow. "Say it ain't so, Lord. Say it ain't so," he whispered, almost as if bargaining, pleading. The words hung in the air long after the door clanked shut, and I could feel the quiet ache in his heart echoing in mine.

I learned, painfully, that consequences from breaking the law doesn't only affect the person who committed the act. They also impact everyone close enough to love them. Watching my father gaze at an eviction notice with my existence and life choices buried inside it taught me that punishment spreads, shame spills out, and sometimes the people who bear the highest cost are those who did nothing wrong. In that moment, with everything falling apart, my parents never abandoned me. Their love didn't erase the consequences, but it gave me the strength to endure them.

The U-Haul ride from the storage unit to my grandmother's house was silent. Guilt weighed heavily on me, making it hard to find words. There was nothing I could say to undo the mess I had caused. Thankfully, the drive was only 15 minutes. Pulling into my grandmother's driveway, my dad finally spoke, but not to me. "Lord, give me strength," he said under his breath.

Together, we unloaded the last of the U-Haul, mostly clothes and small boxes. Once we were done, my dad turned to me and said, "I'm going to the bank. I want to give you something for helping us move today, son."

"Daddy, this is all my fault. Y'all had to move because of me. You don't have to pay me. I caused all this trouble."

"Son, I don't want to hear you say that anymore. We're all in this together."

And that was that. To this day, my parents have never blamed me for the eviction. Not once have they used it as a weapon, not once have they thrown it back in my face. They just kept doing what they've always done—living out the same Christian values that, as a teenager, I thought were out-of-touch and preachy. I didn't understand then that all that "church stuff" was the backbone of how they loved me.

CHAPTER 24

A week after moving in with my grandmother, I stood in her kitchen finishing a call with my probation officer. I gave her my new address and told her about my upcoming appointment to register with the sheriff's office.

I know what you're thinking: *Didn't you just register?* Yes. I did.

My parents' apartment had been inside Houston city limits, so I registered with HPD. My grandmother's house sat outside the city line, county jurisdiction, which meant starting the process all over again with the sheriff's office. The law says every move, every address change, every shift in geography has to be reported and updated. It's not just registration; it's a leash. Wherever I go, the system follows.

My grandmother couldn't wait for the call to finish. She was the sweetest, nicest, but most opinionated woman you'll ever meet. Once, she had me drive across town to pick up some cornbread dressing from a soul food restaurant. I made the trek, got the food, and came back home. After taking a bite, she asked me to hand her the phone. I thought she was about to call one of her church friends, maybe an aunt, anyone! Nope.

"Hello, yes, this is Annie, Annie Laura. I'm sitting here eating some of your dressing, my grandson picked up for me. Did you know you put way too much sage in your dressing? You know, when I make my dressing, I use…" On and on she went, giving the restaurant her opinion on how their cornbread dressing should taste.

I used to tease her, telling her she was two different people. In public, with her good Sunday wig on, she's "Annie", sweet and nice as can be. In the grocery store, she'd pass by people and smile, saying, "Jesus loves you, and so do I." Once, while shopping, a young woman asked her for a product suggestion for a meal, and boy, did she get an earful. My granny looked into the woman's cart and saw frozen and boxed products. She raised an eyebrow and said, "I know you don't plan on using those." Before the woman could say anything, my grandmother was leading her down the aisles, showing her how to make everything from scratch, picking out fresh ingredients and the perfect seasonings along the way.

My grandmother never met a stranger. She's so outgoing, kind, and generous. If she has it, you have it. Her extra rooms were always full. I'm pretty sure every one of her grandchildren has lived with her at some point, but when she's not wearing that Sunday wig, she's Maw-Maw, feisty in that funny, elderly way, and zero filter.

"'Bout time you got off that phone," she said, waving me over. "Come help me skin this chicken."

Now, my grandmother could *cook*. I know everybody swears their grandma is the best cook, but mine really is. We were in the middle of her teaching me how to make gumbo when my probation officer called back. As soon as I hung up, class resumed.

"Now quit playing with that chicken and skin it," she ordered.

Once we skinned and seasoned the chicken thighs, we moved on to deveining the shrimp.

"I don't know why we couldn't just buy the shrimp already peeled and cleaned," I complained.

"You can," she said, "but I'm not going to pay extra for something I can do myself."

"But *I'm* the one doing all the work. Look at my fingers; they're turning yellow."

"You're just rinsing them off after I devein them," I whined, she shot back. "I'm not the one learning to make *my* gumbo," she said, sassily.

We went back and forth the whole time. "Who told you to add that?" she'd ask. "That's not how you cut sausages!"

"Who cares about the shape as long as they're cut right?"

"You can't make gumbo over there playing with that phone," she snapped.

"Chill out. I'm just replying to a text," I quipped back.

"I'm going to chill out alright, all upside your head," she jested.

The whole experience with my grandmother was a lot of fun and full of love. I gave her a hard time, and she enjoyed having me around. As an adult, I never really spent any one-on-one time with her. Aside from family gatherings, I don't think I ever went to her house just to check on her. The only silver lining to being the reason my parents were evicted was that I now had time to get to know her better.

"You answer me one question," she commanded as she sampled the finished product.

"Okay, what is it?" I asked.

She paused, looking over at me with a sideways glance. "You tell me why you want to lay up with another musty Negro." She wasn't playing around.

I had seconds to respond. My first instinct was to dodge. "What are you talking about?"

"Don't give me that," she said, looking at me sideways from under the glasses perched on her nose. "You can lie to your momma and your daddy, but you can't fool me or the Lord."

"Oh, really? So now you're up there with the Lord?" I teased.

"I sure am. Now answer my question."

I felt like I had nowhere to go, backed into a wall, and she wasn't going to let up until I answered. "Guess the same reason why you want to."

"Get out of my kitchen, you asshole!" she snapped.

I burst out laughing. "Maw-Maw, don't curse!"

"That's not a curse word, boy. Everyone has one. Now put some water on for the rice."

"Nope, you told me to leave your kitchen." I said, still laughing.

"I beg your pardon, boy. God, I love you," she said, shaking her head as I walked out.

CHAPTER 25

By the time my next bi-monthly probation visit rolled around, I'd pretty much adapted to the process, psyching myself into "character" before I went in. I knew now that nothing I said would convince my probation officer I was innocent, so I stopped trying. It was easier to play along.

My appointment was at 10:30 AM on a Wednesday. My car had been repossessed, my parents were both at work, and my mom didn't want me driving my grandmother's car, so I was left with no choice but to take public transportation. The bus ride from my grandmother's house to downtown took about an hour. When I arrived downtown, I confidently walked the few blocks to the probation office. Walking down the street, no one would have guessed I was on the state's sex offender registry. I was dressed in slacks, a long-sleeve shirt, my signature Kenneth Cole shoes, and, of course, the matching bag. I blended right in with everyone else.

The only dress code at the probation office was "no shorts allowed." I could have worn jeans and a T-shirt, but I was determined to prove them wrong. I may have submitted to the restrictions, but I was going to fight for my good character by presenting myself professionally.

The probation building was one of the oldest and ugliest buildings in downtown. It sat like an eyesore among glass skyscrapers, a dingy seven-story brick block that always smelled damp and felt like a walk-in freezer. I checked in with the receptionist downstairs. As he time-stamped my appointment sheet, he called my officer to let her know I was on my way up. I rode the elevator up, praying she wasn't running behind on her appointments. If she were on schedule, the entire visit would take about 20-30 minutes, and I'd be back on my way home.

The elevator doors opened to the lobby and, for the first time ever, my officer was already waiting at the front desk.

"Mr. Harris, come on back to my office," she said.

I was a little shocked. She had never seen me so quickly before, which made me all the more eager to get the visit over with. As we walked to her office, she distractionally told me to have my paperwork ready. I fumbled through my bag, passing the upstairs receptionist. She looked at me, smirked, and grunted, "Hmph," like she already knew the punchline to a joke I hadn't heard yet. I wondered what that was about, but I shrugged it off.

The moment I stepped over the threshold into my probation officer's office, two broad-shouldered men appeared like they'd been hiding in the walls. One stepped forward, blocking the doorway with his hulking frame, a wall of muscle and presence that left no room to pass. The other calmly pulled out a pair of handcuffs, his expression as cold as his movements.

"You're under arrest," he said, like he was reading from a script.

My stomach dropped. My legs went numb.

"Arrest?" I cried. "Arrest for what?"

"Mr. Harris," my probation officer said, voice steady, "you have a warrant for your arrest for felony theft-by-check."

"What check?" I yelled, panic rising. The officers tightened their grip on my arms.

"Well, if you'll let me finish," she said, "the check is made payable to an auto dealership for $3,600, dated 2003." She paused, looking at the two officers before continuing, "As my job requires, I notified the court and the judge. He's not going to revoke your probation because the check was written two years ago, but these men are going to escort you to county jail now."

My mind scrambled, trying to flip through that year like pages in a book. Then it hit me, the "hot check" I'd written for a car down payment. The shady salesperson had convinced me not to worry about having the full amount of the check because some check service company would buy the check, try to collect, then eventually write it off as bad debt.

He left out the part where they could file criminal charges.

"Can you at least let me call my mom?" I pleaded, my voice shaking.

She sighed, then nodded toward the officers. "Sure, why not? Let him call his momma," she muttered.

I gave her my mom's work number, watching as she dialed it, ensuring she pressed the correct buttons. She handed the receiver to me, but she quickly realized she would have to hold it herself, so she put the phone on speaker. I could feel my nerves settle just a little, hearing the friendly receptionist's voice come through the phone.

Embarrassment burned my face. My mom worked at a megachurch, and here her son was, getting re-arrested in his probation officer's office.

"Hey, my wife watches that church on TV," one of the officers said as he searched through the contents of my messenger bag.

"Momma, I'm at my probation officer's office, and I'm being arrested again." My voice shook as I tried to explain, but hearing the fear in my voice, she immediately reassured me.

"It's going to be okay," she said. "I'll come by the jail on my way home from work."

Something shifted in my probation officer's demeanor for just a moment. I saw her head dip, her left hand covering her eyes, as if she momentarily saw me not as a case file but as a frightened son reaching out to his mother for reassurance. The brief glimpse of empathy passed quickly, and she spoke up, her voice more businesslike.

"Okay, Mr. Harris, we're going to end this call," she said. Then, to my mom: "If you have questions, I can answer them. Right now, your son is being taken to Harris County Jail. He's scheduled to see the judge in two days." She hung up before my mom could respond.

The officer who had been rifling through my bag threw my belongings back inside and reached for the arrest papers from my probation officer. The two of them flanked me, one on each side, as we walked toward the elevator. They walked me past the upstairs receptionist. She craned her neck, lips smacking.

"Mmm-hmm," she said, satisfied. Then I understood the grunt. She had known what was coming for me, and she couldn't wait to see it.

I thought we'd walk across the street to the jail, but instead they took a freight elevator down to the basement and led me through the tunnels that connect the buildings. For a brief second, I tried to imagine I was some celebrity being escorted through secret passageways to avoid the paparazzi, but there were no cameras. No fans. Just concrete, fluorescent lights, and the familiar chill of county jail, a place I swore I'd never return to.

Everything was the same: the smell, the cold walls still marked with graffiti and curse words, and, of course, the same rude, demeaning guards. The only thing that had changed was the faces, new people, all waiting to be processed and booked into the system. This time, though, I wasn't as scared. The unknown was no longer a fear of mine. I knew what to expect. I found an empty spot on the cold concrete floor and sat down, just like everyone else, waiting for my name to be called.

The process was long and exhausting. Imagine being in a cold, crowded room, unable to get comfortable because every few minutes someone bumps into you or trips over your legs. Then there's the chaos: people irritated, drunk, high, scared, or deliberately trying to pick fights with the guards. Add to that a disgruntled jailer who hates his job, hates you, and hates everyone else in the room. Every opportunity he gets, he curses you out or calls his gangster co-workers to suit up in riot gear and take someone down, all for no reason other than because they know they can get away with it.

Several hours passed before I made it through the worst part of the booking process: the photo, the fingerprints, and the pre-trial arraignment, where the judge informs you of your charge and sets the bond. That's always the longest part. Afterward, it's changing clothes, a tuberculosis exam, and waiting for housing clarification. My name was called to move on to the next phase, changing clothes.

The officer at the counter, clearly annoyed, bellowed, "Look here, I'm only gonna say this once. Shut the fuck up back there. I'm not repeating myself. Oh, you wanna talk? Fine, I'll send you back to the holding room to keep waiting. Don't make a difference to me." The guys who were talking quickly quieted down, realizing the officer wasn't making idle threats.

"Alright," he continued, "no one gets a jumpsuit until everyone's butt naked. One by one, come get a brown bag, put your free-world clothes in it, and I'll give you a jumpsuit. Unless you've got on white underwear, white socks, and a white tee-shirt, you have to turn in any colored underclothes. You can keep your tennis shoes, no loafers or boots."

Having done this before, I tried to hide my blue underwear under my feet. It worked for about three seconds.

"Hand 'em over, slick guy," the officer said.

"Huh?" I asked, trying to play dumb.

"Don't try to play with me, you sonofabitch. Give me those damn drawls under your feet!"

Busted. I couldn't help but laugh as I put the blue underwear in the bag.

"Come on, youngsta, you gotta do better than that," someone teased me.

After changing, we were moved to classification. That's where the intake officer does a brief interview—gang affiliation, mental status, enemies, that kind of thing. While waiting there, I saw a clock for the first time since arriving at the jail. I couldn't believe my eyes. It was 2:37 AM. I had been in that jail for thirteen and a half hours just to get booked, processed, and assigned housing. What's even crazier? Thirteen hours was considered good timing. One guy, relieved to see the time, said, "Man, we made it before 7 AM. Every other time I've been here, it's taken at least 24 hours to get a bed."

"Wow," I thought to myself, "you've gotta love the diligent service of the Harris County jailers." A few moments later, the intake officer called me to his window. He started asking me questions, but I could barely hear him through the glass partition.

I dislike germs and dirty environments. I'm not a clean freak, but I can only stand so much filth, especially when it's someone else's. So, when I had to speak through the small, muffled speaker in the intake area, I nearly gagged. I could smell the last person's breath. The officer noticed my hesitation. "Look, you can sit there trying to be cute, but I don't plan on yelling. This is jail, it's dirty. What do you expect?"

Reluctantly, I leaned in, holding my breath between answers to avoid inhaling any lingering saliva. The questions were standard:

Are you in a gang? Are you suicidal? Are there any people here who might want to harm you? "No, no, no. Not that I'm aware of," I answered smoothly, until he hit me with the one question I didn't expect.

"Are you a homosexual?"

I hesitated.

A few months earlier, in the same county jail I'd prayed and swore to God I was done being a homosexual. Plus between adjusting to life on probation, living with my parents and now my grandmother, there was no time or way to sneak around and be gay.

"Uh… I'm straight," I answered.

He looked at me with a frown. "Are you sure?"

"Yep, I'm straight."

"Okay," he said, clearly unconvinced. "Three months ago, you were here and you self-identified as a homosexual. Now you're straight?"

"Pretty much?"

"Well, that's on you," he shrugged, "but if you're gay and you go into a straight tank and they try to take advantage of you, that's on you."

"Um, I think I'll be alright," I said, trying to mask my nerves.

"Alright," he warned. "Let me see your wrist so I can put your band on."

I didn't remember the exact tank they assigned me to, but I was relieved when I arrived. At least I could finally rest and clear my mind. Every bunk was full, so a trustee brought me a "low rider," a plastic platform with four small legs, just enough to elevate me off the cold concrete floor. The thin mattress barely offered any comfort, but it was something. I lay there, staring at the dim ceiling, exhausted, barely settled, when a guard called my name for court.

My court-appointed attorney turned out to be the same one from my sex case. My expectations dropped. He hadn't done much for me last time, so what were the chances he'd go above and beyond this time?

"Mr. Harris," he said briskly, "the judge is offering you six months in state jail or the chance to make restitution. What do you want to do?"

I was guilty. No way around it. I'd knowingly written a bad check for $3,600 as a down payment on a car because a salesperson convinced me a collection company would eventually write it off. He had made it sound like a loophole. It turned out to be a felony.

"What do you want to do, Mr. Harris?" my lawyer asked again, slightly frustrated.

"I don't want to go to prison," I said.

"You won't be in prison," he countered. "State jail. It's like an extension of the county jail. Non-violent offenders, under two years. There's even a facility in north Houston." He talked like he was selling me a vacation package.

"I'll make restitution," I told him.

"How?" he asked, exasperated. "You're unemployed."

"I'm looking for work," I argued. "How much time will the judge give me?"

He stepped out to talk with the DA. While he was gone, I started mentally listing people I could call. If thirty-six people loaned me $100 each, that would cover it.

When my lawyer returned, I was nearly done with my list. He asked me, "How do you plan on looking for a job while you're in jail?"

"Don't I have a bond? Can't I bond out?" I asked.

"You do have a bond. It's set at $2,000." That was a lot cheaper than the $10,000 bond I had a few months ago.

"Have you talked to my parents?" I asked.

"Yes, they're in the courtroom," he replied. "Well, ask them if they're going to bail me out," I said, somewhat annoyed. I thought that would have been his first move.

He excused himself again and left me in the holding tank. When he came back, he told me, "The judge is willing to give you a 30-day reset. At the end of the 30 days, if you haven't made restitution, he's going to send you to state jail. Do you understand?"

"Yes, I understand," I said.

"Well, good luck," he said, handing me my court reset papers before quickly moving on to the next case.

"Walker, is there a Walker in here?"

I made my way back to the tank, feeling drained. I was too tired to do anything but sleep, and that's precisely what I did.

"Say, look out, hey you, look out." I heard someone shout as I felt my low rider being kicked. Naturally, I jumped up, as this was my first conversation in general population. Trying to look tough, I asked him what he wanted.

"You Harris?" he asked. "If so, they called you for a visit."

"Oh, Aight, 'preciate you," I replied, trying to sound hip.

My parents sat behind the glass, there "to cheer me up." They told me they'd already talked to a bail bondsman; it would take 12–24 hours, but I'd be getting out. I looked through the partition at my dad and told him he could pawn my television to get back the $200 he'd paid the bail bondsman.

"Son, that's not important right now," my dad said with a weary voice.

I spent the rest of our 15-minute visit explaining my plan to borrow $100 from 36 people.

"Son, man isn't your source," my mom interrupted quickly, cutting me off. "You're going to have to seek the Lord and put your faith in action."

I ended up spending four days in jail. Once I got out, I went into hustle mode. I had 30 days to come up with $ 3,600, so I kicked off what I called the "Freedom Pledge Drive," borrowing a tactic from the televangelists I used to watch growing up. I called everyone I knew, the people I partied with, drank with, shopped with. It didn't seem unreasonable; we'd blow $100–200 over a weekend like it was nothing.

Reality arrived around the fourth call. People were happy to hear my voice, concerned about what I'd been through, shocked at the amount I owed. They thought the "Freedom Pledge Drive" was clever, even funny. They offered suggestions:

"Do a car wash."

"Sell your clothes."

"Sign up for medical research and be a guinea pig."

Lots of ideas. No money. Week one ended. Then week two. My total stayed at zero.

I had no idea what to do. I spent all day at the workforce office applying for jobs and attending interviews, but I couldn't get past the criminal background check. The pressure was on, not only on me, but also on my parents. The air at my grandmother's house was heavy. My parents weren't happy living there, and they were looking for a new place to live. Moving to another apartment would've been easier, but they didn't want to leave me behind at my grandmother's.

Most evenings, my dad would get off work and read his Bible, but his study time was constantly interrupted by my grandmother, who always "innocently" needed a hand with something. My dad was frustrated, but what could he do? My mom, on the other hand, would come home, and as soon as the sun started setting, she and I would sit outside to enjoy the evening air. If the mosquitoes were too bad, we'd sit in her car and talk until it was time for bed.

One evening, she said, "Bernard, I'm not being ugly, rude, or ungrateful, but I'm ready to move. I miss my space. I left my mother's house a long time ago, and I'm not used to living like this." If she wasn't sitting outside, she was confined to the guest room she shared with my dad.

One night, I dropped in on her in her room. She said, "I miss my own food. I miss cooking in my own kitchen."

"You haven't cooked since your children moved out." I teased, trying to cheer her up.

We were all stretched thin, financially, emotionally, spiritually.

Between the hurried move to my grandmother's house, my rearrest, and my release on a 30-day court reset while still owing restitution, my parents and I were under immense pressure. In the midst of all this, my probation officer called to inform me that my grandmother's house was located 750 feet from a school, which violated the 1000-feet child safety zone. This meant I would have to move again. She told me to have a new address ready by my next appointment.

Just in case that flew over your head: I had to move again. No job. No money. No $3,600. No idea where to live. Suddenly, six months in state jail sounded less like punishment and more like a twisted kind of relief. No more searching for an address. No more coming up short. No more watching my parents' lives shrink because of me. In my darkest moments, jail wasn't the worst option. Suicide was. The reality of my situation felt suffocating, and seeing the toll it was taking on my family made the guilt unbearable. I was stuck between a rock and a hard place, or in my case, jail and a bridge to nowhere. I didn't want to hurt them any more than I already had, but the thought of ending it all hovered in the corners of my mind like a shadow.

One evening, my mom and I were sitting in her car, having tea, and she asked me, "Do you remember your glasses?"

"What glasses?" I frowned. "You know I've worn contacts since high school."

She continued, "You remember that time when you kept breaking your glasses, and your daddy said he wasn't buying you another pair?"

"Oh, yes, I remember," I said, finally understanding. My mom was right. In junior high, I couldn't keep up with my glasses; I either kept breaking them or losing them. My dad had grown frustrated with having to replace them one after another. Finally, he told me, "This is your last pair. If you break or lose them, it's on you for the entire school year."

And, sure enough, I broke them too. My dad stuck to his word and refused to buy me a replacement pair of glasses. Every Sunday, the local paper would have a coupon for eyewear, and I'd show it to him, hoping for a different response, and every time, he'd say, "Nope, I meant what I said." My glasses were broken beyond repair. Only the lenses were left. In school, I would hold one lens to my eye with my left hand and take notes with my right. That's how badly I needed glasses.

One Sunday evening at church, the sermon was on faith and speaking to the mountain. That night, before going to bed, I prayed with every drop of faith a seventh grader could muster. I spoke to my "mountain" and commanded, as my pastor had instructed, for it to be removed. In my case, the mountain was my dad's unwillingness to give me another chance. As soon as I finished praying, my dad came into my room and asked, "Did you cut any eyewear coupons today?"

"Yes, sir, I did," I replied.

"Well, keep it. Tomorrow after school, I'm going to get you a new pair of glasses."

Praise the Lord, I thought. I would never forget that prayer, because it was the first real prayer of faith I prayed for myself, and God answered it. My mom reminded me of that miracle and told me it was time for me to go pray again, really pray. I was at a point where only God could help me. I had no other address to submit to the courts, and I surely didn't have $3,600. So, I took my mother's advice and prayed. I prayed the way desperate people pray, on my knees, with my eyes closed and my head bowed.

For those who don't know how to pray, I simply and sincerely told God what I was facing and that I needed His help. There's an old hymn that goes, "It's me, it's me, it's me, oh Lord, standing in the need of prayer."

A few more days passed. Still no money. No job. No address. I had only two options left: faith or death. I wasn't afraid to die, but I couldn't be the cause of any more pain for my parents, so I pushed on in faith. My parents were sure that God would make a way. I wasn't as confident, but I kept believing.

A few days before my court date, which was a Wednesday, my dad and I discussed the $3,600 and facing the reality that I would have to move again. In the middle of the conversation, my dad told me, "I'm going to give you the $3,600."

"Huh, what?" was all I could say.

"Well, not give it to you, loan it to you. I'll get a cash advance off my credit card, but buddy, you're going to have to get a job."

"Daddy, I'm trying," I replied.

"I know you are, son, but you're going to have to get a job," he repeated.

That was the moment I realized how combined faith was really carrying this story. I was the one on probation. I was the one on the registry. I was the one who owed the courts, the car company, and the state, but my parents were the ones giving up their home, squeezing into spare rooms, and now swiping a credit card for $3,600 they didn't have.

I thought judgment was my biggest enemy. I thought the system was. I thought the "victim," the judge, and the probation officer were, but standing in my grandmother's yard, hearing my father say he'd go into debt for me *again*, I realized something else:

Sometimes grace doesn't look like a miracle that drops out of the sky. Sometimes it looks like tired parents, maxed-out credit, shared bedrooms, and quiet prayers whispered from our lips to God's ears.

My faith was shaky. Theirs wasn't, and in that season, their belief in God, and in me, was the only thing standing between my despair and the edge I was ready to step over.

I cannot begin to describe how relieved I was when that money came through. Some people might say, "Your daddy was always going to give you the money; he was just holding out." To them I say, *wrong*. My dad hates credit card debt and absolutely abhors co-signing for anyone. He does everything he can to live debt-free. The only time he swipes a credit card is for travel, and if you catch him on the right day, he *might* let you put a birthday outfit on his department-store card. Other than that, it's cash only, so for him to take out a cash advance on his credit card for me was a miracle, especially since I wasn't working and had no way of repaying him. I couldn't thank him enough. Once again, he was being forced out of his comfort zone. Sure, I was going to pay him back, but how could I ever truly repay him for the non-tangible debt I owed him?

As I mentioned earlier, my parents' support was truly humbling. For years, I lied to them I'd kept my life separate because I didn't want to subject myself to their version of how I should live my life. I wanted to be grown and live on my terms, and I thought being grown meant not needing them. Now here they were, with an open house, open hearts, and an open wallet. That kind of love doesn't have a price tag. To my parents, once again, I say: *thank you.*

• • •

Going to court from the *front* door instead of being escorted through an underground tunnel felt strange. Every other time I'd gone before a judge, it was from a holding cell, through the underground tunnel, and into the courtroom, where I'd sit in the back until the deal was done. Most of the time, when you go to court from jail, you have no idea what's happening. Your lawyer goes back and forth between you and the DA, then brings you out just long enough to sign your name on the plea bargain.

This time, I confidently walked in from the street and boldly sat in the first pew. I wanted a front-row seat to witness the judge's face when I presented both a cashier's check for $3,600 and another for court costs, as instructed by my lawyer.

Court was called to order, and my court-appointed lawyer breezed in, spotted me, and asked with a straight face, "Are you prepared to turn yourself in?"

"Turn myself in for what?" I asked.

"Surely you don't have the—" he started, and before he could finish, I pulled the folder from my bag containing the cashier's checks.

The look on his face said it all: *deer in headlights.*

"I'm not even going to ask how you came up with the money," he muttered, grabbing the checks.

I wanted to slap his hand away like my grandmother would if she caught me sneaking food from a pot. He carried the folder to the prosecutor's desk. Even from where I sat, I could see their bewildered expressions. My lawyer shielded his mouth with the folder, so I couldn't hear what they were saying, but the prosecutor nodded.

When he came back, he said, "You're free to go."

"That's it?" I asked, honestly disappointed. I wanted to watch the judge's reaction.

"Yes, Mr. Harris, that's it. You're free to go. The judge says good luck."

Just like that, a six-month state jail sentence evaporated into a "good luck."

CHAPTER 26

A few days after that court victory, there was no time to celebrate. I still had two mountains left: find a job and keep a roof over my head. The biggest one was stepping up my job search. It was early April 2005. I hadn't earned a paycheck since December 2004. My mom covered my cell phone bill, and my grandmother gave me a little cash for errands so I could get haircuts and small things. I was grateful, but I needed a job.

My probation officer required ten job applications a week. I did twenty or thirty. Looking for a job became my full-time job. I spent at least six hours a day at the Texas Workforce, speaking with employment counselors, attending workshops, and applying to every job I could find that didn't involve a school, daycare, or kids.

Late one Friday afternoon, bored and wanting something that felt like *normal life*, I scrolled through my contacts. For four months straight, my life had been court dates, probation visits, and survival: no social life, no friends, no random phone calls, just crisis management.

I ran through my contacts twice before landing on a familiar name: Jeanie, my former boss at the telecommunications company I had quit back in late 2004. I had started there as a file clerk in Central Records, and my job was easy. My initial boss was on a different floor, and Central Records, where I worked, fell under her umbrella. Records weren't a priority for her, which meant I got paid to do almost nothing. I spent my days surfing the internet, talking on the phone, and taking long lunches at the Galleria. I used to joke with my friends that I was getting a "free check."

That all changed when the company restructured, and I got a new manager: hands-on, detail-oriented, worked long hours, and definitely *not* the "sneak out early" type. She knew Records didn't have real work, so she started giving me small projects. At first, I complained, but over time I realized I was actually learning. She moved me from Records to Accounts Receivable and Billing, and along the way, she became a mentor. I went from doodling in meetings under my previous boss to actually participating. Before I knew it, I was fluent in MS Office and the company's accounting software.

One day, during a meeting about company changes, she started peppering me with questions. I was caught off guard, but she didn't let me get away with pretending. She never tried to embarrass me, and only asked questions she knew I could answer. It felt like she was pushing me, but in a good way. By the time the meeting ended, I felt part of the team, something I never felt under my old boss. During the meeting's intermission while everyone snacked and made small talk, she pulled me aside and asked what I knew about the company. I had no idea what she was talking about. I tried answering her questions with more questions, but she wasn't fooled. Finally, she asked, "How long have you worked here?"

"Uh, almost 2 ½ years," I said, thinking I was in trouble.

"You don't have the slightest idea of what this company actually does, do you?" she asked.

"Well, I know we're a communications company, so I assume it's about phones?"

"Almost," she replied, "but not exactly. When the meeting's over, I want you to stay behind. I'll give you a quick overview of what we do."

I waited after the meeting like a schoolboy in trouble. As I waited, I noticed how much food was left from the meeting. I figured I'd make myself a plate for later. There were always tons of leftovers because most people in the department were either too shy to eat or were trying to watch their weight. Not me. No shame in my game.

Once everyone was gone, my manager took me aside. "Ready?" she asked. "Let's go. Momma's about to take you to school." We went on a tour of the company, floor by floor, where she explained the functions of each department and precisely what communication services we offered.

She took me under her wing, becoming my boss, my teacher, and a kind of office mom. I learned so much from her, both about work and about life. One day, I was snooping through a public folder on a shared drive and found a spreadsheet containing everyone's salary in my department. I sat there, stunned, studying the numbers. At the time, I was earning a decent income, but I couldn't help but wonder why everyone else seemed to be making more. I called my boss, hoping for some answers.

When she arrived at my cubicle, I swung my monitor toward her. "You're not supposed to have access to this folder," she said, laughing when I told her it was public.

"Why is everybody getting paid more than me? We're doing the same work," I asked.

"You know what the difference is?" she said. "They have college degrees. You don't. I suggest you get yourself into school."

Right then, I knew I needed to get back into college. She was the reason I went back to school.

All of that flashed through my mind as I hovered over her name in my phone. Finally, I pressed "call."

Jeanie picked up, gave me the latest gossip about the company, and explained that it was short-staffed because people were leaving amid rumors that it was being sold again. She had hired two temps. I joked, "Why didn't you call *me*?"

"Well, you left me for the fancy hotel job, remember?" she teased. "By the way, how's that job going?"

I hesitated. "Well...I was fired."

"What?" she exclaimed. "My children don't get fired. What happened?"

I took a deep breath, and I told her. All of it. The Christmas Eve arrest, the registry, being denied admission in school, my parents' eviction, and getting re-arrested at my probation appointment.

"No way all of that happened in just four months," she said.

"But it's worse; I can't find a job anywhere, no one will hire me with my background," I explained.

"Lord, that's a shame," she said, "How's your mom holding up? I know she's devastated."

We talked for another hour, and then she said, "Hey, I've got to run to a meeting. Stay by the phone."

I didn't expect much, but I did what she said.

Twenty minutes later, my phone rang. It was Carol from HR.

"Norman, this is Carol in Human Resources. I don't know if you remember me, but I just got an email from Jeanie. She mentioned that you and she discussed your returning to the company. Well, I've been asked to extend an offer to you, if you're interested in returning to the company."

I couldn't believe it. I tried to sound calm. "Yes, I'm interested, but what's the position?"

"It's a temporary role, so no benefits, but you'll be a full-time employee. Instead of going through a temporary company, we're going to hire you as a subcontractor. Does that make sense?"

Honestly, I barely heard the details. "Yes, I'll take it," I said quickly.

We confirmed a Monday start date. As soon as we hung up, I called Jeanie.

"I was waiting for your call!" she laughed.

"Thank you so much. You have no idea how much this means to me."

"You better be ready to work Monday, because there's *a lot* of it, and I'm talking about work, not just any easy stuff. You'll be working overtime," she said.

"I need all that money," I joked. "What about the background check?" I nervously asked.

"I didn't think about that," she admitted. "But I'll figure something out. There has to be a way around that."

"I hope so," I replied.

In one week, I'd gone from staring down six months in state jail to keeping my freedom and landing a job. My dad's sacrifice paid my restitution. Jeanie opened a door I thought was shut forever. For the first time in months, things were looking up.

That evening, when my parents came home from work, we all rejoiced. My dad was especially excited because he knew I could repay him. I spent the whole weekend preparing for my first week back at work, creating a budget, getting my mind right, and selecting my outfits. I was determined to steward every dollar, especially since my employment was temporary.

Monday, I walked into that building like it was the promised land. Walking through the building felt amazing. I was back! I exhaled with relief, and as I stood at the elevator, waiting for it to arrive, I was eager to press that button and ride up. The elevator stopped on every floor and every time the doors opened on a floor, I smiled at strangers and said, "Have a good day!"

When I finally got to the 26th floor, I was ready. Unfortunately, I didn't have a security badge to enter. I was left pacing back and forth in the elevator bank. Usually, I would've gotten impatient and frustrated, but not today. Today, I felt thankful. I thanked God for the open door and for supplying the $3,600. As I paced back and forth, I reflected on how everything had come together.

Finally, a familiar face appeared in the hallway. It was Mary, our department administrator. She smiled and mimicked my waving actions, trying to get her attention to open the door. "What are you doing back here?" she asked.

"My new job didn't work out, so I'm back here, on a temporary assignment," I replied.

"Yeah, this place is a ghost town with all the rumors of layoffs. People are leaving left and right."

"Oh, really?"

"Yep. The only reason I'm still here is that I'm trying to ride it out. I heard the company is offering decent severance packages, so I'm just waiting until my name gets pulled."

She pointed in the direction of the "north side" of the floor.

"Your old group is over there now," she said.

"Thanks, I'm sure I'll find them," I said.

With a "Welcome back," she walked off.

I headed toward the north side of the floor, expecting to find my group. All I saw were empty cubicles. The once vibrant office was now eerily quiet. At one point, my group had been 31 people strong, but now, moving boxes filled the space where my coworkers used to sit. I passed each cube and read the nameplates, reflecting on who had left willingly and who had been laid off. When I passed my old cubicle, I was shocked to see my nameplate still there. Five months had passed since I left, and the floor was unrecognizable.

I ran into one of my coworkers in the breakroom, making coffee. "What happened here?" I asked.

"Jeanie told us you'd be back today. As you can see, everyone's gone," she said. "The vendor is supposed to come pick up the machine any day now", she added when she noticed me staring at the empty vending machine. She led me to my new cubicle.

"Is this it?" I asked, looking around.

"Yep," she and another coworker said in unison. From 31 people down to 8. In just a few months.

In classic Jeanie fashion, there was already a sticky note on my monitor with my login information and a message to check my email, no time wasted. I logged in. Her email said she'd be in around 9:30, and I needed to meet HR at 9:00. She ended the email with, "Don't goof off."

I followed her instructions, but instead of working, my coworkers filled me in on the latest gossip as though I'd never left. I assumed everyone already knew about my situation, but surprisingly, no one asked. I'd only told a couple of people about the details, but the silence made me think the word had already spread.

Before heading to HR, I picked up my badges from Facilities. It felt like the moment of truth. When I arrived at the 25th floor, the executive floor, I was immediately struck by how different it felt now, compared to when the company was thriving. It felt almost hollow, like a memory fading away. The once vibrant, bustling floor was now eerily quiet. The hum of computers gave way to the distant sound of boxes being moved.

Carol and I went through my paperwork, and she explained that I was being hired as a subcontractor. "Unfortunately, as a subcontractor, we can't offer you any benefits," she said, her tone matter-of-fact. "But Jeanie and I discussed increasing the hourly rate to compensate for the difference. Is that okay?"

"Of course, that's perfect!" I replied, trying to keep the edge of excitement from creeping into my voice.

She then pulled out my original HR file and said, "You separated from the company less than six months ago, right?"

"Yes, that's correct."

"Well, company policy states that we don't need to do a drug test or background check for rehires under six months. Looks like you're all set."

I tried to hide my relief. No drug test, no background check. This felt like a miracle. I wanted to shout, "Look at God!" but I managed to keep it together.

"Are you okay?" she asked, noticing my reaction.

"Yeah, I'm fine. I'm just delighted to be back at work. Thank you so much," I said sincerely.

After meeting with Jeanie later that day, I thanked her again for everything, especially for the raise she had given me.

"Yep, I'm too good to you. How many people get a raise before they even start?" she joked. "Speaking of which, what did she say about the background check?"

"You mean you didn't know? You're the all-knowing Jeanie, you know everything that goes on around here."

"True, but I don't get involved in HR business," she said with a shrug. I quickly explained the six-month rehire policy. A relieved smile spread across her face. "Well, that's a relief," she said. Then, without skipping a beat, she raised her hand, motioning for a high-five. "Now let's get to work!"

CHAPTER 27

I arrived at my check-in with my probation officer, paranoid and on edge. As I approached the building, I couldn't help but look over my shoulder. I was on high alert, just in case any undercover officers were waiting for me. I wanted to see them before they saw me. I checked in with the desk clerk downstairs, and everything appeared normal, but of course, everything appeared normal the last time, before I was ambushed.

I checked in downstairs, got clearance to go up, walked to the elevator, and moved to the far left, just in case the undercover officers were planning another surprise ambush. When the doors opened, I did a quick scan. Clear! I stepped inside, riding up in the elevator, comparing this ride to the one in my office building. The difference felt like comparing a Rolls-Royce to a Pinto.

Stepping off the elevator into the waiting area, everything seemed as it should. I checked in with the floor clerk. She grunted, "Hmm, wasn't expecting to see you anymore."

I wanted to respond, "Ma'am, shut up and do your work," but I knew better. This was her turf.

"Have a seat," she said, popping her tongue and pointing toward the chairs.

A few minutes later, my old probation officer appeared with another woman.

"Mr. Harris," she called, "I'm no longer assigned to your case. This is your new officer."

I thought, *Here we go again. Another setup.*

The new officer was tall, with a light brown complexion, green contacts, and eyelashes that looked like she'd glued feathers to her lids, and judging by the smudge, it was evident that her beauty mole was self-made. Her office was decorated wall-to-wall with Tweety Bird: posters, calendars, stickers. Professionalism clearly wasn't her gift.

"Give me a minute to review your file," she said, patting her blonde wig. She patted it a little too hard and it slipped back, exposing the wig cap. I tried to gesture discreetly, but she didn't catch it.

The receptionist popped her head in. "Knock, knock, girl, you busy?"

Obviously, I thought.

"Nah, not really," my new officer responded.

All I could do was roll my eyes.

"Oh, okay," the receptionist continued, "I was just seeing if you had something planned for lunch."

Lunch? It was barely 9 a.m.! I thought, waiting for her to leave.

"Nah, I don't," the officer replied. "Why? You want to go somewhere?"

They spent the next five minutes discussing their food preferences and the distances to nearby restaurants. I couldn't believe how unprofessional and disrespectful they were to my time, but what could I do?

"Girl, let me finish him up and I'll get back with you," the officer said, suddenly paying attention to me reaching for my check-in form, as if it were my fault she couldn't plan her lunch date. Then, her office phone rang. Again, I rolled my eyes at the interruption. "Girl, you silly. Bye!" she said, hanging up the phone. It seemed like the receptionist had informed her about her wig, because as she hung up, she tried adjusting it while I pretended not to notice. I almost wanted to tell her, but I held back.

At last, she looked at my file. "I see here you and your parents petitioned the court about your address?" She looked at me, and I couldn't tell if she was asking a question or stating a fact.

"We didn't petition the court," I explained. "We just wrote a letter asking the judge if he could approve my grandmother's address since it's within the 1000-foot child safety zone. I don't have any other place to go."

"That's petitioning," she corrected. "Did your previous officer give you permission to write to the court?"

"No, ma'am, we did it on our own. We didn't know what else to do, and when I accepted the plea bargain, the judge stressed that only he could amend the terms."

"In the future, do not petition the court," she said sharply. "I am the liaison between the court and you. I will forward your request to the court as I see fit."

I bit my tongue. I'd written that letter in desperation, not rebellion.

"The judge did reduce your child safety zone to 750 feet, allowing you to live with your grandmother," she added.

I exhaled. First the $3,600. Then the job. Now an approved address. One by one, the boulders I'd been pushing started to move.

"Are you still unemployed?" she asked.

"No, I started working a few days ago," I said, ready with the company information. She flipped through my file, looking for the proof I had given my previous officer.

"Well, I don't see anything here. Give me the address again," she said. "You know, you have seven days to update your new home address with the sheriff's office and your job address as well."

"Yes, I know. Both tasks have already been completed." I was confused as to why she was being so sharp with me. She continued her questioning with an attitude, as if she were trying to prove her authority.

"What about treatment?" she asked.

"What about it?" I responded, matching her energy.

"Are there any problems or issues you want to discuss regarding your treatment?"

"Nope," I replied. "I just don't like it."

"It's not for you to like; it's for you to learn your triggers and get the treatment you need."

"Treatment I need? None of this is my fault. My 'victim' lied to me," I said, feeling my emotions rise. I was about to break down when she spoke again, almost too calmly.

"It may not have been your fault, but it's your problem now, and you have to deal with it."

Her words stung, but not in the way I expected. For the first time, someone in the system acknowledged that what happened to me wasn't as black-and-white as the paperwork made it seem.

That day, something subtle but essential shifted. I wasn't suddenly "fixed." The registry didn't vanish. The debt to my dad, the rules, the stigma…they all stayed, but the ground under my feet felt a little less like quicksand. My father had stepped into debt for me, even though he hated it. Jeanie had risked her professional credibility to bring me back. The judge had quietly adjusted a boundary line so I could keep a roof over my head, and now, a probation officer, wig slipping, lunch-planning and all, had admitted what nobody else in the system would say out loud: I might not have been innocent, but I also wasn't the villain the label "registered" painted me as. That one sentence, It may not have been your fault, but it's your problem now, became fuel. Not because I liked it, but because it forced me to decide who I was going to be under all these labels. I couldn't control the registry, the background checks, or the gossip, but I could control how I showed up: in court, at work, in treatment, with my family. From that point forward, whether anyone believed me or not, I was determined to live in a way that proved I wasn't the monster they'd already decided I was.

Before long, my life fell back into a routine, and boredom set in, but this time, it was a welcome respite. It meant my life was returning to normal. I was working full-time again, which felt like a miracle. Thanks to Jeanie and her project, my temporary contract was extended. Whenever something needed to be done, Jeanie volunteered me to complete the task. She had a tactical approach to everything.

Since Central Records, my old department, was now under her direction, she convinced HR and Facilities to let her review the files of departing employees to decide what should be shredded and what should be archived. She was also in charge of clearing out empty cubicles and offices. Guess who got assigned to that part.

There were days Jeanie would email me lists of cubicles to clean, files to pack, and equipment to prepare for IT retrieval. As the company's executives realized they were leasing floors with less than 20% occupancy, they decided to consolidate everyone into a smaller area and sublet the unused floors. Jeanie, always involved, oversaw the moving process and the budget. To save the company money, she volunteered her team to assist with the move. The team being her and me. One day, Jeanie showed up in torn jeans and beat-up tennis shoes. "Today, you and I are moving file cabinets, boxes, and microwaves," she said.

At first, I was annoyed and questioned her, "Why are you volunteering me to be a mover? We work in finance!"

She put down a moving box, looked me dead in the eye, and said, "My boss wanted to pull your contract weeks ago. He said billing was slow, and you were no longer needed. Therefore, I must justify keeping you on payroll. To do that, I need to keep you busy. Don't you want to pay your dad back?"

I nodded.

"Well, help me load this box on the dolly and get back to work."

I never complained again. Some days I spent the morning at a desk entering invoices and the afternoon hauling boxes and cleaning offices. It wasn't all bad. In some of the executive offices we found expensive gadgets and personal items abandoned like a corporate estate sale. Work gave me purpose. Paying my dad back gave me a goal, and for a while, that was enough.

Outside of work, life was scheduled around the system. I had my monthly probation visits, which had become routine. The probation appointments rarely lasted longer than fifteen minutes. The longest part was sitting in the waiting room while my officer finished whatever she was doing. More than once, I'd walk in and see her portable DVD player paused, movie ready to resume the second I left. I'd think, *This lady is watching movies while I'm taking off work to be here.* I stopped fighting her authority, but it was apparent that my time, my job, and my schedule meant nothing to her.

Thankfully, Jeanie understood. On probation days, she gave me a two-hour lunch so I could get downtown and back without losing pay. Treatment was $35 a week, which I could finally afford. In my heart, I still didn't believe I was a sex offender or had deviant proclivities, but I went through the motions and actively participated in class. If I'm being honest, there were times I thought I was better than some of my classmates. Not in terms of financial status, but because the facts around our cases were entirely different.

My facilitator recognized this and moved me to a class with participants of a similar age. I felt a little more at ease, but despite being in the same age group, their victims' ages ranged from 5 to 14. It was hard for me not to judge them, but some of their stories didn't make sense to me. *You mistook a twelve-year-old for an eighteen-year-old?* I kept my opinions to myself, though, and focused on the coursework and assignments. I realized that, regardless of whether I had an assignment to present, I still had to pay the $35 every week. The quickest way through the program was to present every week, so I treated it like a job: do the homework, work ahead, always be ready in case someone else wasn't prepared to present.

At first, I didn't agree with the treatment; naturally, I felt like I didn't belong there. The assignments on thinking errors, passive-aggressive behavior, control, and manipulation forced me to look at patterns in my everyday relationships. I started seeing places I could actually grow.

Most importantly, I learned to empathize with my victim. I had always felt remorse for his mom and younger sister, for having to witness their son/brother caught in a sexual act. To me, they were the victims. Their Christmas was ruined. Even though I blamed him for being stuck in this predicament, I came to see my role and how my choices also contributed to the situation.

My facilitator kept insisting there were signs he was underage and that I chose to ignore them. I clung to the fact that his profile said eighteen and he told me he was eighteen. In my mind, that was the end of it. Still, I adopted a simple philosophy to get through class: *If it doesn't apply, let it fly.* I took what I could use, left what I couldn't, and kept turning in homework. Even if I didn't fully buy the process, the process was still changing me.

CHAPTER 28

That became my life: work, treatment, and monthly probation visits. I didn't have much of a social life, but I'd meet up with my friends Tonya and Monique for dinner or ride with them while they ran errands. I previously mentioned how my friends worked hard, but they also partied harder. Now that I was on probation, I couldn't afford to hang out or risk violating the conditions of my plea agreement. There was no fun being the only sober one, watching my friends take shots and down mixed drinks.

I pulled away from my gay friends and the scene altogether. Inside, I knew I wasn't straight, but I had made a promise to God, and I was trying to keep it.

The truth was simpler: I lived with my parents. Sneaking out to hang with my gay friends wasn't realistic. My parents considered them good people, but they also viewed them as distractions from my walk with the Lord. After everything I'd put my parents through, denying who I was felt like the least I could do to honor their sacrifices. I also dreaded being confronted by them. I didn't want another speech or scripture marathon. And a part of me wondered if they were right, maybe the $3,600 miracle, my old job returning, and my grandmother's address being approved were all tied to me not living what they considered a "sinful" life.

I didn't want to violate my probation, nor did I want to disappoint my parents any further. I didn't want to tempt fate, so I decided to play it straight (no pun intended). I spent my weekends renting movies and ordering my favorite wing combo—five barbecue and five lemon pepper. It was boring and lonely, but it felt safe. I felt I had no other choice. The routine became my escape from the chaos, a small bubble of comfort in an otherwise uncertain and overwhelming world. While everyone else seemed to be out living their lives out loud, I stayed in the quiet, clinging to the small comforts that helped me make it through each day. Security came at the cost of myself.

One Sunday at church, while browsing through the weekly announcements, I came across information about the revamped college and young adult ministry. There were weekly events where participants would meet at the church and then go out to eat. To make the event lively, each participant randomly pulled a number, and each number corresponded to a specific restaurant. It was a great way to meet new people each week. After dinner, everyone would meet back at the church for board games, dessert, and drinks (coffee, tea, and soda, of course). Desperately needing some form of social life, I decided to attend the event.

I arrived, pulled my number, and met with my group and we headed to the restaurant. We sat around doing introductions and icebreakers until the waitress came for drink orders. Everyone at the table ordered water, soda, or tea .However, one member of our group broke tradition and ordered a virgin daiquiri, explaining that she liked the slush-like taste of the drink. In my opinion, no big deal, but judging by the looks around the table, she might as well have ordered a line of shots and a side of adultery.

Noticing her discomfort, I spoke up. "It's a virgin daiquiri, meaning non-alcoholic. Relax."

"True, but the Bible warns us to refrain from the appearance of evil" (1 Thessalonians 5:22), someone preached from across the table. Another person chimed in, "We are representing the church; it doesn't look right." The rest of the table agreed, passing judgment.

I couldn't take it. "Look, I grew up in this church and have been a member all my life. I feel you guys are trying too hard. Your holier-than-thou attitude is unbecoming of the values taught here. We're here to meet new people and have fun, so once again, relax."

An awkward silence fell over the table, but we ate our food, all of us pretending to enjoy ourselves.

Upon arriving back at church, I got the same vibe from everyone. Maybe I was wrong, but it felt like everyone thought that because we were at church, we had to be constantly "saved and sanctified." Every conversation felt forced, with phrases like 'Praise the

Lord, Amen this, God is good that.' It didn't feel natural. Surely, you could be a Christian and have fun, but clearly, these young adults hadn't gotten the memo, or maybe, I thought, I wasn't as "saved and sanctified" as I believed.

The next weekend, I skipped the ministry event, rented a movie, and ordered my wings. I couldn't deny myself that small comfort anymore. It wasn't exciting, but at least it was honest.

CHAPTER 29

By early August 2005, life had settled into a steady rhythm. With the fall semester approaching, I wanted to go back to school. I called campus police to check on my appeal to re-enroll and, to my surprise, the university had approved it. I could come back, but on probation. I had to maintain at least a C average and report to campus police at the start and end of every semester.

During my monthly probation visit, my officer informed me it was time to schedule my first polygraph test. She explained that there were three types of polygraph tests. The first was an instant offense test, specifically designed to focus on my case and determine if I had denied or omitted any information. She didn't recommend I take this one, as I never denied having sex with the victim. The second was a sexual history test, concentrating on past and present sexual encounters to identify any other victims or history of deviant behavior. The third was the monitoring version, which I would take. This version focused on questions relating to the terms and conditions of my probation to see if I had violated any stipulations.

The cost was $300…out of my pocket.

I couldn't understand the point. Polygraphs aren't admissible in court. Passing doesn't prove innocence, but failing can absolutely be used against you. To me, the only purpose was to scare people into confessing and to generate revenue for the county. But I didn't have a choice, so I took the referral slip for the administrator who would administer my test.

A week later, I arrived for my first polygraph test. I was nervous and unsure of what to expect. All I could picture was sitting in an empty, dark room under a glaring light, like something out of a TV show. A member of my treatment group advised me to regulate my breathing by taking deep breaths and exhaling slowly between each question. He also suggested I take a muscle relaxer to stay calm, but I decided against it. I had nothing to hide, so I figured I'd breathe and answer the questions.

The administrator was a pale, ghostly-looking man. I had never seen someone so white. He looked like he had never seen daylight. Tall with strikingly clear blue eyes, he wore a pressed white Oxford shirt, perfectly creased slacks, and shoes that shone as brightly as his face. His hands were freshly manicured, buffed, not polished. His entire appearance was magazine-cover worthy. Between the manicured hands and the $300 price tag, I could see he was doing just fine.

His office was minimal: mahogany desk, laptop, and the machine.

He shook my hand and briefly explained the testing procedures to me. He was going to wrap a wire around my chest and attach another to my middle finger and one around my arm like a blood pressure cuff. He would ask me a series of questions, repeating them in a different order. My only job was to answer "yes" or "no." No explanations, no stories.

"Are you ready to start the test?" he asked.

"Yes, I guess so."

He shook his head in disapproval and repeated his question, "Are you ready to start the test?"

"Yes."

"Good, very good."

He attached the wires and instructed me to relax, to stay as still as possible. I did the opposite. I sat straight up in the chair, and the more I tried not to move, the more I did. Out of nowhere, my leg would itch, or something seemed to get in my eye, making it harder to stay still. My eyes started to sting from trying not to blink. Despite my best efforts to regulate my breathing, I struggled for air.

Very patiently, he told me to relax. "Everything will be fine. As long as you're truthful."

He started with easy questions to establish a baseline.

"Is your name Norman Harris?"

"Yes."

"Do you live in Houston?"

"Yes."

"Are you sitting down?"

"Yes."

Once I settled, he said, "I'm going to start the test."

"Have you had any contact with your victim?"

"No."

"Have you been alone with any person under 17 years old?"

"No."

"Have you accessed the internet?"

"No."

"Have you consumed any drugs or alcohol?"

"No."

"Have you viewed any pornography?"

"No."

"Have you had sexual contact with anyone under the age of 17 years?"

"No."

He asked about 10 questions in total, all of which I answered "no." After finishing, he released the pressure cuff.

"Very good. You can relax now."

Before I could fully relax, he was ready to begin again. "Remember, these are the same questions, just in a different order."

I answered "no" to each question again, just like I had before.

"This concludes the test," he said. "Now I'll analyze the data to see if you were being honest."

He studied the graphs for a few minutes, then paused. He looked at me and asked, "Is there anything you would like to tell me?"

Fear and alarm flashed through me, but I tried to hide it. Did I fail the test? I wanted to ask, but I decided to stay calm and respond, "No."

"Are you sure?" he pressed, frowning.

"Yes."

"Very good," he said, starting to smile. "Your test showed no deception. You passed."

The words hit me like a weight lifting off my chest. It felt like music to my ears. For a split second, I almost couldn't believe it. A rush of relief flooded through me as the tension I was carrying melted away. He unhooked all the wires, his voice fading into the background as my mind raced. I couldn't shake the feeling that I had somehow cheated the system, like I had just dodged a bullet. The battle wasn't over, but for now, I had won that round.

Technically, I had been online, but only for job searches. My mom summed it up this way: "You passed because God gave you grace. He knew you had to be online for work. If you'd been on there for anything else, the test might've said something different."

Maybe she was right. Maybe she wasn't. Either way, I passed, and I wasn't going to waste time dissecting it.

Later that week I was on the phone with Daymond. We hadn't seen each other in a while, and I missed him. Daymond is my best friend, for real, ride-or-die. I could write a whole book about our adventures. I call him my best audience because I've performed every one-man show, spoken-word set, monologue, and concert in front of him. He always laughs and joins in. Anyone else would've had me committed; he just calls me crazy and keeps it moving.

While we were catching up, he asked if I would attend his birthday party at the end of August. "Well, you know I don't have a car," I responded, already reaching for excuses.

"Shut up, Norman, you know I'm going to pick you up. Or, do you not want to come? I know you're trying to play straight, but it's my birthday."

"Goose (don't tell him I told you his nickname), you know I want to, but my parents aren't going for that."

"You're grown; you can't let them dictate your life forever."

"Easy for you to say, you don't live with your parents. I'll call you in a few days to let you know for sure. I promise."

"Sure, whatever, tramp," he joked before hanging up the phone.

Of course I wanted to go. Weeks of wings, boredom, and waiting on Netflix to mail me my next three DVDs like a lifeline had me crawling the walls.I had new clothes, a job, and a desperate need to see and be seen. I decided to hint around with my parents and sort of test the water, gauging the chances of them letting me go. I was 24 years old, so technically, I could have gone regardless, but I didn't want the lecture or the tension. Pretending to still be on the phone, I walked into the living room where my parents were watching television.

"Okay, bye, I'll talk to you later," I said, making sure they heard me.

"Who was that?" my mother asked.

Yes, my plan was working. "It was just Daymond," I said nonchalantly.

My dad, overhearing, looked up and frowned. Let me set the record straight: my dad didn't hate Daymond. He would eventually admit that Daymond was a good friend. My dad's position on homosexuality, however, was firm. He 100% believed it was a sin. His disdain wasn't personal toward Daymond or anyone else. It was a deeply rooted belief he held.

"Oh, what was he talking about?" my mom asked.

"Nothing much, just seeing how I was doing," I replied. I wasn't really lying.

"Son, I don't see why you're holding on to that friendship," my dad injected.

Daymond and I had been through thick and thin, things my dad would never understand, and I tried to explain and defend my friendship. "Son, if you're trying to change some things, you just have to let go," my dad said.

I almost blurted out, "I'm done trying to change," but I knew better. The truth was, I had no problem with being gay. Sure, I made a promise to God that I was trying to keep. I could change things like slowing down, not partying as much, and eliminating casual sex, but at this point, I only wanted to change for my parents, not for myself. I didn't want to respond to his comment about letting go, so I tried changing the subject.

"His birthday is coming up, and he's having a little get-together," I said, attempting to minimize the significance of his party.

"Oh, okay," my mom said, switching her attention back to the television.

My dad, however, knew exactly where I was going. "You're not thinking about going, are you?"

"Well, I want to."

"Son, that's going to pull you off track. God has been working in your life, and you don't want to tie His hands," he continued.

I wanted to tell him, "Point taken," but instead, I chose to go to my room. I couldn't tell Daymond I wouldn't be able to attend his birthday, so I texted him instead. On the night of his party, he sent me a text: "Wish you were here. Everyone says hi. I understand." His grace just made me feel worse. I wasn't only on probation with the court. I was on probation with my parents and, in my own mind, with God.

CHAPTER 30

As the saying goes, all good things must come to an end. My time with Jeanie ended in mid-September 2005. I couldn't even be mad. She'd already stretched that temporary contract as far as it could go. I qualified for unemployment, so at least I had some income. Outside of my dad's loan, probation fees, treatment, and basic living costs, I didn't have many bills. Financially, I was steady.

I was also back in school and taking it seriously this time. After almost losing the chance to get a degree, I had a new respect for education. I participated in class discussions, joined study groups, and, believe it or not, did my homework.

Socially, I kept things light. Sometimes my study group met at restaurants to study over appetizers. I even treated myself to solo movie dates—always matinees, when most kids were in school, because I still wasn't sure how movie theaters fit into the child-safety zone rules. When I asked my officer about the mall, she said I could go as long as I entered through major department stores with separate entrances from the food court and the general mall area would be okay.

That didn't make much sense to me. For one, I didn't shop at major department stores; for two, there were kids everywhere in the mall, but I followed the guidelines and, when in doubt, I exercised my judgment. I didn't see myself as a pedophile or someone with deviant tendencies, so I had to find a way to both comply with the law and still live some kind of life. So far, I'd managed to do both.

I was progressing in treatment, though I still wasn't comfortable presenting myself as a "sex offender" during our weekly introductions. I'd cringe when one of my groupmates would say things like "us sex offenders" or "people like us." The statements made me sick to my stomach, and I had to resist the urge to ask not to be included in those generalizations.

But I kept my mouth shut. I knew if I pushed back too openly, it would be labeled "resistance to treatment," and that could be used against me. I'd cross my fingers under the table in defiance each time I had to identify as a sex offender, a silent protest only God and I knew about, and kept turning in my assignments. My goal wasn't to become the poster child for treatment. My goal was to finish the book, finish the program, and finish probation.

During treatment, I'd hear horror stories from my group members about their experiences with their probation officers. Thankfully, I wasn't having major problems with mine. I checked in once a month; she would review my file, go over my treatment summary, and schedule my next appointment. My biggest complaint was that she took her sweet time. Appointments never started on time, but there was nothing I could do about it.

Around Halloween, the outside world made sure I couldn't forget my label. News stations ran endless specials on how to "keep kids safe from predators." Every segment seemed to include a reminder and warning to be vigilant and on the lookout for sex offenders.They reported on the restrictions placed on "us"—curfews, rules about porch lights being turned off, bans on passing out candy or even putting up Halloween decorations.My probation officer had me sign an affidavit acknowledging I had to be home all night and couldn't turn on my porch light until after 10 p.m. She warned me that field officers would conduct random checks and that if I wasn't home, a warrant would be issued immediately.

To me, it felt like overkill.

Growing up, my family didn't celebrate Halloween like that anyway, but we did celebrate Hallelujah Night at the church. I don't remember ever going trick-or-treating. I do recall carving a pumpkin as a family once or twice. The best part of Halloween was buying discounted candy the days after.

Because of all the media coverage on sex offenders, I nervously anticipated whether my grandmother's house would be on the list for a routine check-in. I spent Halloween evening ping-ponging between the living room and the kitchen window, watching the news and listening for vans. Some stations even sent reporters door-to-door to offenders' houses for their own "compliance checks." I couldn't tell if they cared about safety or just wanted a sensational story. In the end, my street stayed quiet. No trick-or-treaters, no cops, no news vans. At 10:10 p.m., I turned on the porch light, exhaled, and went to bed. Living under suspicion meant even a quiet night felt like a win.

As soon as Halloween passed, treatment shifted into holiday mode. According to our therapist, the holiday season is high-risk. Some of my groupmates had restrictions and couldn't be with their families at all, which made loneliness and depression dangerous. For those of us who *could* attend family gatherings, the question was: "How will you handle being around minors?" Our assignment was to list ten hypothetical situations and write out exit plans or thought-shift strategies for each one. My real plan was simple: keep looking for a job. That's where all my mental energy was anyway. Unemployment checks were still coming, but I knew they wouldn't last forever.

In mid-November, I was on the phone with Daymond, laughing about the "good ole days," when he told me one of our friends was coming back to town for Thanksgiving and throwing a birthday house party near my grandmother's house.

"Oh really? When is it? I might bless y'all with my presence," I joked.

"Yeah, right. Don't play. You don't hang with us anymore, remember?"

"It's not like that," I tried to explain. "It's hard. You just don't understand."

"You can't keep trying to play straight for your parents forever. You have to want to change for *you*, not for them."

"It's not that easy. I'm dependent on them right now. Their house, their rules. Plus, I promised God."

"Chile, don't you think God already knew you weren't going to keep that promise? You made that promise because you were scared in a jail cell. I can't tell you how to live your life. Only God and you know what's in your heart, but you can't be afraid of your parents forever. This is your life. However you decide to live, you can count on me being there for you, tramp."

Deep down, I knew he was right. I was living scared…of my parents, of the court, of God, and of myself, but fear didn't change the reality that I still lived under my parents' roof and under my parents' rules.

I still wanted to go to that party.

Lying didn't feel like my best option, but it felt like my only one. At twenty-four, I was back to using teenage tactics. I knew lying was disrespectful, especially after all I'd put them through. I didn't want to disappoint them. I knew if I presented the idea of being gay or wanting to hang out with my gay friends, it would be a disappointment to my parents and would be met with disapproval.

I came up with a plan. The week of the party, I started dropping the host's name—a woman—into casual conversation.

"I talked to my friend Keisha today," I told my mom.

"Oh, who's that?"

"Some girl I know through Tonya and Monique. She's going to forward my résumé to her HR department." That part was true.

The next day: "I was on the phone with Keisha again. She bought a house in that new subdivision up the street. She said I should come see it sometime." I kept that up all week.

"Hey, Mom, Keisha is having a small get-together at her house tonight. Can I go?"

"Are you sure you need to be around that environment?" she asked, her concern obvious.

"It's nothing big, just a little housewarming," I said, downplaying it. It was technically true—it was a house party at Keisha's. I just left out that it was for my gay friend's birthday.

"Well, we know you can't stay cooped up all day. Go ahead and go, but remember, you're on probation."

I didn't wait for any extra commentary. I grabbed my phone and texted Daymond: *Bitch, I'll be there.*

"How'd you pull that off?" he replied.

"Same way I did when I was younger and told them I was going to your sister's house."

"That's a shame, Norman. You need a ride?"

"Nah, Granny's letting me use her car since it's close."

Driving over, I was paranoid. I kept expecting sirens, headlights, something. I couldn't shake the feeling that something bad was going to happen. I rationalized my thoughts, trying to assure myself nothing would go wrong. It wasn't as if I were sneaking; I had my parents' approval. Besides, *I'm grown*, I told myself. I was going to Keisha's, as I said. I just conveniently omitted that it was in celebration of a gay friend.

It took only five minutes to get to the party. By the time I reached the front door, I was over my fears and anxiety and ready to get the party started. I loved house parties. Unlike packed clubs, they were relaxed, and you could truly converse and enjoy yourself. It didn't take long for me to work the room. If you didn't know any better, you might have thought I was hosting the party. I loved attention, and that's what made me shine at these types of events.

People rushed me with hugs and questions. "Oh my God, how have you been?" "I heard what happened—do you want me to burn his house down?" Their jokes and outrage made me feel seen, covered, loved. For the first time in a long while, I was surrounded by people who weren't judging me, just *holding* me with their presence. I was reminded of how much my friends cared.

There was no bartender, so naturally, I slid behind the counter. I'm no mixologist, but I can mix a drink that gets you where you're going.

Around midnight, I turned to Daymond. "You want to hit the club?"

"You already know the answer," he said.

"Oh really?" I raised an eyebrow, feigning shock.

"I already know you're not going. I'm not wasting my time asking."

"Says who? You don't know what I have planned."

"Don't play, Norman."

"I got that gin in my system, somebody's gonna be my victim!" I said, snapping my fingers in the air to a New Orleans bounce track.

He knew I was serious. "Alright, let's hit it."

Standing in line for the club felt like stepping back into my old life. It had only been eleven months, but it felt like years. I was buzzing, part nerves, part excitement. Daymond kept telling me to calm down, comparing me to an underage queen sneaking into the club for the first time.

As we neared the door, I blurted, "What if my probation officer is in there?"

"Are you serious?" he laughed. "Why would your probation officer be here? Is she a lesbian?"

"I don't know. What if she's hanging with gay friends or something?"

"Does she have gay friends, Norman?"

"Again, I don't know," I said, my voice filled with unease. He chuckled at my heightened sense of paranoia. "Easy for you to laugh," I shot back, "you're not on probation."

He just smiled and shrugged. "True, but if you're this scared, maybe you shouldn't have come in the first place."

He had a point, but fear wasn't enough to send me home. Not that night.

As soon as the neon lights and lasers hit my eyes, the fog rolled over the dance floor, and the bass shook my chest, everything else faded. I felt...home. I hadn't realized how much I missed the club until I was back in it. Instantly, all the drunken memories flooded my mind, the good, the bad, the sloppy, reminding me of the fun I used to have and who I used to be.

Daymond and I did our infamous "club walk-through." Every group of friends has its version of this. It's walking through the club as if you own it. It's all about letting your presence be known. You don't make eye contact on the first walk. You glide. You're grand. You're the moment. As NeNe Leakes would say, "I have arrived, and the spotlight is on me, honey."

You don't stop to talk to anyone on your first walk. If someone tries to grab your attention or starts talking to you, you smile vaguely or act like you didn't see them. When they call you out for acting all high and mighty, you brush it off with an "Oh, I didn't even notice you," and keep moving, like you're on a mission. We had it down to a science. Our route: walk the perimeter of the dance floor, pass the bar, through the patio doors, up the stairs, past the second-floor bar, down the stairs, and back to the bar downstairs. We'd been doing this routine so long it was muscle memory.

People were shocked to see me.

"Where have you been hiding?"

"They said you caught those alphabets."

"Bitch, were you really in jail?"

I tried to keep it cute and moving, just enough shade to stay mysterious, just enough warmth to stay loved, but everyone kept stopping me, wanting to know where I'd been. The idea was to be slightly shady but graceful, like walking down the red carpet. I received a lot of attention that night. Old acquaintances telling me how much they missed me or asking when I was having another house party. There were also a few new faces, people who thought I was a new guy or an out-of-towner, since it'd been 11 months since I'd last been to a club. I worked that to my advantage.

"Nothing like that," I'd say. "Just been going through some things and needed to clear my head."

Daymond and I danced, laughed, and showed out, even breaking into our ridiculous "white girl" routine to "Salt Shaker" by Lil Jon and the Eastside Boyz. At one point he leaned into my ear and yelled over the music, "You can take the queen out the club, but you can't take the club out the queen. Welcome back, bitch!"

By the time I crept into my grandmother's house, it was late. The alarm chimed "front door" loud enough to wake the dead, and I held my breath, waiting for someone to flip on a light. Nothing. Everyone stayed asleep. I closed my door and finally exhaled. I'd gotten away with it.

I sat on my bed, ripped open my Jack-in-the-Box bag, and inhaled my Sourdough Jack, egg rolls, and bacon cheddar potato wedges with a large orange soda. Then I passed out, full and exhausted, the scent of the club still clinging to my clothes. For one night, I had been my old self again, and nobody knew but me.

As 2005 came to a close, I spent New Year's Eve at home with my parents and grandmother. No parties, no countdown, no kiss at midnight. They were all asleep long before midnight. I sat alone in my room, letting the year replay in my mind.

I thought about being released from jail, registering as a sex offender, getting fired, getting my parents evicted, being suspended from school, going back to jail, starting treatment, facing rejection after rejection, taking a polygraph, living with loneliness and shame, all from one night with someone who lied about his age.

But I also thought about the miracles. My grandmother opening her home. Jeanie bringing me back to work. My dad loaned me $3,600 he didn't really have. Being approved for unemployment. Getting back into school. Somehow, between my bad decisions and everyone else's grace, I'd survived the first year of probation.

With God's favor, my parents' love, and a stubbornly determined streak a mile wide, I had made it through year one.

Only six more to go.

To mark the event, I threw a small barbecue, just my parents, my grandmother, my aunt, Monique, and Tonya. Nothing big, just burgers, laughter, and a quiet sense that I'd crossed some invisible line. The first year had been the hardest. My whole life had been flipped upside down, and now I was walking around with a permanent X on my back: Sex Offender. You can't imagine how heavy those two words feel until they're attached to your name.

Once the plates were thrown away and everyone headed home, reality tapped me on the shoulder. Celebration over. Time to get back to business. I needed a job.

CHAPTER 31

I went after work like it owed me back pay. Every day I camped out at the Texas Workforce Commission: applying for jobs, attending job fairs, sitting through résumé workshops, and practicing mock interviews.

One day at TWC, a Marine recruiter approached me, full of confidence and a sales pitch. I cut him off early.

"Just so you know, I'm on felony deferred probation," I said. I figured I'd save him some time.

"We work with certain convictions," he replied. "What was your charge?"

"Sexual assault of a child," I said, boldly, for the first time.

His face fell. "Yeah, um, we won't be able to do anything with that. Thanks for your time."

I walked away thinking, *Well, at least my background is good for shutting down a sales pitch.*

My probation officer signed me up for a department-sponsored job fair, which turned out to be a joke. The material was outdated and basic. Everyone in the room looked like they'd rather be anywhere else. I remember sitting there thinking, *I could teach this better than they can.*

At TWC, I started helping other job seekers fill out applications, polish résumés, and complete online assessments. Before long, people were asking *me* for help instead of waiting on a job coach. One woman even suggested they should hire me. I didn't think I was doing anything special, just using what I'd learned in high school and a few semesters of college, but it felt good to be useful to someone.

Despite my efforts, I couldn't land anything for myself. I was averaging three to five interviews a week, and the script was always the same:

"I hate that happened to you, but unfortunately…we can't move forward. We wish you the best of luck."

No matter how I told my story, the felony conviction was a wall I couldn't climb. I knew I was qualified, but the sentence followed me everywhere. It was frustrating. I understood employers have the right to choose who they hire, but it felt like discrimination dressed up as "policy." People say they believe in second chances until they're the ones who have to give it. I wasn't giving up. I couldn't.

Even though I wasn't working, I stayed busy. I was enrolled in night and weekend classes to complete my associate's degree. Not working gave me more time to focus on my studies, and I devoted myself to my homework, determined to succeed. I couldn't control my background, but I could control my GPA.

Meanwhile, my mother stayed on her own mission: to find a new place to live. She'd been ready to leave my grandmother's house the day we moved in. By February 2006, she'd had enough. Despite not wanting to leave me behind, my parents packed up and moved out. As Daymond would say, they "hit it."

Now it was just my grandmother and me. In some ways, I was more excited about my parents moving out than they were. At this point, my grandmother was working as a Home Healthcare Provider from 4 p.m. to 12 a.m. I would often tease her, "How are you taking care of patients when you need someone to take care of you?" She always had a witty comeback. "I do have a provider, in fact, I have two," she'd say.

"Oh really, please tell," I'd respond.

"I have Jesus, and I have you. Now go get me some water."

And she wasn't wrong. Since I still wasn't working, I became her driver and errand-runner. I handled her banking, took her grocery shopping, and sat with her at doctor's appointments. She was the worst backseat driver, "Did you signal? Why are you driving so close behind that truck? The other lane is moving!" On and on it went. I never minded being her chauffeur. She was too busy praying and holding onto the door, "Lord, please let me get there in one piece."

While she was at work, I had the house to myself. I loved the quiet, but I also missed having true freedom. The upside of my parents moving out was that I could hang with Daymond more without feeling like I was sneaking out of a dorm.

Friday nights, Daymond would come to pick me up, and by the time my grandmother came home from her shift, I'd be well on my way to the club. Saturdays were routine: help her pick greens, watch *Wheel of Fortune*, and by the time the show ended, she'd be in bed, giving me the car for the night.

The hardest part of that double life was dragging myself to church on Sunday after two hours of sleep, then heading straight to treatment from 1 to 2 p.m. I'd sit in group with club smoke still in my clothes, talking about victim empathy and relapse prevention. Somehow, both pieces of me existed side by side.

Treatment was going well, and after my first year, I was voted into Phase II where the focus was developing empathy for victims. Emotionally, I still struggled to see him as a victim in the way the program wanted. My heart always went first to his mom and sister. Still, one assignment got under my skin in a way I didn't expect.

The assignment required me to create 40 flashcards, each one detailing a loss that my victim had experienced because of me. These weren't supposed to be direct, personal reflections since I couldn't reach out to him, but I did my best to step into his shoes. I thought about the inner turmoil I'd faced at 16, hiding my attraction to men from my family, questioning whether my feelings were wrong, or worse, sinful.

As I worked on the assignment, something shifted. I started to see him less as the victim who lied to me and more as a teenager drowning in his own confusion. I began to feel more profound empathy for him. I pictured the shame he must have felt when his mother walked in, the terror of being outed in the worst possible way, the pain of being caught in something so deeply personal. I thought about the comfort he might have sought, engaging with men at that age, the same way I had sought refuge in my private world.

Did I *feel* like I'd taken advantage of him? No. I also knew saying that out loud could be counted as "not accepting responsibility," and that could threaten my progress, or my freedom. So, for one hour every Sunday, I put on the mask they needed to see. I expressed empathy, even when I had to work to feel it. It wasn't fully honest, but it was survival.

My monthly probation visits were generally smooth. The biggest concern my officer had was that I wasn't employed; however, as long as I submitted a job search log showing that I had completed a minimum of 10 applications or submitted resumes, she considered me compliant. My "random" drug test came every three months, but drugs weren't my thing; alcohol was. To play it safe, I stopped drinking after Sunday, the week of my office visit.

The real battle was still work. No matter how many interviews I went to, my record shut the door. No company was willing to hire me once they discovered my criminal record.

By mid-March 2006, I'd lost count of rejection letters. Part of me wanted to quit trying altogether. It felt ridiculous to keep banging on doors that never opened. To cope, I turned the process into a game. I pretended interviews were talk-show appearances and I was the celebrity guest promoting my latest project. I had my lines memorized: my experience, my strengths, my polished "tell me about a time when…" stories. I knew when to joke and when to get serious. If they weren't going to give me a job, I was at least going to give them a performance.

One interview stands out. The interviewer was gay, and the whole time I felt like he was flexing his power. The conversation was dry. After a quick overview of the company, he spent most of the time talking about himself. Finally, exhausted, I cut in.

"Look," I said, "I have a criminal background. I'm on probation for sexual assault. Your company isn't going to hire me. Sorry for wasting your time."

I stood up, thanked him, and walked out. It wasn't my proudest moment, but I couldn't picture myself working under him anyway.

With my unemployment benefits about to run out, I knew I needed something, anything, fast. One morning, my phone rang from an unknown number.

"Queen, you got a job yet?" a voice shouted.

"What? Who is this?"

"It's Erma Jean, Chile!"

Brodrick, also known as Erma Jean, was my gay mother and a loyal friend.

"No, I'm still looking," I said. "What about you?"

"I got a job, and the company is hiring people. Boots!"

"Oh really? Where at?"

He told me about his job and gave me his supervisor's contact information. I set up an interview, but I tried not to get my hopes up. I'd been disappointed too many times to start celebrating early.

When I arrived, I learned the company had a contract with a major cable provider in Houston. The field techs went out, installed new cable modems, and then called in for activation. Our job was to answer those calls and handle the activations.

I'd be hired as a subcontractor. They made it clear that, even though we worked with the cable company, we were *not* their employees and were not to mix with their full-time staff. It wasn't glamorous. It wasn't permanent, but it was a chance. At that point in my life, a chance was everything.

The pay was decent, especially compared to nothing, and the application was only half a page long. There was no mention of a background check, so I didn't bring it up. We shook hands, and I was scheduled to start the next day.

Too good to be true, I kept thinking as I drove in. Training lasted thirty minutes. After that, they put me on the phones.

Erma Jean wasn't lying; it was effortless. A technician would call in, read off the serial numbers, and I'd enter them into the system and click *Activate*. Most calls took two minutes, maybe three if someone couldn't read their own handwriting.

Even though the job was temporary, it felt *so* good to be working again. I've never liked being dependent on anybody. A job meant freedom. It meant control. My parents had never held anything over my head, but still, who wants to rely on their parents forever? I was young, and once you get a taste of living on your own, it's hard to swallow going backward.

I didn't have many major bills, so I started saving, and every month I gave my grandmother $300. It wasn't "rent," but my way of putting something in her hand for letting me stay. For the first time in a long time, I felt complete again. Even with the monthly probation visits and the weekly treatment classes, my life felt normal. I was proud of myself for not giving up. I'd taken rejection after rejection and still kept moving.

Life was good, and somehow, I could feel it, like the air before a storm breaks, life was about to get even better.

About two months into my temporary contract, Jeanie called. It was early June 2006.

"You want to work?" she asked. No greeting, no buildup. That was Jeanie. "When can you start?"

"Immediately," was my reply.

I don't burn bridges, so I submitted a resignation letter and explained to my supervisor that a better opportunity had come up and that I needed to start right away. It was professional. Clean.

Still, I couldn't help but think, *Wow.* I had gone from desperately needing a job to being in a position where I could leave one for something better. I had history with the company, and although most of my old coworkers were gone after the merger, a few familiar faces remained. The place felt different, leaner, quieter, but the work hadn't slowed down.

The department was small, which meant there was a lot to do, and a lot of overtime. Many nights, Jeanie and I worked past eleven, sometimes until midnight. I didn't complain. The pay was good, and for the first time in a while, I felt financially steady. It was summer. I was only taking one Saturday morning class. I had no reason *not* to work.

More than anything, having a job made me feel normal again. Between work and school, my life finally resembled that of a typical twenty-six-year-old. I wasn't the monster society had reduced me to. I was a working adult, pulling long hours, paying bills, and building something.

The only times I felt like a sex offender were Sundays, for one hour in treatment, and once a month when I sat across from my probation officer. The rest of the time, I was just living.

The more I worked, the more I longed for independence. I wanted my own apartment again, my own car, the ability to come and go without explanation, but yearning for something doesn't make it possible or always plausible. Legally living in an apartment was no longer an option for me, not even worth entertaining the thought. Most complexes had swimming pools, playgrounds, or shared common areas, which were automatic violations of child-safety zones. Nearly all of them ran background checks anyways, and a criminal record closed doors before they ever opened. If I wanted a place of my own, I would have to buy a house.

I wasn't ready to buy, not financially, not emotionally, and certainly not with a job that was still temporary. That realization alone should have stopped me. Still, curiosity got the better of me. A new townhome subdivision was going up near my grandmother's house, and one Sunday after treatment, I decided to take a look.

The saleswoman was older, friendly, and aggressive in the way only seasoned professionals can be. She reminded me of my grandmother almost immediately. Within minutes, she insisted I call her "Granny" and pressed warm chocolate chip cookies into my hands, followed by a perfectly tart glass of lemonade.

Once inside the model home, she went to work painting a vivid picture of my life there: friends gathered in the living room, me working diligently in a home office, weekends spent barbecuing in the backyard. Somehow, she even guessed that I liked to grill. Everything she said felt personal, intentional, as if the house had been waiting specifically for me.

I tried to explain that my job was temporary. Granny waved it off with a knowing smile. A young, smart, good-looking man like me would have no trouble finding another position, she assured me, and if money ever got tight, I could always rent out a room to one of my friends. She said it as though it were the simplest solution in the world. Against my better judgment, I found myself listening. I began mentally listing friends who *might* need a place to stay, even though I knew I couldn't afford the townhome. Every concern I raised, Granny countered with confidence. Her reasoning sounded logical, responsible, even. Only later did I recognize it as the same optimism that would help fuel the housing collapse years later.

By the time she finished, homeownership felt attainable. Not reckless. Not premature. Just one bold step away. Before I fully understood what was happening, I was signing papers and handing over a $500 check as earnest money.

My mother was stunned.

"You're not ready to buy a house," she said, disbelief and restraint fighting for dominance. "You don't even have a full-time job. What were you thinking?"

"I don't know," I admitted. "Granny just kept talking. She made it sound like I was ready."

"Who is Granny?" she asked.

"The sales rep," I said. "She sold me my house."

My mom insisted on meeting her.

The cookies didn't work this time. My mother explained my situation plainly, without embellishment. Granny promised that if I lost my job before closing, the deal would be canceled and my earnest money returned.

The next day, I told Jeanie what I'd done. She laughed, harder than my mom had, and agreed to write a letter explaining my employment status. She joked that she could have saved the company a fortune if she'd known warm cookies were all it took to convince me of anything. As funny as it was, the experience clarified something important. I wasn't chasing a house; I was chasing permission to feel settled. The paperwork just gave that longing a shape.

CHAPTER 32

My independence was still conditional. As long as my employment was temporary, so was my stability. If I wanted real autonomy, I needed a permanent position, one that didn't expire, relocate, or disappear without warning. The difference now was that I was already working, which made the job hunt feel less desperate. Even on borrowed time, I wasn't panicking the way I had before.

Jeanie and the rest of the team were job searching too. Everyone knew the move out of state was coming, and no one wanted to be left behind. Job hunting had become a group effort. None of us pretended otherwise. We passed along leads, forwarded postings, and quietly rooted for one another to land something solid. There were days when half the group was out interviewing simultaneously.

One of my interviews was with a small audiovisual company with about 75 employees and offices across Texas. They specialized in projectors, smartboards, and the installation of AV equipment in conference rooms and classrooms. I met with the finance manager and the CFO.

The CFO was in his late sixties and looked like he'd stepped straight off a ranch, weathered face, plain suit, firm handshake. He was warm and disarming. The finance manager, a Vietnamese woman, was professional and friendly, sharp without being intimidating. From the start, the interview felt easy. Natural. Like a place I could belong.

At the end, the CFO shook my hand and said, "Young man, you did an excellent job presenting yourself."

No one had ever said that to me before. I walked out confident, certain, even. That simple sentence did more for me than he could've known. After months of being reduced to a label, painted as something dangerous, something to fear, his words felt like permission to breathe again. For a moment, I wasn't a registry entry or a cautionary headline; I was just a capable man being seen for who he was.

His compliment didn't erase what I was carrying, but it lifted me enough to stand a little straighter, to remember that confidence wasn't gone, just buried.

As soon as I returned back to work, I sent thank-you emails to both of them. I wanted that job, and I wasn't going to be passive about it.

Two weeks later, the finance manager called and offered me the position. I thanked her, trying to match her enthusiasm, but my stomach tightened as she confirmed my address so she could send the offer letter, start date, and employment application. She told me to sign and return everything and ended the call with, "We look forward to seeing you on your first day."

I hung up and went straight to Jeanie's office. We celebrated first, quietly, cautiously, and then the reality set in. The background check. I hadn't brought it up in the interview. The conversation had gone too well, and I hadn't wanted to derail it. Now I was stuck between excitement and dread.

If I quit my current job and the background check became an issue, there would be no coming back. Jeanie knew it too. She'd already pulled strings to keep me as long as she had.

Earlier, the department director had warned her my contract was technically expired. He wasn't pressing the issue, as long as payroll stayed quiet and his superiors didn't ask questions. His advice had been simple: *stay busy and stay invisible.* There I was again, working hard, doing everything right, and still living on borrowed time because of my record.

My life had become a series of temporary permissions, granted, extended, or revoked depending on how quiet I could stay. The fear was suffocating. I knew what unemployment meant. I'd lived it: financial instability, rejection, and starting over...again.

Do I accept the new position and risk the background check, or do I stay where I am, hoping no one notices my contract has expired?

Once again, Jeanie found a way through.

"What if you accept the position," she said, "and work here part-time? Come in from six to ten. If the background check comes up, you can come back full-time. If it doesn't, you put in your notice once you're settled."

The relief was immediate.

"Thank you, God, for Jeanie," was all I could manage. One problem was solved, temporarily, but the bigger question remained. The application.

The box. *Have you ever been convicted of a felony?*

Checking "yes" felt like disqualifying myself before I even began, but I couldn't bring myself to lie and say "no," only to be fired when the results came back. At that point, honesty and survival felt like opposing forces, so I left the box blank and put the outcome in fate's hands.

I started the position in mid-November 2006, and every day felt like walking a tightrope. One wrong step, one question asked at the wrong time, and everything could unravel. Still, for the first time in months, hope crept in. On my first day, I was introduced to my new coworkers. Everyone was warm, kind, and welcoming. The office itself surprised me; it doubled as the company's headquarters, yet the entire Houston staff numbered only twenty-two people. I'd come from departments twice that size. This place felt intimate, almost familial. On the outside, I was thrilled to be there. On the inside, I was bracing for impact.

I expected it any moment, the call to the office, the quiet look, the polite dismissal. Surely this was too good to last, but the first day ended, and the background check never came up.

After work, I went straight to my part-time job. Day after day, I showed up expecting to be fired. Every time my manager emailed me, my chest tightened. Every time she walked past my cubicle, I waited for the tap on the shoulder. I avoided her office, avoided eye contact, and avoided breathing too deeply.

For weeks, I lived under constant stress, holding my breath—present, productive, and entirely on edge. By my third week, Jeanie told me to relax. "If it were a problem," she said, "you'd know by now." I tried to believe her, but I couldn't unclench until a month passed. Background checks don't take thirty days, right?

Wrong. My desk phone rang. It was the CFO.

"Do you have a minute?"

Here we go. I considered walking straight out the front door, sparing myself the humiliation, but my legs carried me to his office anyway. Inside, both he and my manager were waiting.

"Go ahead and close the door, son," he said. He didn't waste time. "Your background check came back, and we'd like to ask you a few questions."

The air thickened. Sweat gathered at my hairline.

"If you don't mind," he continued, "can you explain what we found?"

"I'm on probation for sexual assault of a child 14-17," I said.

Then I panicked. Fear took over, and I lied. I told them I'd met a woman in a club, and said she'd lied about her age. I reshaped the story into something more familiar, more socially acceptable. I told myself it was survival. I told myself it made sense.

In that moment, honesty felt like a luxury I couldn't afford. Fear doesn't always make you silent. Sometimes it makes you strategic, which is why I felt it was safer to change the gender of the victim, especially given how homosexuality is already misunderstood, sensationalized, and weaponized in public narratives. I wasn't trying to rewrite the truth; I was trying to prevent the story from being reduced to stereotypes that would distract from the real issues I was trying to examine.

The CFO listened quietly. His office was filled with Christian symbols: crosses, scripture, a Jesus fish. When I finished, he smiled.

"I bet you learned your lesson," he said. "These girls today can really get you in trouble."

He shared a similar story about a young man from his church. I nodded, unsure whether I was being forgiven or misunderstood.

Then he said, "To be honest, we were more concerned about the theft-by-check charge."

I almost laughed. That, *that*, was their concern? I explained it away, too. Carefully. Incompletely. I didn't confess intent. I framed it as a misunderstanding that had already been resolved.

He nodded.

"Given your role in accounting," he said, "we needed clarity. Now that we have it, we're comfortable moving forward. We've hired people with complicated pasts before. We'll give you a chance too." He stood, extended his hand, and said, "Get back to work, son."

I walked out of his office stunned.

I didn't know whether to thank God or ask for forgiveness. I'd survived, but not cleanly. Sometimes survival looks like grace. Other times, it seems like a compromise wearing a halo.

Still, I had done it. For the first time since everything fell apart, I had a full-time, permanent job with a company that knew my past and kept me anyway. At that moment, I couldn't ask for more.

The holiday season arrived quickly, and at my new job, excitement was building around the annual Christmas party. Our CEO was Jewish, so it was officially called a "Holiday Party," hosted at his private country club. He spared no expense, even arranging hotel accommodations for employees traveling in from out of town.

I invited Tonya as my plus-one. As a precaution, and, honestly, as armor. We both wore wedding bands. Naturally, most of my coworkers assumed we were married. I was the only Black employee in the room, so Tonya and I stood out. When people asked directly, I told the truth: we were just friends. When they didn't ask, I let their assumptions sit undisturbed.

As the night went on, the open bar flowed, and for once, I allowed myself to relax. I talked, laughed, and genuinely enjoyed getting to know my coworkers. The food was incredible. There was even a magician performing table-to-table. For the first time in a long while, I felt light.

What made the night truly freeing was knowing I didn't have to hide. My employer knew my background and still welcomed me. That alone felt like a quiet miracle.

The highlight of the evening came when I won a door prize: a flat-screen computer monitor. As I walked up to accept it, someone shouted, "The new guy always wins!" The room erupted in laughter. I smiled, holding the box, overwhelmed by gratitude. I really couldn't ask for more.

Acceptance doesn't always arrive with applause. Sometimes it shows up as a seat at the table—and stays.

As 2006 came to a close, I sat alone in my room one night, counting my blessings. The year had tested me in every possible way: rejection, fear, probation, and the heavy stigma of my record replayed in my mind, but I had endured. By the grace of God, I found a way forward.

The second year of probation felt different from the first. The constant paranoia had eased. I understood the rules now. I knew what was expected of me and how to live within those boundaries. As my probation officer once said, it might not have been my fault, but it was my problem, and I was learning how to live with it.

CHAPTER 33

I started 2007 busy, working full-time, still helping Jeanie part-time, and taking three college classes. Jeanie adjusted my schedule so I could attend school two evenings a week. I didn't want to let go of my job with her, even though I didn't need it anymore. My full-time employer knew my criminal background, trusted me, and I was thriving in my role.

For the first time in years, my life didn't feel like damage control. It felt like momentum.

January 12, 2007, marked the completion of another year on probation. Two down. Five more to go. My parents had moved out of my grandmother's house, and by coincidence, my grandmother was out of town. The timing felt intentional, almost generous. I decided to host a small house party to celebrate making it another year. Nothing wild, maybe fifteen or twenty people.

As the undisputed king of Pitty Pat, I dominated the card table that night and walked away with everyone's money. It felt good to host again. To open the door and welcome people in. With my grandmother gone, it almost felt like I had my own place, something I'd been craving more than I admitted.

Independence doesn't always announce itself loudly. Sometimes it arrives quietly, disguised as a borrowed house and a card table.

In 2007, I started dating again.I reconnected with someone I'd known before probation. At first, it was innocent, two bored people killing time with movies, dinners, and drinks, but familiarity has a way of softening into something else. The more time we spent together, the more obvious it became that this wasn't casual anymore.

That's when the fear crept in. I knew I had to tell him about my criminal background. I just didn't know how. I'd met him online through the same site I'd used years before. Surely he would understand, but understanding and judgment are close cousins. What if he saw me the way the media did? A predator. A liar. A walking head-line.

When do you tell someone you're dating, *By the way, I'm a regis-tered sex offender. Want Chinese tonight?* There's no good timing for that. One Saturday night, we were at a Mexican restaurant, drinks on the table, talking about how strange life is, how people drift apart and circle back years later. We'd first met in 2002, but back then, we were in completely different places. Sitting across from him now, nearly five years later, I felt like I was withholding something sacred and dangerous at the same time.

"Hey," I said, "I need to tell you something, but I honestly don't know how."

"What is it? You can tell me anything," he replied.

"It's deep. I don't think you can handle it."

"Tell me. It can't be that bad."

"Yes, it is."

"Well then tell me."

"I don't know where to start. Just…guess."

"Norman, stop playing."

"Is it something bad?" he asked.

"Yeah. But not *that* bad."

"You make me sick. Tell me now or let it go. Are you sick? Do you have that 'lick' or something?"

"No, I don't have HIV. Don't put that on me," I said, half-laugh-ing, half-relieved.

"Then what is it?"

I couldn't say the words out loud. Instead, I sent him a text.

He looked at his phone. "Really? Are you serious? All this dra-ma?"

"Shut up and read."

His eyes widened. "You're on probation? For what? Hot checks?"

"Now you know I'm not a check-writing queen," I said. "And it's worse than that."

I texted him everything. The whole truth. I watched his face as it shifted from confusion to disbelief. He thought I was joking until I started filling in the gaps out loud.

He was relieved when I mentioned treatment classes. Apparently, he thought I was spending Sundays with someone else. I answered every question he asked. Still, it stung when he laughed.

"It's your fault," he said. "You never wanted to settle down."

He asked why I hadn't told him sooner. I told him the truth; I didn't know where we were headed, and I wasn't about to share something that personal just to have my business spilled at the club. That offended him. He thought I knew him better than that. Said he wasn't a "messy queen."

Eventually, we moved past it. Once again, life felt normal. I had a stable job. I was in a committed relationship, one I kept hidden from my parents. Probation visits were smooth. My employer knew my status and let me leave early on appointment days.

School was going well. On the surface, no one could tell I was a registered sex offender.

For a while, that illusion was enough. I wanted to move out of my grandmother's house, but I wasn't financially ready to buy. Renting felt risky: one slip, one job loss, and I'd be right back where I started. Instead of saving, I spent. Happy hours. Club nights. Restaurants five or six times a week. Shopping just because I could.

My expenses were minimal: $300 to my grandmother, $35 a week for treatment, $25 a month for probation, and my cell phone bill. The rest of my paycheck? I wasted it. At the time, I told myself I deserved it. Time was passing quickly, and life was beginning to resemble something I hadn't felt in a long time: normal. I keep using words like *normal* and *routine*, and I know that might sound trivial to someone who hasn't lived through what I have, but imagine losing everything at once: your possessions, your dignity, your stability, and being forced to start over from nothing. Not because of a natural disaster or some uncontrollable force, but because of a single line on a record. Everything you planned, everything you assumed was secure, was suddenly gone.

Probation was my personal disaster. Not loud or visible like a hurricane or wildfire, but just as destructive. It stripped away my freedom, my identity, and any certainty about my future. The devastation wasn't just material; it was internal. Knowing my name lived permanently on a list. Knowing that no matter how hard I worked, that label would always come first. Stability, once you've lost it, stops feeling ordinary. It becomes sacred.

Little by little, life rebuilt itself. With each small win, I allowed myself to believe, cautiously, that a future was still possible. Because I knew how quickly everything could be taken away, I stopped taking peace for granted.

So we fast forward to August 2007.

By then, I was bored in my rekindled relationship. I knew it wouldn't last. According to Daymond, the problem was that I hadn't experienced real love yet. He swore that once I did, boredom wouldn't even be an option. It sounded poetic, but at that moment, I just wanted out.

I hate hurting people. Mostly because I don't like being hurt myself. I've never been good at breaking up with someone, so instead of being honest, I did what I'd always done; I became passive-aggressive and waited for them to leave.

It started small. I stopped engaging in conversation. I seemed distracted and preoccupied, then I got "busy." I promised to call back only to follow up the next morning with an apology about falling asleep. Eventually, I stopped answering calls altogether and hoped he'd get tired and walk away.

Now that I'm older, I know that behavior was cowardly. At the time, it felt easier than saying the words out loud.

He put up with a lot. Too much, honestly. The breaking point came one Wednesday night. There was a popular Vietnamese restaurant that offered $2 frozen Cosmopolitans, a regular spot for my friends and me. Wednesdays worked perfectly because my monthly probation visit was that day, which meant I could get my urinalysis done and still make it in time for frozen drinks.

That night, I decided to show out. He'd been too patient and too forgiving, so I flirted with everyone in the restaurant. I disrespected him openly, so openly that I exchanged numbers with someone right in front of him. Even Daymond was offended.

"Stop the foolishness," he texted me from across the table. "Just break up with him. You're putting him through hell."

He was right. My boyfriend stormed out of the restaurant. I chased him into the parking lot, pretending I had no idea why he was upset. We argued for nearly an hour while I played innocent.

"You must forget I know you," he said. "We were friends before this. You've been ignoring my calls, canceling our dates, and pulling stunts like tonight because you're scared to say you don't want me. Stop being a bitch and just say it."

All I could manage was, "I enjoy spending time with you. I just don't want a relationship. If you take the 'boy' out of 'boyfriend,' you get a friend."

Even saying it now makes me cringe. He wasn't trying to hear any of it.

"I'll make this easy for you," he said. "Don't call me anymore."

Then he got in his car and drove off. I didn't watch him leave. I went back inside.

Daymond asked how it went. Of course, I played the victim.

"He broke up with me," I said, pretending to be hurt. "Can you believe that?"

At the time, I told myself I'd won. In truth, I'd just repeated a pattern: choosing avoidance over honesty and calling it kindness.

"Guess I'm single again. Round on me!"

At work, I never confirmed nor denied being gay. It wasn't shame; it just wasn't anyone's business. My coworkers and I got along well, but we didn't socialize outside the office, and I preferred to keep it that way. Still, for some reason, my manager seemed determined to figure me out. She joked often, sometimes crossing lines, once laughing that my "ass was so big you could set a drink on it." Coming from a usually reserved Vietnamese woman, it caught me off guard. I laughed it off, but it felt unprofessional and unwanted.

One afternoon, our group went out to lunch. As a favor to a relative, my manager had hired her niece, a college-age woman. The young woman had only been in the U.S. for a few years. She was smart and quickly picked up our procedures, but she struggled with American social norms. She dressed conservatively: long gloves, a scarf even while driving, and, though no one wanted to say it outright, her hygiene had become a topic of concern.

During lunch, the women steered the conversation toward fashion and personal care, hoping the message would land gently. The girl turned bright red, covered her face, and asked, "How can you discuss these things in front of a man?" pointing at me.

"Don't worry about him," my manager laughed. "He's one of the girls. Aren't you, Norman?"

Now it was my turn to feel exposed. The young woman looked confused. "How can he be one of the girls?" she asked quietly.

"Look at him," my manager said, waving her hand. "He's a woman, like you and me."

Then, without hesitation, permission, or assurance, she began explaining my sexuality to her. I sat there frozen. I wasn't ashamed of who I was, but I'd always believed that disclosure should be my choice, on my terms. Reporting it wasn't really an option. I needed this job, so I laughed weakly, swallowed the discomfort, and let it pass.

Silence can feel like survival, but it always costs something.

Later that day, the CFO called a meeting. We were reviewing a change in procedure after multiple customers refused to pay invoices without approved purchase orders. The directive was clear: no order would be processed without a purchase order in hand. No exceptions. No promises from sales to secure one later.

A few weeks later, on the Friday before Labor Day, I received an order from the office manager at one of our out-of-town locations, managed by the CEO's brother-in-law.

When I reviewed the paperwork, there was no purchase order attached. I followed protocol, called his office, and left a message with his assistant. Hours passed. I called his company cell. Voicemail. I sent an email to the entire Austin office explaining the delay and cc'd my manager.

That afternoon my manager took us out to lunch, as that was our Friday norm. We didn't return until after 2 p.m. When I got back to my desk, my phone was blinking. Multiple voicemails from the Austin manager, all urgent.

As I was deleting the messages, my manager called me into her office. The Austin manager was already on speakerphone, shouting. He demanded to know why his order hadn't been processed. The project was scheduled to start the following week. With Labor Day on Monday, this was his last chance to meet the vendor's same-day 2 p.m. processing deadline.

I explained that I'd tried repeatedly to reach him and had followed up with emails. I looked to my manager, hoping she'd confirm it. She said nothing.

"How could you be so stupid?" he yelled.

Still nothing from her.

I stayed calm. I knew I was right. I'd followed the CFO's instructions to the letter. After a string of insults, I picked up the receiver, paused, then gently placed it back in its cradle, ending the call while he was mid-sentence, still hurling insults. Because, who are you talking to like that?

He called back immediately and continued yelling, baffled that the call ended. When there was a pause, I said evenly, "I followed instructions, and you're not going to speak to me like I'm your child."

That didn't go over well. He accused me of insubordination and hurled more insults. By then, we were going word for word. The entire time, my manager hadn't said a thing. I knew why: this was the CEO's brother-in-law, and she didn't want to upset him, but this guy was being extremely disrespectful.

I stood my ground. "No matter how much you curse, the order won't be entered without a purchase order. If you have a problem with that, take it up with the CFO."

This time, he hung up. My manager stared at me, stunned. I asked why she hadn't said anything. "I just couldn't believe he was that angry," she replied.

That was it. I left at 5 p.m., ready to enjoy the long weekend. For the first time in a long while, I didn't fold. I followed the rules, defended myself, and walked out with my dignity intact.

Tuesday morning before work, I arranged for a coworker to meet me at a mechanic's shop. My truck needed new brakes, and I planned to drop it off before work and pick it up during lunch. The day began like any other: warm kolaches, doughnuts in the breakroom, emails answered, tasks lined up. Everything felt normal. I assumed the Austin manager had used the long weekend to cool off; there were no angry emails, no hostile voicemails.

Around 10:30 a.m., the CFO called me into his office for a "quick chat."

Here we go, I thought.

When I walked in, my manager was already seated. That alone put me on edge. She was usually joking, always lightening the mood. Today, her face was still and unreadable. She wasn't even blinking.

"Have a seat, young man," the CFO said.

"I'll get straight to the point," he continued. "Mr. Harris, it's come to our attention that you lied about your criminal background. You told us your case involved a sixteen-year-old female. The report states a sixteen-year-old male. Care to explain?"

I stared at him, my mind scrambling. I hadn't signed any statement. For a moment, I considered denying it outright. You *must be mistaken*, but I knew better and didn't want to insult his intelligence. The silence stretched, thick and uncomfortable, the three of us locked in a quiet standoff. Finally, he spoke again. "It's clear you misrepresented yourself. We're offering you the option to resign, or we can terminate you effective immediately."

The words landed hard. I took a breath.

"Look," I said carefully. "This is a small company. I thought if I presented myself as straight, the details of my case wouldn't sound as bad. I didn't want to be seen as a predator. That's what people assume in cases like mine."

I paused, then continued. "And I don't believe this is new information. When you ran my background a year ago, the gender was already there. I think this is about what happened Friday with the Austin office. I followed instructions, and now my record is being used against me."

The CFO said nothing at first. My manager was silent. I could tell she was uncomfortable.

"Son," he finally said, "this has nothing to do with Austin. You lied, and now there are consequences. So, are you resigning, or are we terminating your employment?"

I weighed it quickly. Resigning meant no unemployment. Termination might give me a chance. He added, almost like he was reading my mind, "Either way, you won't be eligible for unemployment."

I sighed, knowing I'd lost. "Well, I'll take my chances," I muttered. "You can fire me."

"Effective immediately," he said, "your services are no longer needed. Had you resigned, you could've left with dignity. Since we're terminating you, your manager will escort you out."

"I need to get my things," I said.

"No," he replied. "She'll pack them for you."

As she left the room, the CFO looked at me and said, "I'm disappointed in you, son."

That sentence hurt more than losing the job. I knew my feelings were hurt because I felt it in my chest, tight, constricting, like the air had been pulled from the room.

Losing a job hurts. Being told you've disappointed someone cuts deeper. It taps into every old wound you thought you'd outgrown. When my manager returned with my belongings, another reality hit me.

My truck.

I had dropped it off at the shop that morning, planning to pick it up during my lunch break. Now I had no car and no job. I felt like a fool.

The CFO shot me a look, like he was thinking, "Why are you still here?"

"I don't have my car; I dropped it off at the shop. Am I supposed to walk home? How does this work?"

The CFO glanced at my manager. "Can you take him?"

He glanced at my manager, who was waiting to escort me out of the office. "Would you mind taking him to his car?" he asked.

How embarrassing. Thankfully, the mechanic was only a 10-minute drive away. At least I wouldn't have to walk home. The ride felt longer than it was. It seemed like we hit every red light, and every minute dragged on. Looking out the corner of my eye, I caught her glancing at me, and I couldn't even begin to imagine how uncomfortable this must have been for her. I didn't know who was more relieved when we finally pulled into the repair shop parking lot.

"Is this it?" she asked.

"Yes," I replied, barely holding it together. "Okay, thank you," I added, quickly jumping out of her car. I didn't bother to watch her drive away. God, how did this happen? How did I go from working at a company to being fired all over a long weekend?

Maybe I was being punished for being gay. My parents were right. As long as I am gay, I will always have setbacks. I'd never get ahead in this life. I wallowed in my self-pity for a while, but then I decided to call my sister and Daymond to break the news. I didn't want to tell my mom at work and ruin her day, so I waited until later that evening.

When I got my truck back from the shop, I was hit with another reality check: the bill. Over $300. Ouch. Another reminder that unemployment doesn't pause real life.

There I was, back at square one, unemployed again. Why was it so hard for me to keep a job? I couldn't blame it on my background. The company knew about it. It wasn't my performance either, for I'd received a performance raise after completing my first year.

They fired me for a lie I told, but I knew that wasn't the real reason. The more I thought about it, the angrier I got. I wanted to get even.

I began to consider filing a wrongful termination lawsuit against the company. Since I was going to sue anyway, I figured I might as well throw in a claim for sexual harassment. After all, I had been harassed at work, especially by my manager. I knew I would need a witness to substantiate the harassment claim, and I knew which coworker I would call.

I'd formed a good relationship with one of my coworkers, a woman who, like me, was frustrated by the nepotism in our department. She was a white woman and wasn't used to being the minority in the workplace. Our manager's relatives and friends were constantly given cushy positions, and she wasn't shy about voicing her dissatisfaction.

We went to lunch together often, mostly taking walks at a nearby park, talking and venting about work. One walk I got too comfortable and told her everything about my background, my sexuality, everything. She understood me and was the only person who knew the whole story.

"Hey, it's me," I called her.

"Oh my God, what happened?" she whispered into the phone.

"I'll tell you, but first, what are they saying?" I asked.

She explained that our manager wasn't giving her any details but mentioned that I was a "good example" of why you should always tell the truth.

I laughed a little. "Well, that's not so bad."

I then went into detail about why I had been fired. "Wow, I can't believe they fired you for that. Do you think it had anything to do with what happened in Austin?" she asked.

"I sure do. In fact, I'm convinced that's the reason they let me go," I replied.

I explained my plan to file a complaint with the EEOC and possibly seek compensation. At first, she was reluctant to testify or write a statement on my behalf because she still needed the job, but she said that if I absolutely needed her, she would be a witness.

Before we ended the call, she mentioned, "Oh, yeah, they ate all your food. I couldn't do it. I felt bad, like I was betraying you."

I had completely forgotten about the fruit, yogurt, deli meats, cheese, and snacks I had brought to work that Tuesday to eat for lunch during the week. Since they wouldn't let me pack up my desk, I never made it to the breakroom to retrieve it.

"We'll keep in touch," I promised before ending the call.

My next stop was downtown to the EEOC. I was pumped, mentally counting what I'd do with my settlement money, but was quickly disappointed.

Because I hadn't provided an explanation about the details of my offense on any formal documentation, it was essentially my word against theirs. If I went to arbitration and it came out that I had lied about the gender of my victim, I could face perjury charges. As for the sexual harassment claim, since I never formally complained to HR about the inappropriate jokes, I didn't have grounds for a lawsuit. The way the EEOC explained it was simple: if I had told anyone to stop the jokes, then they could be considered harassment; but because I never said 'stop,' I essentially welcomed the harassment.

Next up was unemployment. I filed my claim the day I was fired, but, of course, the company disputed it. I appealed the decision and was assigned a mediator. I'd lost my first appeal back in 2005, so I didn't expect much this time either, but I went through with the conference call, hoping for the best while knowing systems don't bend for nuance. They reward paperwork, not truth, and certainly not survival.

I wanted revenge. Plain and simple.

In my mind, my termination wasn't justified. Some readers may think that sounds delusional, Texas is an at-will state, after all, but here's what I knew: I wasn't fired because I lied about the victim's gender. I was fired because I pissed off the wrong person, and the lie became a convenient excuse.

If the altercation with the CEO's brother-in-law hadn't happened, I would've accepted the termination as entirely my fault. But timing matters. Power matters. This wasn't about integrity; it was about retaliation.

Why am I explaining this to you, the reader? I needed to convince the mediator.

During the appeal call, the mediator gave both sides time to present their case. The company went first. The CFO spoke calmly, confidently.

"If you look at the criminal background check performed on Mr. Harris," he said, "it clearly states that the victim was male. When questioned, Mr. Harris told both myself and our finance manager that the victim was female. Therefore, he was terminated for lying to us. We cannot trust a liar."

I wanted to shout, *Objection! Character attack!* like the lawyers on television, but I stayed quiet.

"Thank you," the mediator said. "Mr. Harris, you may now present your case."

My heart raced, but I was prepared. I'd written everything down.

"When I was hired," I began, "I didn't check yes or no on the application regarding a felony conviction. About a month into my employment, I was called into a meeting with my CFO and manager to discuss the background check. We reviewed it verbally. I never signed any statement agreeing to specific facts."

I explained the incident with the Austin office, how the manager had cursed me out over the phone in front of my supervisor, and how she chose not to defend me, despite knowing I was following company policy.

"I was also pressured to resign," I added, "and told that either way, I wouldn't receive unemployment."

Then I made my final point.

"If you look at the date the background check was completed, you'll see that the printout from the state's sex offender registry was included. The company knew the victim's gender when the background check was first run. The victim's gender isn't a new revelation. The printout, thankfully, had a web address and a date at the bottom, which shows when it was printed online."

I felt a slight relief after speaking up. It was out there now, all the details, the truth, and my defense.

The mediator paused.

"Give me a moment to review the dates," she said. "Mr. Harris, you're correct. The background check was completed shortly after your start date. The company was aware of the victim's gender at that time. Any concerns should have been addressed then. Because of that, I'm overturning the denial and approving your claim."

I don't remember anything she said after that. I'd won.

Victory doesn't always feel like justice. Sometimes it just feels like survival, like proving you weren't completely powerless after all.

I never admitted, or denied, what I'd said about the victim's gender. Television had taught me one thing well: stick to the facts, and the fact was, they knew his gender before calling me into the office to discuss the results of the background check.

Still, winning unemployment didn't erase reality. I was back in the job market. You'd think I'd be numb to rejection by now, but nothing prepares you for it. Every interview, every polite smile followed by silence, it still hurt. No bruises, no blood, just repeated blows to the psyche.

Four weeks had passed since I'd been wrongfully terminated (in my eyes), and while I wasn't expecting to land a job overnight, I still had hope. I hoped that finding work would be easier this time around, but that wasn't the case. I'm not trying to play the victim here. Yes, I was wrong for lying to my company. I felt guilty because I knew I had probably made it harder for the next person with a criminal background to get hired. The company took a chance on me, and even though my performance was never an issue, I started questioning whether they would now doubt the integrity of every other applicant with a similar background.

To try to right my wrongs, I sent the CFO an email apologizing and thanking him for the opportunity. I even saw my old position posted online and, with some nerve, applied for it again. What harm could there be in asking? I had nothing left to lose.

He never responded, and that was my answer. Sometimes accountability doesn't come with forgiveness. Sometimes the best you get is the chance to walk away knowing you told the truth, at least the parts that mattered.

CHAPTER 34

Despite my lack of success in the job market, I was thriving in other areas of my life. Academically, I was doing well—well enough that I was only two or three classes away from completing my associate's degree. That mattered. It felt like progress when so much else felt stalled.

My relationship with my probation officer had also stabilized. Our visits were routine. She checked for violations and never found any. I passed another polygraph, and my random drug and alcohol tests were spaced out every ninety days. To be safe, I avoided drinking the week of my check-ins until after my appointment.

Once, she surprised me with additional testing. Along with the urine test, she conducted a pupil scan meant to detect drug use, followed by a saliva swab that would change color if alcohol was present. That one made me nervous, even though I knew alcohol leaves the system quickly. I passed.

She seemed almost disappointed. On paper, my file was spotless. I was the model client. Did I bend the rules? Yes. I used the internet for work and school. I went to clubs. I drank alcohol. But none of that showed up on paper. And in my mind, I justified it. I was on probation for a sex offense, not for drinking or socializing. Alcohol was legal. I wasn't using drugs. As for the internet, it was becoming impossible to function without it. I wasn't on any social media sites, I stayed out of chat rooms, and the world was increasingly moving online, making it impossible to function without internet access.

This was 2007—smartphones were starting to make their mark, and while technology was evolving, the system I was caught in felt stuck in the past. As Denzel Washington famously said in *Training Day*, "It's not what you know, it's what you can prove." And while my probation officer probably suspected I was slipping up, thankfully for me, she couldn't prove it.

Some readers may wonder why I'm admitting this now, especially since I was never caught. The answer is simple: the system doesn't account for reality. It looks functional on paper but collapses under the weight of real life. Once you're labeled a felon, once your name exists on a list, you carry invisible chains that affect every aspect of your existence: employment, housing, education, relationships.

That was the story I wanted to tell. Not perfection, not innocence, but the weight of navigating a world that never lets you forget who it has decided you are. I don't want to portray myself as perfect or undeserving of my consequences. I know what I've done, and I'm not trying to excuse it. However, I wanted to share something more profound: the systemic barriers and unintended consequences that come with having a criminal record, encompassing employment, housing, education, and all other aspects of life. These are topics often overlooked in criminal justice conversations. It's the untold story of how those labels don't just follow you; they define you in ways that impact every part of your life. I also wanted to highlight the specific struggles of being a registered citizen, the daily realities, the constant weight of that label, and how I navigated them, just trying to make it through the cracks of a system that didn't leave much room for people like me.

I still needed a job, but my search wasn't going anywhere. I was actively pursuing every opportunity I could find. I spent so much time at the Workforce Center that I began referring to it as my office. Every Sunday, I'd buy a newspaper and scour the employment classifieds. My resume was posted on every job site I could find, and I even made cold calls to businesses that weren't advertising job openings.

One afternoon, fresh from an interview, I spotted a massive *NOW HIRING* sign waving above a building I'd passed earlier that morning. My heart jumped. The sign hadn't been there before. I took it as a sign, maybe even divine timing, and pulled in.

Inside, I met an older man in casual clothes. His office was sparse.

"I operate a small staffing agency," he said, "specializing in industrial and heavy warehouse work." He looked down at my resume, then back at me. "Mr. Harris, I don't think this type of work is for you. It involves heavy lifting and back-breaking work. I just don't see you performing these kinds of jobs."

"You're right, sir," I responded. "I've never worked in a warehouse, but I'm not afraid to get dirty and put in a hard day's work," I said, partly out of optimism, partly to make myself sound tougher than I felt.

He smiled. "I've met a lot of people like you, down on their luck, desperate for a job. I understand bills need to be paid, but every time I staff someone with an administrative background, it doesn't work out. They're hardworking, no doubt, but once a better opportunity comes along, they leave. Then I'm stuck with a vacancy and an upset client."

I couldn't argue with him; he had a point. I didn't see myself doing back-breaking labor for long, either. "Could you possibly use my services around your office?" I asked. "I could help with your filing and manage your office tasks."

"You're determined, I'll give you that," he said, waving his index finger in the air with a grin. "There really isn't enough work for two people around here," he said, "but I appreciate your offer, and if things pick up, I'll be glad to take you up on that." We shook hands, and I thanked him for his time.

"You have a bright future, young man. Don't give up; things will turn around for you."

As I drove home, I didn't know how to feel. Had I been turned down for a job, or was I saved from accepting one I didn't want? It felt like a breakup scene from a movie: the classic "It's not you, it's me" speech. A little rejected, yet also thankful that I at least tried. I hoped he was right in that things would get better.

CHAPTER 35

The holiday season always brought a sense of reflection during treatment. It was a time when we took a step back and examined our progress, especially as it related to high-risk situations we might encounter during the holidays. As was customary, our group facilitator led us through hypothetical scenarios, guiding us on how to handle potential triggers, whether we were with family or spending the holidays alone.

One scenario that stuck with me went something like this: "Everyone is gathered for dinner in the family room. You excuse yourself to go to the restroom, but when you walk in, you find a younger relative alone in the bathroom. All the adults are busy enjoying their dinner elsewhere, leaving you alone with this child. What do you do?"

For me, the answer had become second nature. By my third year in treatment, I had learned to anticipate these kinds of hypothetical situations. Deep down, I knew I didn't have any sexual attraction to children. Still, even so, I had learned that it was easier to play along with the process, to give the correct answers and show that I understood the importance of treatment, even if I didn't always feel the need to be reminded. It was a constant balancing act going through a process that felt forced, while knowing it was unnecessary and didn't truly reflect who I am.

I raised my hand and gave my answer: "I would let it be known that I'm going to use the restroom. Prior to dinner, I would have already made a plan with my accountability partner (my parents), and they would know that if I'm not back from the restroom within a reasonable time, they should come and check on me. I would also be sure to close and lock the restroom door while I'm inside. If there happens to be a child who needs help, like reaching the light switch or washing their hands, I wouldn't help them. I would immediately find another adult to handle the situation."

"Very good," she responded. "The key is prevention. You have to think of all possible situations because you never know what scenario you might find yourself in. I want you all to enjoy your families, but you have to do it in ways that are safe and compliant with treatment and probation, and, most importantly, safe for your family and friends. What about those who planned to spend the holiday alone?" she asked.

My facilitator had a genuine concern for our class. She knew when to be tough and break us down, but she also had the sensitivity to recognize our struggles and knew how to lift us back up. I still wasn't thrilled about the $35 weekly cost of treatment, but hey, she has to eat, right?

As for my real plans for Thanksgiving, they were simple. When I was younger, my dad would take us to the Thanksgiving Day parade, then we'd return home for a meal prepared by my mom. These days, Mom doesn't prepare the big traditional Thanksgiving feast. She'd buy sliced turkey breast from the deli, make a pan of cornbread dressing, and say, "You know your daddy loves my dressing," she'd boast. She'd also prepare a small potato salad and a pot of greens. My dad would bake his famous sweet potato pie and buy a cake from the bakery.

I would spend a few hours with my parents before heading to my sister's house to visit her and the kids. Once my parents had eaten dinner, they were ready for their naps. My sister, my nephews, and I would watch holiday movies and play games. Just like my parents my sister would eventually doze off. I enjoyed spending time with my family, but I was different; I didn't want to sleep.

As usual, Daymond and I ate our fill at his mother's house. Later in the evening, we'd meet up with friends for drinks and game night. Of course, I was a natural champ at the card table and racked up some big winnings. It was a fun holiday, but it was back to business as usual on Monday. Monday always came.

Despite interviews and callbacks, I couldn't clear the background check. Desperation crept in. I emailed my former CFO again, begging for my old position back. A few months had passed since I was fired, and I noticed that my position was still posted on job boards. I took that as a sign that the company was struggling to fill the role, which to me meant the job was practically mine. I explained this in my email, convinced that meant something.

When he finally replied, his message was brief:

"Mr. Harris, you are not eligible for rehire."

That was it.

I was out of solutions. I was doing everything in my power to secure a job, but nothing was happening. Outwardly, I remained strong, positive, and ensured a glass-half-full outlook, but inwardly, I was starting to feel the weight of it all.

I was a wreck. I took each rejection personally and started to feel inadequate and insecure. My friends were all living their lives, working, and doing things that made them happy. Meanwhile, there I was, stuck at my grandmother's house.

I loved and appreciated my grandmother, but she was becoming more demanding. She stopped asking for help and began to expect it from me. The small things she could do for herself, she no longer did because I was there. At first, I enjoyed helping her because we got to spend time together. However, it soon felt like a burden because every time I walked in, she had a list of tasks for me to complete. For example, she'd send me to the grocery store with a list of items, and as soon as I got home, she'd say, "My prescription is ready," sending me out again to pick it up. Then, I'd return home to yet another errand.

One day, out of frustration, I asked, "If I wasn't here, who would do all this?" She smiled and replied, "You're here", with a big smile on her face.

Eventually, I started spending my days at my parents' and my nights with friends, escaping until I could breathe again.

And slowly, a dangerous thought returned.

Maybe my parents were right. Maybe being gay was blocking my blessings. Maybe God wasn't answering my prayers because of who I was. I wrestled with it constantly. Perhaps homosexuality was blocking my blessings. I wrestled with this thought every day, but it was like trying to hold on to smoke. No matter how hard I tried, I couldn't catch it. What were my choices? Pretend to be straight? Date a woman I wasn't attracted to, only to betray her and myself? How was that fair to either of us? Was I supposed to live my life in celibacy, hoping the desire to be with a man would vanish?

If I didn't choose to be gay, why was I being punished for it? It wasn't something I asked for or brought upon myself, so why did it feel like my breakthrough and blessing were unattainable for me for something so intrinsic, so out of my control? I buried these questions deep inside, pretending like I had the answers when I didn't. The weight of them was suffocating me, and I couldn't escape it.

The crazy part? I even thought that maybe if I ended it all, I could come back as someone else, someone the world would accept. Someone without this burden. I knew how twisted that thought was, but in those dark moments, it felt like the only way out, but I couldn't bear the idea of putting my parents through that kind of pain. So, I buried it. I suppressed the thoughts and drank myself to sleep every night, mixing Tylenol cough syrup with Gin to drown out the noise in my head. It was the only way to numb the confusion, the rejection, the feelings of worthlessness that I couldn't escape.

I didn't want to die; I just wanted the pain to stop, but when the world keeps telling you that who you are is the problem, it becomes hard to imagine a version of yourself that's allowed to stay.

CHAPTER 36

The weekend before Christmas, a friend hosted a surprise birthday party for her husband. Not the cliché kind where everyone hides in the dark waiting to yell *Surprise!* Those kinds of parties only work in theory because more often than not, the birthday person always finds out.

Like the year, my sister and I planned a surprise party for my mom, but the surprise was blown when we asked her for money, and she ended up planning her own party. She still had a great time, and that's what matters.

Anyway, my friend rented a penthouse for her husband's surprise party, and let me tell you, this place was something else. The penthouse had six rooms, a game room, and a viewing deck. One room was entirely dedicated to exotic jacuzzies and spa bathtubs, with stripper poles, ropes, and swings hanging from the ceiling, extending down into the shower. The main suite was located on the second floor, featuring all-glass walls that offered a clear view of the entire lower level. The ceiling was completely mirrored. I'm not exaggerating when I say this penthouse looked like it belonged to a celebrity.

My plus-one was my boyfriend. I probably should've mentioned that earlier; I'd met him a few months before, around Halloween

We parked in the garage and were met with a mile-long line as we walked to the elevators. We complained, of course, then joined it like everyone else. After fifteen minutes without moving, I turned to the woman in front of us.

"This must be a big surprise party."

"Party? What party?" she asked, clearly confused.

"You know, Lisa's party," I replied.

"We don't know Lisa. We're in line for the Musiq Soulchild concert," she said, sounding equally puzzled.

That explained everything.

I spotted a security guard nearby and walked over. "Excuse me, we're here for Lisa's party. Are we in the right place?" I asked.

"Oh, you guys are going to the penthouse," he replied, his voice carrying a touch of exclusivity.

He pulled out a clipboard and asked for my name "just to make sure." After confirming that we were indeed on the guest list, he instructed us to get out of the line and follow him. He led us to the front, treating us like we were VIPs. I could feel the eyes of the concertgoers following us, trying to figure out who we were.

"I have Mr. Harris and guest en route to the penthouse," he said into his radio.

As we rode up, my boyfriend leaned over. "What kind of friends do you have?"

"Wouldn't you like to know," I smirked.

The elevator doors slid open to the penthouse lobby, and we were immediately greeted by a photographer who offered to snap a picture of us. After a few clicks, we made our way into the party. And let me tell you, this was hands down the best party I had ever been to. I felt like a celebrity, like I belonged among the A-listers, and it was hard not to get caught up in the glamour of it all.

The open bar was impossible to miss, just waiting to be explored. Bottles of wine, champagne, and "spirits" (because we don't say liquor in a penthouse, right?) were neatly arranged, and without hesitation, I made my way to it. I ordered my usual, a gin on the rocks with a twist of lime. Cheers indeed.

As I walked around and mingled with the guests, my eyes kept drifting to my boyfriend. He was in his element, entertaining a crowd of people like a pro, and I couldn't help but feel even more attracted to him. It was something about seeing him hold his own among strangers, confidently navigating conversations with ease. I couldn't help but watch him, mesmerized by the way the colorful disco lights highlighted his face, making his smile shine even brighter. Was it his smile that made him look amazing, or was it the gin?

Regardless, he was everything. He had been so supportive of me, never once judging me when I shared my struggles. When I told him about my case, he didn't flinch or look at me differently. Instead, he assured me that what had happened to me could have happened to him just as easily, as he once had a profile on the same website. It made me feel understood in a way I hadn't realized I needed.

I didn't want to interrupt his conversation, so I pulled out my phone and sent him a text instead. I thanked him for his unwavering support, letting him know how much his presence in my life meant to me. I told him how amazing he looked, even in that moment when he was surrounded by others, effortlessly drawing attention without even trying. I was falling for him, and I couldn't keep that to myself. The words spilled out, and I ended the message with a simple yet heartfelt, "I'm so glad you're here." As I hit send, I felt a mix of relief and vulnerability. Maybe it wasn't the perfect way to say it, but it was the truth.

We danced. Drank. Danced more. Drank more.

Around 12:30 a.m., we decided to leave for the club. I loved partying with straight friends, but being around my own felt different. Lighter.

We wandered the parking garage for twenty minutes trying to find the car, laughing the entire time. Eventually, we did, and he mentioned that he needed to stop by the ATM.

"There was an ATM in the lobby. Why didn't you use that one?" I asked.

"I don't want to pay the fee," he replied.

"Oh my God, you're so cheap, what's $2? I'll give you $2".

"How you don't have a job?" he teased, a playful grin on his face.

"Oh really, you're hitting below the belt now?" I shot back, pretending to act hurt, though I knew he was just joking.

"I'm sorry, I was only joking!" he quickly begged for forgiveness, reaching out to me with a sheepish look.

"Don't touch me, I'm trying to drive," I said, trying to keep my focus on the road, but there was a hint of laughter in my voice. "You're lucky your bank is on the way to the club."

"Really? Where?" he asked.

I gave him the location of the bank, but he was adamant that there was no bank right there. "How long have you lived in Houston?" I asked.

"About 7 months."

"Exactly," I said. "I've been here 25 years. I know my city, and I know there's a bank right off the freeway."

"No, there's not," he insisted.

I knew I was right, so I stuck my hand out toward him with a smirk. "Let's make a bet. Bet me."

"Alright, what do you want to bet?"

I paused for a moment, thinking. Well, my mama might read this book, so I'll keep our wager to myself.

Long story short, I was right; the bank was right on the corner where I said it would be. As we drove out of the bank parking lot, I couldn't help but relish in my victory, taunting him with a playful grin.

Driving on the feeder road, merging onto the freeway, I accelerated, still teasing him about how I was going to collect my debt. We were laughing, enjoying the moment as we headed to the club, completely unaware of what was about to happen.

Out of nowhere, I heard him shout, "The wall!" and before I could even react, he grabbed the steering wheel. In that split second, I lost all control of the car. Panicking, I overcorrected, and the car slammed into the wall off the freeway. The impact jolted us, sending the car into a violent spin. It collided with the guardrail, which acted like a ramp, launching the vehicle into the air and causing it to pop a wheelie.

Time seemed to freeze as the car flipped, landing upside down and skidding for what felt like an eternity on its roof. The screeching sound of metal scraping against the road filled my ears as we slid until the car finally hit the curb of the feeder road. I swear, it felt like a scene from an action movie.

Once the car came to a complete stop, I turned to him, my heart racing in my chest. "Are you alright?" I asked, trying to assess the situation.

He could barely talk.

"Can you move?" I asked.

He tried to shrug his shoulders, but we were still upside down. I unbuckled and crawled out through the shattered window, then helped him out. Somehow, we were both mostly fine, just a small gash on my knee from crawling out of the window, and he had a small piece of glass stuck in the palm of his hand. All the windows were busted, and the windshield and rear window glass were shattered.

We stood there, staring at the wreck.

"Why did you grab the wheel?" I asked.

"I thought you were about to hit the wall and panicked," he said.

"Are you two alright?" an elderly female motorist asked, pulling over.

I looked at her, confused and thinking to myself, *Lady, it's way too late for you to be out.*

"Is there anyone else in the car? What happened?" she asked again. "Are you guys alright?" she repeated, concern written all over her face. It was clear she was genuinely worried, but her questions were starting to annoy me. I was on probation. I had been drinking. If I failed a breathalyzer, this wouldn't just be a wreck; it would be a violation. Maybe worse.

"I've already notified the police," she continued. "I'm so glad no one was hurt."

The police arrived quickly, followed by an ambulance and tow trucks circling like vultures, ready to claim the vehicle. The cold front that had swept in was relentless. The temperature had dropped dramatically, biting into our skin as we stood there, shivering uncontrollably.

The officer, wearing short sleeves, was clearly miserable. His bare arms were exposed to the chill, visibly stiffening as the cold air gnawed at him. I saw him rub his hands together in a futile attempt to generate warmth, but he didn't waste any time rushing through the report to return to the relative warmth of his squad car. His urgency wasn't lost on me, and I couldn't help but notice how the cold seemed to add a layer of tension to the situation, as if everyone, me included, just wanted to get out of the freezing air and back to something warmer.

I stood frozen, my breath visible in the cold, as I processed these events in slow motion. The reality of what had just happened hit me harder than the freezing temperatures around me. My boyfriend and I had already agreed that since it was his car, he would say he was driving. Frankly, the wreck was his fault for grabbing the wheel, and we wondered if his insurance would cover the wreck if I were the one driving.

As the cop talked to my boyfriend, I stood a few feet away, hoping the strong wind would keep him from smelling the alcohol on our breath. The officer took our statements and let the EMT check us for any injuries. He was too cold to ask about alcohol and finished his investigation in 20 minutes since there were no other cars involved or injuries. No breathalyzer or field sobriety test. My boyfriend did get a ticket for failure to control speed. Relief washed over me so hard I almost collapsed.

Standing on that curb, watching the wreck get hauled away, I understood how thin the line was between surviving and losing everything again. One breath test. One extra question. One wrong decision, and my life would've snapped right back into chaos. I'd been living on borrowed mercy longer than I cared to admit.

We stood in silence, knowing how close we'd come.

I called a friend who had been at the party, and she came to pick us up and take us back to my boyfriend's apartment. Once we got there and the adrenaline wore off, my boyfriend had a mild panic attack. We were both shaken up.

CHAPTER 37

The following weekend was Christmas. Even though *Jesus is the reason for the season*, I couldn't shake the heaviness. I had no money for gifts for my nieces and nephews, and that hurt more than I expected. I'd promised myself that when they were born, I'd be the kind of uncle I never had: present, dependable, someone they could count on.

I didn't grow up with uncles. Two of my mom's brothers had passed before I had the chance to meet them, and her remaining brother lived out of state, so I never spent much time with him. My dad had one brother who also lived out of state, so I never really got the chance to experience what it was like to have an uncle.

Like Thanksgiving, my family's Christmas plans were modest, so I prepared to do what I always did, bounce from house to house. Before the wreck, my boyfriend had already been homesick. After it, that longing intensified. Since Christmas fell on a Sunday, he planned to drive to Louisiana to spend the weekend with his family. He asked me to come, more than once. I didn't want to.

The main reason was simple: I wasn't allowed to leave the county. It was one of those rules that reminded me my freedom wasn't really mine. I couldn't just go where I wanted because I felt like it. A few days before his trip, he asked again if I had changed my mind. I reminded him, "I can't leave the county."

"So now you're all worried about your probation?" he asked.

"What's that supposed to mean?" I replied.

"Well, you go to clubs; you drink, and you use the internet. You do everything you want without thinking about the restrictions the court put on you. So remind me again why you can't go with me?"

I sighed. "I'm online looking for a job."

"Let me guess, clubbing is your idea of networking?" he sarcastically added. "I bet if Daymond wanted you to go, you would."

"Nope, he wouldn't ask me to break the rules."

"Norman, that's bull. Dallas trip, hello!"

He was right. I went with Daymond to Dallas before. "That's different," I said. "Dallas is in the same state. You want me to cross state lines. What if something happens, and I end up going back to jail?"

"Something like what? You wreck my car again?" He shot back, and now I was pissed off.

"You're the dummy who grabbed the wheel, so technically, you wrecked your own car."

"And the cops? I took the blame for you."

"No, you took the blame so your insurance would replace your car."

We continued going back and forth. He was right; I was using probation as an excuse.

In a way, I was scared.I knew if I brought another man home, my dad wouldn't exactly roll out the red carpet.

"What are your parents going to say?" I asked.

"My parents aren't like yours. They accept me and love me for who I am. They want to be part of my life," he responded.

"Can we get a room instead? I'll feel more comfortable if we stayed in a hotel rather than at your parents' house."

"You have nothing to be afraid of or uncomfortable about. My parents have met all my boyfriends and friends."

"Oh, so what is this, a tradition? You bring a guy home every year?" I said, attempting to pick a fight and divert his attention, but he caught on.

"I'm not falling for that. I want you to come. I'm asking you to come."

On Friday, he was on I-10 heading to Louisiana, and where was I? In the passenger seat like a fool.

"Wake up," he said when I tried to sleep.

"If I sleep, nothing happens," I muttered.

He turned the radio up.

"I'm serious," I said. "I'm not supposed to be on this road."

"Talk to me," he pleaded.

"I'm risking my freedom for this trip. Do you understand that?"

That landed. His smile faded.

"Fine. I'll wake you when we get there."

Between you and me, he was cute when he pouted.

Deep down, I was excited to be on this trip. I wish I could introduce my boyfriend to my parents and spend the holidays together, forming one big, happy family like in the movies. Of course, I couldn't let him know how much I was looking forward to meeting his family.

I grew tired of pretending to sleep. I lifted the armrest and took out my flask from the inside compartment and took a pull. Don't judge me!

"What are you doing?" he asked.

"I'm trying to calm my nerves."

"Thought you were so worried about us getting pulled over."

"I am, that's why I need a drink."

We both laughed, and a few hours later, we were pulling into his parents' driveway.

"Do you want me to give them 'trade' or queen?" I asked as we took our bags out of the trunk.

"You couldn't pull off trade if you wanted to," he shot back. "Just be yourself."

"Okay, queen it is."

"My baby, my baby home!" his mother screamed from the front door. Her Cajun accent was heavy. At her announcement, his father and two younger brothers also jumped to greet him. His youngest brother, a sophomore in high school, ran out of the house and jumped into his oldest brother's arms. I stepped aside to give them room to love each other. It became clear that they were a close family, and now I understood why he insisted that I meet them.

"Who this be, baby?" his mother asked him as she pulled me into her arms. She hugged and squeezed me as if I were her child. I melted. She felt like home. I saw and felt so much of my mother's love in her; she was warm and welcoming. I was glad I came. Even his brothers hugged me as if I were a family member. I was expecting his dad to be standoffish with me. It's only natural, but to my surprise, he was just the opposite.

"I'm glad you could come," he said, hugging me. "Any friend of my son is a friend of mine and my family. Make yourself at home."

This was a scene from a fairytale. His brothers took our bags into my boyfriend's childhood room as we followed them inside. Inside his room, his mother told us she had moved out all the boxes and changed the linens on the bed earlier that day.

"Baby, why your friend got that look on his face?" she asked my boyfriend, who turned around to examine my expression.

"He 'fraid to be in the bed with me."

Suddenly, her accent kicked in hard and heavy. "Chile," she laughed, "don't y'all be in the bed together in Houston?" she asked me.

Blushing, I didn't know if I was supposed to answer. "Is this a setup?"

"You don't be ashamed in this house," she instructed me.

"Yes, ma'am, I'm just trying to be respectful."

"Chile, I know what my son does in the bed. Same as me and his daddy," she laughed, clapping her hands.

Soon, we were all laughing. We spent the rest of the night eating, drinking, and being merry. His aunts and cousins came over, and we ate and drank some more. Somehow, a deck of cards got pulled out, so we played spades and $1 games of Pitty Pat.

"You gonna take all my money back to Houston?" one of his aunts asked as I reached across the table, pulling in my winnings.

"I told y'all he's lucky with them cards," my boyfriend explained again.

After everyone left, I helped his mother wrap up the leftovers while my boyfriend did the dishes. Once the kitchen was cleaned, we sat in the living room, where his brothers asked questions about living in the city. His mom wanted to know all about her baby and her baby's friend, how we met, when I'm coming back, etc. His dad nodded off in his lazy chair, occasionally reminding his wife that she was getting too personal.

Later that night, I confessed to my boyfriend that I was glad I had come and how much I was enjoying myself.

"I knew you would," he replied.

"Oh, I never paid my debt."

"What debt?" I asked.

"You know, the bet from the ATM."

"Boy, that got canceled in the car wreck."

"Nah, I want to pay," he insisted.

"Stop it, this is your parents' house."

"You heard her, she already knows." (Mom, please turn the page).

Early the next morning, Christmas Eve, his mother was busy in the kitchen. It was the smell of food that woke me up. After I showered and dressed, I joined his mother and aunts in the kitchen. Since we were leaving after Christmas Mass on Sunday, his family wanted to have Christmas dinner the day before.

"If you don't know what you're doing, get out the way," his aunt teased.

I didn't know what I was doing, although I'd picked up a few pointers from cooking with my grandmother. So, I left the kitchen and chose to sit on a bar stool. Everything smelled so good, Cajun, seasoned,and deep-fried.

That evening, after the rest of his family arrived, we all stood around the dinner table, holding hands while his father blessed the food. He ended his prayer by saying, "God bless my son's special friend." I peeked out of my right eye to see if everyone knew he was talking about me! I felt so accepted and loved. I didn't realize how hungry I was to be accepted until I felt it. Not tolerated. Not ignored. Accepted. It felt like stepping into a life I wasn't sure I was allowed to have.

The next morning, we all headed to church for the Christmas service. I'd never been to a Catholic service before, so I didn't know what to expect. As ignorant as this may sound, I didn't even know that Black people could be Catholic. It blew my mind to see a Black priest. "Is that the Pope?" I asked my boyfriend as we sat down in the small church. The way he rolled his eyes let me know the answer.

The first time someone crossed their heart to pray, I got excited. "Oh my God, just like they do on TV," I whispered to him. One thing I learned about the Catholic church is that they do a lot of standing. As soon as I got comfortable sitting, it was time to stand again. It was like a workout.

I didn't participate in communion because I wasn't about to drink out of the same cup as everyone else. When my boyfriend came back to his seat, I joked, "I'll take communion when we get back to your parents' house."

He raised an eyebrow, "How?"

I grinned, "Easy, mix a little gin with some cranberry juice."

He chuckled, shaking his head. At the end of the service, everyone hugged and wished each other a Merry Christmas. For the first time that weekend, I missed my family.

Back at his parents' house, we ate one last meal before leaving. During the meal, his mother began to cry because her baby was leaving again. Her tears were contagious, and soon everyone was tearing up, even I held back a few. His mother packed him about a month's worth of food, and as we loaded the car, she handed me some leftover mac & cheese. Hands down, her macaroni and cheese was the best I'd ever tasted.

Once the car was packed, his family said their final goodbyes. It was a sad moment. All my family lived within minutes of each other, and we were never apart for more than a few days. This was my first time witnessing something like this, and it made me realize how much I take my own family for granted. I thanked his parents again for their hospitality and for making me feel like part of the family. As they walked us to the car, his mother called out, "Naw'man, take care of my baby, you promise?"

All I could say was, "Yes, ma'am."

Returning home, I decided to take the last week of the month, well, the year off. There was no point in going to the Workforce. Due to the holidays, no job fairs or workshops were scheduled, and most employers were waiting until after the New Year to post new job openings. Typically, the holidays were a time of good food, fun with family, and a break from everything else. I wasn't the type to get depressed during the holiday season; in fact, I usually looked forward to reflecting on the past year, thanking God for my accomplishments, and setting new goals for the upcoming one, but by the end of 2007, I wasn't resetting.

I was sinking.

That Christmas gave me a glimpse of what life *could* look like: love, belonging, and ease, and somehow, that made returning to my reality even harder. Hope is a dangerous thing when you don't know how long you're allowed to hold it.

CHAPTER 38

My sinking wasn't just about being unemployed; it was that everything in my life felt like it was on pause, like it was standing still. I felt like a failure, watching everyone else move forward while I remained stuck. I was 25 years old, living with my grandmother, hiding away in the room that used to be my sanctuary. It wasn't a space I felt comfortable in anymore. Living with her felt more like a sentence than a home. I was ashamed to be there, ashamed of what my life had become. My days felt like I was moving in a loop of uncertainty, waiting for something to change but not knowing how.

I felt like I had no control over my own life. I was trapped in her house, sneaking in and out like a teenager, even though I was an adult. I had become her personal butler, constantly running errands and fulfilling every request, big or small. At first I did things willingly. I told myself I was being kind, but kindness can turn into a contract when you keep paying it out without boundaries. Soon, she didn't ask; she expected, and I felt the weight of it in my chest every time I walked through the door, bracing for "one more thing."

It wasn't that I hated helping her, but it was like my entire life had been swallowed up by her needs. I had no space to breathe. When I was home, I felt like I was constantly on the edge, knowing she'd hand me another list of things to do. I retreated into my room, hoping that by staying out of sight, I could escape the pressure to do more.

I hated myself for resenting her. She was the person who took me in when I had nowhere else to go, and I wasn't blaming her, not really. I blamed myself for training the dynamic, spoiling her at the beginning, saying yes to everything, then waking up one day burnt out and trapped inside my own goodwill.

I hoped and prayed that the New Year would bring change, that somehow, things would get better, but as the clock ticked down, and I sat alone in my room once again, I didn't feel hopeful. I felt lost, caught between a rock and a hard place, unsure of how to take the first step toward making things right again.

Burnout doesn't always come from hard work. Sometimes it comes from living without choices. When you can't control the big things: housing, employment, freedom, you start choking on the small things too.

As New Year's approached, I kept telling myself the calendar would do something magical. That midnight would carry me into a new version of my life, but sitting alone in my room again, I didn't feel hopeful. I felt stuck. I didn't even know what the first step was anymore.

I spent New Year's Eve at a house party with my boyfriend. When the countdown started, he disappeared into the backyard. In my heart, I knew he was a good boyfriend, patient, supportive, and steady in ways I wasn't. I wanted to thank him for staying by me through a season that had nothing glamorous to offer.

We did the kiss-at-midnight thing. Part of me was happy, and part of me wanted out.

Happy New Year.

"Life is great in 2008!" became my theme, half affirmation, half dare. I was still unemployed, but other areas were holding. In a few weeks, I'd hit another probation anniversary. Three down, four to go. On paper, I was a model case. No violations anyone could prove. I learned to live in the gray without triggering the system's alarms.

I rationalized it the same way I rationalized everything else. I wasn't on probation for drinking. Alcohol wasn't part of my offense. It wasn't illegal to have a drink. Clubs were eighteen and up, and my stipulations only banned sexually oriented businesses and places that catered to children.So I convinced myself that going out still fell within the lines. When I used the internet, it was strictly for school and job searching. That was it. No social media. No dating sites. No chat rooms. It was okay to use the internet, as long as it stayed within those limits. Again it was 2008, the internet was becoming part of everyday life.Not using it at all would've been almost impossible.

The Louisiana trip was the most significant risk, but it happened without a hitch. As long as I stayed under the radar, my probation officer mostly left me alone.

My probation officer had only visited the house once in three years, and of course I wasn't home. My grandmother gave me the full report of how she told her off for "harassing" me and making it harder for me to find a job. After that, my house visits were handled by a field officer, who would mostly knock on the door and leave a card before either I or my grandmother could answer.

In my treatment program, I was on cruise control, coasting along. I was just a few assignments away from being voted into Phase IV, Maintenance. In Phase IV, I would only need to attend treatment once a month, instead of weekly. The cost of the monthly visit was $75, which was another incentive for me to complete the course.

As I mentioned before, there were parts of the program that I found beneficial. The assignments on thinking errors and impulse control were helpful, and I made an intentional effort to apply them to my everyday life. However, what I didn't agree with was how the program lumped all sex cases into the same category.

In the program, we were all treated the same, as though we were all pedophiles. It also taught that homosexuality was deviant and went against societal norms. Since all my sexual experiences had been with men, I found it difficult to relate to the assignments that focused on sexual experiences with women. Regardless, I made sure to complete and present all my weekly assignments. To stay ahead, I would often complete two weeks' worth of work in one week, just in case someone else didn't have an assignment to present, allowing me to move forward in the program.

College was the bright spot. I was two classes away from my associate's degree. My friends were solid. My parents helped me financially. They didn't know I was back in the gay scene and in a relationship. I wanted them in my life, but I didn't have the energy for another fire-and-brimstone sermon, so I kept that door cracked, open enough to breathe, closed sufficient to survive. I often described it as being "in the closet," but with the door wide open.

As I'd done the previous two years, I planned a small party to celebrate another year down on this seven-year probation journey. My grandmother was leaving town for a few days, so I didn't ask permission. A family friend picked her up early that afternoon, giving me enough time to straighten up the house and get things ready. I probably should have asked, but I'd had company over before and she never made a big deal out of it—and she wouldn't even be there. I ended up inviting about twenty people.

The party was going smoothly when the alarm announced, "Front door."

We all froze.

Who walks into a house without knocking? The homeowner, my grandmother.

She played it cool, walked straight to her room and called me in. "Oh, Bernie… come talk to me." She explained they'd run into car trouble and the trip would be delayed one day. She told me not to worry and said I could keep enjoying "your little party." We'd talk later.

When she returned a few days after that, her biggest complaint wasn't the people. It was that I had "folks in my house and you didn't dust".

February hit, and my unemployment was set to expire in March. I was exhausted; interview after interview, confidence boosted, compliments poured on, then the same ending: "Unfortunately, due to your background…" One day, driving home from another interview, I passed a Jack-in-the-Box with a NOW HIRING sign.

Out of pure desperation, I turned in. I sat in the car and talked myself into filling out an application. *Within a month I could be a shift leader. Just suck it up. It's temporary.*

I went inside, filled out the application while munching on 99-cent tacos, and when I turned in the application, I slyly filled my empty water cup with orange soda like a teenager stealing a thrill.

Then I got back in my car and just… broke. I remember thinking, "What has become of my life? All these obstacles, all these setbacks, because of one choice, one night. I sat there, gripping the steering wheel, imagining myself in a fast-food uniform, working at a job I never thought I'd end up at. The thought of it was suffocating, and I couldn't stop the tears from coming. I was exhausted, mentally, physically, and emotionally. It felt like I was standing at the bottom of a mountain, looking up at a peak that seemed unreachable; the distance between where I was and where I wanted to be felt infinite.

I had no job, no stability, and no plan. I had a pile of diminishing hope and broken dreams. Each setback felt like a weight pulling me deeper into a hole I couldn't climb out of. I tried to fight it, tried to remind myself that things would get better, but in that moment, it seemed impossible. It wasn't the job that crushed me. It was the realization that one night had rerouted my entire adulthood, and I still didn't know how to get back to the road I was supposed to be on. I had done everything in my power to secure suitable employment, but no doors were opening.

Defeated, I drove home.

As with any storm, the clouds of self-pity passed later that afternoon. I was pulling weeds from the plants I had planted for my grandmother around her mailbox when I felt my phone vibrating. I didn't recognize the number, but I assumed it was a call about a job. I ripped the gloves off my hands, my heart racing, and answered the phone.

I was right; it was a job. A bright, courteous voice asked if I had time to discuss my resume. "Sure, I'm just doing a little gardening for my grandmother," I bragged, hoping to score some extra points. It worked. She mentioned that she also needed to take advantage of the nice weather and tend to her own gardening. When she asked what kind of flowers I planted, I stumbled for words, trying to find the plant labels. They were nowhere to be seen, so I blurted out, "seasonal plants. Just adding some color around the mailbox."

At the end of the call, she invited me to meet with her and the finance director to discuss a billing position they were trying to fill. We scheduled a time for the next day. I was so excited that I rushed into the house and picked out an outfit for the interview, leaving the gloves and gardening tools in the yard.

The rest of the day was spent preparing. I reviewed my interview script and resume. I was meeting with both her and the finance director, so I knew I had to bring my A-game.

Despite having gone through numerous interviews and answering the same questions in different ways, I didn't want to leave anything to chance. This was a tag-team match, and I was without a partner, well, except for God, and that's the best partner I could ever have.

The interview went well. I made a strong connection with both the hiring manager and the finance director. The topic of my criminal background didn't come up, so I chose not to mention it. Along with my resume, I filled out an application, and I didn't see any questions related to a background check. At the end of the interview, they mentioned the need for a drug test and that they would be calling my references if I were offered the job. I had no issues with either the drug test or the reference checks.

As I left the company, I noticed it was across the street from a high school, but I didn't think much of it at the time. On the way home, I received a call from Jeanie, who told me the company had contacted her for a reference. That only made me more excited. As soon as I ended the call with Jeanie, I got another call from a former coworker who said she had also been contacted. Wow, they called two of my references; this had to be a good sign! By the time I got home, the company called again and asked how soon I could take a drug test. "I can take it today!" I exclaimed, trying to hide my excitement. She told me she'd need to fax the paperwork to the lab so the test could be done the next day. She also told me that, pending the results, I had the job.

Yes! Finally, "life is great in 2008".

A week later, I began my new job. Not only did I have my own office, but the salary was far above my expected hourly wage. This was my dream job. I saw this as my ticket to independence, my chance to finally move out of my grandmother's house. I pictured myself building a future here, maybe even retiring from this job. During my first week, I met with Human Resources and completed all new-hire paperwork; there was no mention of a background check. I thought, if they needed to know, they would ask, but they never did.

During my monthly meeting with my probation officer in March, I told her about the job. I gave her the address and mentioned that it was near a high school. I used her own words, "you can't refuse a reasonable job offer," to justify my acceptance. I showed her my offer letter, and the look on her face when she saw my salary was priceless vindication. It took everything in me not to gloat. She told me to continue working while she contacted the courts for approval of the address. I felt like I was on top of the world, that things were finally turning in my favor.

About a week after the meeting with my officer, she called to inform me that the court had not approved the address due to its proximity to the high school. It was deemed a blatant violation of the 1000-foot child safety zone. I was in shock. How could they not allow me to work? It didn't make any sense. I remembered the housing barrier back in 2005 when the court had initially denied my grandmother's address, and how my family and I wrote letters to the judge to explain that it was either my grandmother's house or the streets. I asked my probation officer if it would be possible for me to write directly to the judge. She gave her approval and suggested that I gather as many character letters as possible, including one from my treatment provider, to show support for my case. She assured me she had no issues with the job, but ultimately, the decision was up to the court.

I was devastated. Surely, my judge would be reasonable and allow me to continue working. I gathered letters from my parents, friends, and treatment provider, all supporting my request and asking the court to allow me to keep my job. All I could do now was submit them and wait.

I had a friend who managed a small tax office. She suggested that I tell the courts I quit the job and was offered a position at her tax office. She offered to produce an offer letter and provide me with check stubs to show proof of gainful employment to my probation officer.

I found myself stuck between a rock and a hard place. My mind raced as I tried to weigh the consequences of the right choice. I had been trying for so long to get back on track, to find stability, and now, it felt like everything I'd fought for could slip away. Should I do the right thing or take my chances and lie, hoping that my plan would keep me employed and out of trouble?

The idea of quitting my job felt like admitting defeat. I had worked hard to get where I was, and it felt like taking a step back in my journey. Her offer, while not ideal, was a lifeline for me. The thought of going back into an endless job search, where rejection seemed inevitable, was enough to make me want to grab hold of the opportunity, no matter the cost.

My friend's offer to fabricate new hire paperwork and pay stubs made it all feel so easy, so tempting. The plan made sense in a way. If I took the job with her, I could keep my dream job, and I wouldn't have to go through the miserable cycle of being unemployed, but the cost was high. My moral compass was screaming at me, and the consequences could be dire if I got caught. It was a risky game, one that could lead to more legal trouble and jeopardize everything I was trying to rebuild.

Then there was the issue of registering her address with the police. While it seemed unlikely that my probation officer would visit the office, as they typically avoid checking up on clients at work to prevent unwanted attention, there was still a chance that HPD could conduct a compliance check. It would be just my luck to get selected for a random visit, and someone unaware of the plan might report that I didn't work there. Failure to update my registration would carry the same legal consequences as actually committing an offense. The weight of that risk hung heavily on me, knowing that one misstep could lead to severe repercussions, and the possibility of being caught in a lie made the stakes even higher. I was standing in a familiar place: the place where fear makes lying look like a lifeline.

Either way, I'd lose something. If I quit, I'd lose the stability I fought for. If I lied, I'd be gambling with my future.

The plan had risks: registration, compliance checks, the kind of bad luck that always seems to find you when you're already tired.

One misstep could carry consequences as severe as committing a new offense. Still, the temptation was real.

This is what people don't understand about "second chances." Sometimes the system offers you a door and then punishes you for walking through it. After a while, you start believing the only way forward is sideways.

The truth is, I believed the judge would use common sense. My probation officer and treatment provider weren't objecting. I didn't want to lie, not again, not after everything, so I kept showing up to work like nothing was wrong, holding onto hope while I waited for the court's decision.

CHAPTER 39

I used my second paycheck to throw a crawfish boil to celebrate all my hard work and perseverance.

I wanted to honor myself for never giving up, and with my boyfriend being from Louisiana, I thought it would be fun to give him a taste of home. He agreed to host the party at his apartment. He invited some of his friends, and we all had a good time, until…

I was outside tending to the BBQ pit, cooking skewers and wings for those who didn't eat crawfish. I spotted a familiar face; unbeknownst to me, my boyfriend's neighbor was someone I had casually dated - nothing major, just movies and dinner. Both of us were caught off guard seeing each other, and started talking, catching up. Of course, I had been drinking and might've gotten a little too friendly in my conversation.

My boyfriend walked up and saw how friendly I was being and went completely off. When dark liquor was involved, he had a way of losing control. We started yelling at each other, he in both English and Creole, while I shouted back, acting like a fool. It got so loud that Daymond, trying to calm things down, reminded me that I was on probation and needed to cool off before someone called the cops.

Daymond was right. I needed to de-escalate the situation, so I decided to take a walk, but I invited the neighbor to join me. As we took off walking down the sidewalk, my boyfriend, feeling disrespected, ran up and pushed me into the bushes, a prickly one at that. The sharp thorns poked and stung my skin. It hurt like hell. Daymond tried to pull me out of the bush but kept getting poked himself. "I told you about playing with people's emotions," he laughed, trying to help me.

Back inside the apartment, my boyfriend was commanding everyone to leave. "Party's over, go, go!" he screamed. "Ignore him," I shouted over him, "y'all know he can't handle his liquor!" My arms were still itching from the bush as I yelled, "He's just putting on a show."

I knew I was wrong for what I had done. All he ever wanted from me was love, but I had already moved past the infatuation stage. The relationship no longer felt fun and had lost its spark. I had never been good at maintaining a relationship. For me, it was always about meeting someone, getting to know them over drinks and dates, having fun, and then moving on to someone new. Now here I was, stuck in a dilemma. I didn't want to break up with him right after landing my new job. I didn't want him to feel like I had used him to have someone by my side while I was unemployed. I began to subtly frustrate him, hoping he would be the one to end things. I didn't want to be the bad guy, but I couldn't shake the feeling that I was no longer invested in the relationship. It felt easier to push him away than to have the difficult conversation of breaking up. I wasn't proud of it, but I figured if I made things difficult enough, he would be the one to walk away, sparing me the guilt of ending it myself.

Meanwhile, work was going well. I was in my second month of employment and starting to settle into my role. I had begun building relationships with my co-workers and learning the ins and outs of the office and accounting system. Once a week, I called my probation officer to check if the court had decided whether I could keep my job. Her answer was always, "Not yet, keep working until I tell you differently."

In April, I was able to buy a new car. Back in high school, I had fallen in love with Hondas and picked out a brand-new Civic straight off the showroom floor. It was a deep green, and I only told my mother about it. A week later at school, my high school best friend, who didn't know about the car, told me to follow him to the parking lot to show me his new ride. My heart sank when he triggered the alarm on a green Honda Civic, the exact car I picked out. I was crushed. Eventually, I got over it, but my pride wouldn't let me look at another Civic. I had to do better, so I fell in love with the Accord. I came close to buying one, but my mom convinced me otherwise. A year later, I bought my first car, a Laser Red Mazda 626.

Four cars later, I was still in love with the Accord. This time, I finally had the chance to buy one, so I purchased a Honda Accord Coupe EX-V6, which was fully loaded. I had the job, the good salary, my own office, and the car to match. My life finally reflected what I thought a 25-year-old's life should look like. Life had turned completely around.

For Easter, my boyfriend went back home. He begged me to come with him, but this time, I stood my ground. I had my own money, a new car, and a free weekend to myself. "Have a safe trip," I told him, dismissing his invitation. I think he knew what I was up to, which is why he tried so hard to get me to go, but I wasn't giving in. Sure enough, that weekend at the club, I met someone new. We spent the entire weekend together, and I even had him over at my boyfriend's place because he had given me a key. I know it's wrong, and I own that. I continued seeing this new guy after my boyfriend returned to town. Maybe a week after Easter, I broke up with my boyfriend via text.

• • •

Splash weekend (first weekend in May) was always the biggest weekend in the Houston Black gay community. It was our version of Pride. It usually took place the last weekend of April through the first week of May, attracting Black gay men from all over the country. The highlight was always the big beach party in Galveston. Before I could dive into the festivities, I had business to take care of. I was preparing for my finals, and my probation visit was the weekend after Splash, so I wanted to enjoy myself without worrying about any surprises. In treatment, I was about to be voted into Phase IV, which meant only attending therapy once a month instead of weekly, so I made sure to have my homework done before the weekend.

To ensure my Splash weekend was drama-free, I asked my recent ex-boyfriend if he planned to attend any of the parties. Knowing how he was when he got hold of dark liquor, I didn't want any drama, so I wanted to know which parties or clubs he would be at. I figured I could go somewhere else to avoid him. This aggravated him.

He didn't understand why I was celebrating Splash while he was still struggling to cope with our breakup. Before hanging up on me, he reminded me that I was no longer his concern and told me to enjoy my weekend, "Remember, being a hoe got you into this situation."

Friday night of Splash weekend, I spent some time with my new guy before heading out to the club to meet Daymond and the crew. We had a blast that night. Everything was going great until I ran into my ex, who was drinking dark liquor. "Why did you do this Splash weekend?" one of his friends asked me.

"Look at him, he's a mess. He's been drinking since he got off work," she explained. She was right; he was a mess. I asked if she could get him to step outside so I could talk to him. As the drag show began, I stood outside with him while he cried about his hurting heart. He called me all sorts of names, accusing me of lying. He started reading some of the saved text messages I had sent him, like the one from the night of the penthouse party, in which he asked how my feelings had changed so quickly.

Looking at him, I felt so bad. I still had feelings for him, but I didn't want to be in a relationship. "I'm going home," he yelled. I begged him to let someone drive him home, but he refused, saying he needed to clear his head. I suggested walking him to his car, but I saw that familiar look in his eyes, the same one he had when he had pushed me into the bushes. I decided to stay where I was.

After he left, my friends and I went back inside the club. Around 3:30 AM, I decided to head home. I had finals in a few hours and needed some sleep. As I walked to my car, I called my ex to see if he'd made it home safely. He was sitting in his car, crying. Without saying a word, I drove to his apartment. Sure enough, he was still in his car. I begged him to let me help him inside and get him to bed, and then I immediately left once he was settled.

The next morning, I woke up in someone's hotel room, but that's a story for another time.

I had a final exam to take, so I quickly scrambled to find my clothes and left. On the drive to class, I tried to piece together how I ended up in that hotel and, more importantly, whose hotel it was. I called my classmate, who teased me every Saturday for coming to class smelling like "last night," as she called it. She immediately started lecturing me, sharing that the professor had said I could still take the final if I got there before it ended. I arrived at class twenty minutes late, finding my seat next to her. She glanced over her shoulder and pretended to sniff me, her way of letting me know the Gin was coming out of my pores, "Oh Lord," she mouthed, rolling her eyes.

My professor was kind enough to grade the papers on the spot. We both passed. After class, my classmate and I went to the admissions office to complete our graduation applications. We still needed one more three-hour class, but we could apply as long as we registered for the last course. As we left the office, I suggested we celebrate our success. "I'm not going to let you turn me into a lush," she laughed, declining my invitation.

On my way home, I called my grandmother to see if she needed anything. Once I got home, I planned to sleep undisturbed. I couldn't remember much from that night, but I knew I had a good time.

Looking back, that weekend captured a pattern I didn't want to name yet—achievement and chaos running side by side. I could hold a job, pass exams, and still unravel socially without slowing down. As long as nothing officially fell apart, I told myself everything was fine.

Sunday was the big beach party. I was still undecided if I was going or not. I told Daymond I'd let him know after church. Yes, I still went to church. I had to give thanks for my blessings. After church, I went to treatment. I wasn't able to present my last assignment for Phase III because one of my group members had a breakdown, and the facilitator spent most of the hour attending to him. My facilitator promised that next week I'd present first, and the group would vote me into Phase IV.

After leaving treatment, I decided I wasn't going to the beach. Galveston was in another county, and I didn't want to take any risks. As I mentioned before, I felt I could bend specific rules, but God's grace can only cover so much, I would tell myself. I didn't have any reason to be in Galveston other than to break the rules willfully. I couldn't justify it, so I stayed home. Nearly everyone I knew was either at the beach or on their way, so I needed to find something to do alone.

As I was driving home from treatment, I remembered that it was a friends' birthday. I called to wish him a happy birthday, and like me, he wasn't going to the beach for Splash. Instead, he was going to a Buddhist exhibit at a local university. I decided to join him. The exhibit was new, and I enjoyed the wine, cheese, and hors d'oeuvres, which made the experience even better. After the exhibit, we went to a Cajun restaurant where he convinced me to try frog legs and alligator. It does taste like chicken. We had a good time at the bar for a few hours, and after a quick change of clothes at his place, we hit the club for the last night of Splash. We called it an early night around 2 AM, since we both had work the next day.

As I lay in bed that late night-early morning, I thought about how crazy the weekend was and how much my life had changed. All I needed was my own place, and my life would finally feel normal. I told myself, "Soon."

Monday morning, sitting in my office (I love saying that), I was tempted to shut my door, close the blinds, and sneak in a quick power nap. The weekend adventures had worn me out. Instead of sneaking in a nap, I decided to listen to music, hoping to get a boost of energy. I'd had enough of club music for a while, so I switched to my gospel playlist—same upbeat rhythm, minus the urge to drop it low.

Before I knew it, I was making my way through the invoices in my inbox. At this rate, I'd be done before lunch. "If God's been good to you, say amen," the artist sang out. "Amen," I murmured under my breath. "Take a moment to think about where you were and where you are right now."

I followed her instructions, reflecting on all the disappointments, rejections, and feelings of failure I had faced not too long ago. Then I looked around my office. I pulled open my desk drawer and picked up my keys to my new car. She was right. I was in a much better place. God had truly blessed me. I had the perfect job, where my background never came up, with an excellent salary and a new car. A few weeks ago, I was filling out an application at a fast-food restaurant; now I was working in my own office.

My cell phone, vibrating against my desk, interrupted my praise break. I thought it was Daymond calling to talk about our weekend, but when I checked the number, I saw it was my probation officer. As the phone continued to vibrate, I turned down the music and braced myself for whatever she was about to say. There were no pleasantries, no "How was your weekend?", just, "Can you come see me tomorrow?" My appointment was scheduled for Wednesday, but now she was moving it up a day.

"Is everything alright?" I asked, my heart racing. She assured me everything was fine, just that she'd overscheduled her appointments, but something didn't sit right. I agreed to meet her at 11:30 AM the next day, but as I sat back in my chair replaying the conversation, I couldn't shake the feeling that something was wrong.

Then it hit me. One day at work, I noticed a police car parked across the street from my building. He was sitting right outside my office. Looking at him, I wondered if he could see me, or if he was even watching me. My suspicions were confirmed when he pulled out a camera and started taking pictures of my building. Could he see me through the mini-blinds? Maybe the court had sent him to investigate the distance between my office and the school, or perhaps he was from the sheriff's office verifying my address for registration. Either way, I knew he was there for me.

With that memory in mind, I called my mom. I didn't want to call from inside my office, so I stepped outside to my car.

"Momma, I'm going to jail," I cried out, overwhelmed with fear, as soon as she answered the phone. I explained the conversation with my officer and the cop taking pictures outside my office, but she insisted I calm down. She tried consoling me, but it wasn't working. I knew. I just knew. I was going to jail.

She offered to take the rest of the day off work and meet me at my job, but I agreed with her that I was probably panicking. Back inside my office, I called my sister and Daymond to let them know what was going on. They both agreed with my mom, telling me I was overthinking the situation. Deep down, I knew something wasn't right.

That evening, I locked myself in my room, trying to regain control of my emotions. My parents, sister, and Daymond did their best to convince me I was overreacting. I explained to them that my appointments had never been rescheduled. My officer had always made me wait hours if she was running behind, never caring about my time or schedule. This was different. They were convinced I was just overthinking, but I couldn't shake the feeling I was about to be arrested. That night, I had a panic attack and couldn't sleep.

Tuesday morning, I sat in my office, contemplating what, if anything, I should tell my manager. Usually, my probation meetings were during my lunch hour, so I never had to explain anything to her. If the meetings had gone longer, I would have had the flexibility to make up the time. I considered writing a letter detailing everything, including my background and the situation, and leaving it on my desk, just in case I was going to jail, but what if I was wrong? What if my officer just had a scheduling conflict, and she found my confession letter only to find out everything was okay? Would I be fired? I didn't know what to do.

At 10:45 a.m., I shut down my computer and stood in my office. Before turning off the lights, I took one last look around. I pulled the door shut behind me and stared at my nameplate. I prayed I would be back to see it again.

For the first time since getting the job, I let myself consider that it might already be over. Not because I failed at the work, but because stability, for me, had always come with conditions.

Driving downtown, I listened to Israel Houghton's "I Am a Friend of God" on repeat. The plan was to call my sister when I arrived downtown and then again when I left. Inside the building, I did my best to contain the paranoia. I looked over my shoulder with every step, worried that I might be followed. When I checked in with the receptionist, I watched him pick up the phone to call my officer.

"Harris is here," he said, emphasizing the name like it meant something.

I sat down, as I always did, and waited. However, after thirty minutes, I began to feel restless. A part of me wanted to leave, but I kept thinking about the consequences. What if they were waiting to issue a warrant for my arrest? What if I left and they broadcast my photo on the news as a wanted sex offender? Would leaving be considered a missed appointment?

I paced the lobby, trying to calm my nerves. It was going on an hour now, and still no sign of my officer. I asked the receptionist to call her again. After he hung up the phone, he said, "She told me to tell you she'll be with you soon." I couldn't take it anymore. I started shaking uncontrollably and even began to cry. It didn't feel right. I called my sister.

"I told you, you're panicking," she said, trying to calm me down.

"Not really," I replied, still shaking. "I haven't seen her yet. I'm still waiting."

"Just keep your cool," she reassured me. "Everything will work out. Call me when you're done."

The more I thought about jail, the harder it became to breathe. I told myself to pray, but my mind was too tangled in fear. It was too late to pray, I thought. No, pray. What do you have to lose? If I were going to jail, I had nothing to lose.

At 1:30 p.m., the receptionist called me to the window. "You can go back now," he said.

My heart was pounding in my chest as I walked down the hall. As I stepped into my officer's office, two undercover officers appeared out of nowhere, again.

CHAPTER 40

I knew the routine. All I could do was turn around and put my hands behind my back. Goosebumps spread over my arms as the cold handcuffs tightened around my wrists. A chill ran through my entire body. It took everything in me not to break down and cry. I wasn't going to let my officer see me cry. Not now. Not after everything I had been through.

Once the handcuffs were on, one of the officers released his grip on my arms and backed into the doorway to block it, just in case I tried to run. My probation officer pulled out a legal-size document with "Motion to Revoke" written across the center.

"Mr. Harris, you have a warrant for your arrest," she said, her voice calm but cold. "Your probation is being revoked because you violated your child safety zone of 1,000 feet set by the court."

She slid the motion across the desk, and I stared at it, dumbfounded. "I thought you said I could work there?" I asked, confusion and anger rising. "You set me up," I shouted, looking deep into her eyes. Hate surged within me. Every part of me wanted to react physically, but fear and the handcuffs restrained me.

Feeling somewhat guilty, she offered to allow me to call my mother. I explained everything to her, and she calmly reassured me that she and my dad would support me, no matter what. My probation officer allowed me to leave my car keys with her so my mom could pick up my car from the metered parking lot. Then it was off to jail.

I was back in jail for the third time. I had promised myself I would never return to this place, but there I was again. Tears of disappointment filled my eyes, mixed with a sense of betrayal by my officer. Inside the packed holding cell, I found a clean spot on the floor and let despair take over.

In the booking process, I met a drag queen. She was sitting alone in the corner of the cell. Her calm demeanor stood in stark contrast to the smirks and taunts of the straight men who were mocking her. I wanted to say something, but instead, I just walked over and sat next to her.

She was arrested on prostitution charges and for a bag with cocaine residue in it. Very calmly, she said, "I'll be out within 45 days or less. I could use this mini vacation."

I didn't think I could ever refer to jail as a vacation, but she seemed to be at peace with it. We didn't go into all the details, but I told her I violated my probation. She nodded and said, "So, which tank are you trying to get into?"

I looked at her, confused. "What do you mean, which tank?"

"There are three tanks for the 'girls,'" she explained. "I'm going to try to get into one of the ones on F-pod."

I had no idea what to say, so I just nodded. The reality of where I was and where I had ended up began to sink in more deeply.

I had never been in a "gay" tank before. The last time I was locked up, I told them I was straight. The time before that, I was in isolation. "Oh, I have a friend who goes into the straight pods all the time," she said, with a smirk. "She wants all the attention for herself, being the only 'girl' among all the trade. I tried it once, but all trade wanted was my commissary. I work too hard for my coins to let jail trade get over on me."

We both laughed at the absurdity of it all. She went on to explain that the gay pod was like being at the club. "All the 'girls' are up in there," she added. "It's just like being at the club. Sometimes, I don't even remember I'm in jail." Her words stuck with me. It sounded like fun, being surrounded by people I knew from the club, with whom I could vibe. So when I met with housing, I finally decided to tell them I was gay.

"Are you sure this time?" the officer asked, glancing at his monitor. "Every time you come, you change your orientation." I didn't like the way he said "every time," as if I were some career criminal.

At around 2 AM, I walked into 5D2. Except for the emergency lights, the tank was dark. I scanned the bunks, hoping to find an empty bottom bunk, but as expected, they were all taken. "That's the only empty bed," someone said, pointing to a top bunk in the center of the room. I reluctantly walked over, threw my mattress on it, and climbed up, hoping to get some sleep. Just my luck, the bunk was directly under the A/C vent. The temperature in the county jail is so cold you could hang meat. I froze under that vent that night.

The pounding of a bass drum startled me. I nearly jumped off the top bunk. It wasn't a bass drum. It was a fist beating against the cold steel of the bunk. "Count time," someone yelled. "They're coming in for a count." It took a few seconds to realize what was going on. As I popped out of my bunk, I noticed everyone else sitting on the steel benches in the dayroom. Seeing that I was the only one still in bed, I jumped down and found a place to sit.

An officer walked in and started his security check. All the inmates' eyes followed him as he went from bunk to bunk, checking underneath the worn mattresses for contraband. When he got to my bunk, he hit the mattress hard with his fist to point out my bunk wasn't made. "He just got here," someone spoke up in my defense, but the officer wasn't having it. "I suggest someone let him know how we do it around here," the jailer barked.

Once the officer finished his rounds, he stood in front of the dayroom and took a headcount. "Y'all know what it is," he said. "I'll give you the newspapers and turn on the TV after the dayroom is cleaned up." He walked out, slamming the door behind him.

I climbed back into bed, pulled the blanket over me, and tried to sleep, but it was freezing. The sound of the officer's fist pounding on the plexiglass from the control booth broke the silence. "You can't be under the blanket after 6 a.m.," someone yelled at me. I jumped down from the top bunk and tucked my sheets under the mattress.

Once back in bed, I tried to sleep again, but the cold made it impossible. It didn't make sense to me why we weren't allowed to be under the covers between 6 a.m. and bedtime. It wasn't as if anything productive was happening. I jumped down once again and decided to sit in the dayroom on one of the cold steel benches, staring at the blank TV screen. It was cold, I was tired, and the scent of dirty mop water filled the room as someone pushed the mop back and forth.

In the back of the room, two people began their morning work-out routine, which included push-ups, sit-ups, and jumping jacks. There was someone in the shower and another person on the toilet. I couldn't believe someone could sit on the toilet with 30 other people in the room. In the corner, a sheet draped down from the top bunk to the floor, hiding the bottom bunk. I knew what was going on, but I couldn't believe they were so bold. It was surreal. I was in jail.

As time passed, the tank started to come alive. People were playing dominoes, lovers were fighting and making up, only to fight again. Everyone had their way of passing the time, whether it was cooking, reading, writing letters, or exercising. I was literally in a cage with 30 other people, and I couldn't help but notice that I didn't recognize anyone from the club. There were more straight men in the tank than gay ones, which I found confusing.

There was an older queen who introduced himself as Miss Ross, as in Diana, but insisted, "My friends call me Diana." Then there was a toothless, elderly queen who pranced the perimeter of the tank, speaking to herself in low, mumbling conversations. There was a transgender woman who looked days away from death; both of her wrists were scarred from failed suicide attempts. I looked around the room, thinking about what I had gotten myself into.

I soon discovered that half of the people in the tank were on psych meds. Later that day, one of the 'straight' men returned from court, having accepted a plea deal for 15 years. He was sitting on the floor, tears streaming down his face, talking to his wife on the phone. I watched real tears fall from his face as he expressed how much he would miss her and their kids. The whole time, he was comforted and caressed by a man - his jail lover who gently assured him that everything would be alright.

I have many stories from my time in 5D2: two men fighting over a queen, two queens fighting over a man, and couples arguing. The tank was a constant soap opera. You may be wondering, *What about you, Norman? What did you do every day in the county?*

Somehow, I had earned the title of 'renegade'. I refused to play house or submit to some fake husband telling me what I could and couldn't do. One of the girls suggested I shave my facial hair to look more feminine. That tripped me out. I had never considered myself masculine, but I took it as a compliment. The truth was, these straight men were in the gay tank looking for a free ride: headhunters, booty bandits, truck drivers, or whatever you want to call them. I wasn't about to give my commissary away, compromise my self-respect, or create an illusion of being female to make some confused down-low man feel better about the fact that he was gay.

I met a man in his late 40s who had the body of a 20-year-old. He reluctantly opened up to me about his struggles with crack cocaine, how he stole and committed other crimes to feed his addiction. He had served time before, but this time, he was facing 25 years. It was easy to connect with him because he accepted that I wasn't in jail looking for sex or love. He assured me that he wanted nothing from me, and his daughter sent him money, so he wasn't using me for commissary. He provided me with a great deal of valuable advice during my time there. He took me to the law library and taught me how to research my case. In a place like that, he was a much-needed friend.

Unfortunately, I wasn't in jail to make friends. I was here because I was waiting for my court date on a motion to revoke my probation. Sadly, I had become all too familiar with this routine.

Walking through the underground tunnels that led to the courthouse, I felt disappointed in myself. I had accepted this situation with an unwelcome familiarity, as if I had become too comfortable with the system. I even found myself coaching first-timers through the steps to getting to court, explaining each step. *Have I really become a pro at this?* I thought to myself as I coached another inmate through the ordeal.

When I got to the holding cell behind the courtroom, I was disgusted at the sight of the same court-appointed lawyer who had represented me twice before. He wore the same dingy brown blazer, which looked as if it reeked of stale cigarettes and coffee. To my surprise, he called my name, and I couldn't believe it. Surely, there had to be another lawyer besides him. I raised my hand, making myself visible among the other men, and he walked over to me. He sat on the stool opposite me, introducing himself with all the enthusiasm of someone who had done this far too many times. I thought, *Really? You don't recognize your clients?*

Just like the entire criminal justice system, he was going through the motions, with no regard for my future. He didn't care about me or the man next to me. It was all about conviction rates, backdoor deals, and securing business. I couldn't help but feel it was all a game to them. I was just another Black man, another case in a legal folder.

He reviewed my charges and explained that the court was prepared to offer me a sentence of two years in state prison. I looked at him in shock, as if the wind had been knocked out of me. "Two years?! For what?!" I shouted through the speaker, disbelief flooding my veins.

Behind me, someone yelled, "Two years ain't shit, young brother!" He continued reading from my case, detailing how the distance between my job and the school violated the child safety zone. He wasn't explaining anything to me; he just read from the court documents, and the entire conversation felt like it was happening in a haze.

One of my group members in treatment had violated his probation and was sentenced by his judge to serve 90 days in weekend jail. I mentioned to my lawyer, "Will the court consider that? What about reinstating my probation?" I begged him for some hope, but he was convinced the court wouldn't reinstate it. He dismissed my concerns, saying weekend jail wasn't an option for me. He excused himself, promising he'd be right back.

After 45 minutes, the bailiff informed me that my case had been reset and directed me back to the holding cell. I cursed under my breath, feeling completely helpless. Back in the tank, the others thought I was foolish for not taking the two-year sentence, but I defended my actions. "My probation officer knew I was working there," I argued, "She gave me permission." I couldn't sleep, haunted by nightmares of prison. Most nights, I would be woken by someone knocking on my bunk, telling me I was talking in my sleep. Eventually, I resorted to buying psych meds from someone in my dorm who sold them for food and hygiene. One pill knocked me out for two days. I knew it wasn't a solution, but it was easier to escape that way.

My parents were worried and wanted to help. We agreed to fire my court-appointed lawyer and hire a private one. This new lawyer came to visit me in jail and listened to my side of the story. I explained everything to him: from the time I notified my officer about the job to the day I was arrested in her office. I even presented the legal statutes I'd found in the law library. I stressed that this was my first violation in three and a half years. I had passed all my annual polygraph tests, attended treatment regularly, and was about to enter Phase IV. I had never failed a drug test, and here I was, locked up for working. It made no sense.

I started crying, overwhelmed by the injustice. He sympathized, but then explained that my probation officer's testimony would be crucial. Unfortunately, he didn't believe she would testify that she went against the court's orders. He said I had two options: I could accept the two-year sentence or go to trial, but with a judge alone making the decision, no jury involved.

The thought of a judge deciding my future left me shaken, but I was willing to fight. My lawyer reassured me he would subpoena my treatment provider, bring in character witnesses, and argue my case. After that visit, I was determined to go to war. My parents continued to support me, reminding me that we were putting our trust in God, not in any man.

As the days dragged on in the county jail, I became more comfortable with my environment. I could no longer stay on my high horse, so I began engaging with the people in my tank. It rotated often. Some were released, and new faces appeared, but over time, I began to connect with many of the men. I learned their stories of addiction, broken homes, violence, and survival.

These young Black men shared painful accounts of their childhoods: mothers turning to drugs and prostitution, fathers absent or abusive, siblings left to care for each other. Some were molested, and some had committed petty crimes just to feed their families.

As I heard these stories, I reflected on my upbringing. Despite our struggles, my family had been different. We weren't rich, but I had two parents who provided for me. I never went hungry, and, to my knowledge, our utilities were never disconnected. My parents weren't on drugs, and I never went to school with holes in my clothes. I realized how blessed I had been, and my respect for my parents, especially my father, deepened.

One Sunday morning, I woke up in tears. A fellow inmate asked why I was crying, and I sobbed uncontrollably. "I miss my daddy," I whispered. I compared my father to the men in the tank, especially the ones who considered themselves straight. They were selfish, petty, and gossipy. They preyed on the weak, using others for their own gain, and if they did anything kind, they expected something in return.

My father had never asked for anything. He showed up every day, working hard, sacrificing for our family.

I turned 26 in county jail, and despite the attempts of everyone to cheer me up, I was deeply depressed. I thought back to how I'd celebrated my birthday in the past, dinners at nice restaurants, good food, and good drinks, all replaced by Ramen noodles and hooch jail wine.

At my next court appearance, my lawyer informed me that my offer had changed to four years. The judge was upset, feeling that I had blatantly violated his orders by accepting the job. He told me he was still prepared to fight for me and then left to return to the courtroom. When he returned 30 minutes later, he had a big smile on his face.

"Your probation officer can't find your check stubs," he said.

"What do you mean she can't find my check stubs? I turned them in to her," I replied, confused.

The lawyer's smile widened, and it was only then that I realized what he was getting at. He explained that if they couldn't produce the check stubs, it meant I had never worked there, and therefore, couldn't have violated my probation.

It clicked. I smiled too. In that moment, I realized what had happened: my probation officer, likely knowing the court would have a hard time proving I had violated the child safety zone, must have thrown away my check stubs to help me out. I never had evidence, but I somehow felt that this was her way of silently helping me.

The bailiff called me into the courtroom, and the prosecutor agreed to reinstate my probation due to a lack of evidence. The judge began reading the motions, and I started smiling with relief, thinking I was going home, but then, out of nowhere, another prosecutor yelled, "Why don't we call the company?"

I didn't know who this person was or where he came from. My mom said he was a prosecutor who had appeared out of the back offices. Whoever he was, he ruined everything. The judge immediately banged the gavel and reset the hearing. I turned to look at my parents, who were just as shocked as I was. Even my probation officer looked confused. We were all blindsided.

How could I have come so close to going home, only for it to be snatched away by someone who wasn't even working on my case? I spent the rest of the afternoon crying, feeling like everything I had worked for was slipping away. When my parents came for their visit, they tried to console me, reminding me that this was a spiritual fight and that the devil comes to kill, steal, and destroy, and that this was just an attack from the pits of Hell.

I couldn't see the devil. My anger was directed at the judge and that mysterious prosecutor. After the visit ended, I went back to the tank, and thankfully, someone had pills for sale. I took two of the psych meds, which quickly knocked me out.

In the middle of the night, I woke up in a cold sweat, shaken by a vivid dream. I was in a heated argument with the judge, begging him to listen to me. "Look at the facts," I pleaded, but my words fell on deaf ears. I felt helpless, knowing the court didn't see it as just a matter of working; it was a violation of the child safety zone.

A few days before my next court date, my lawyer came to strategize for the trial. I knew my only defense was logic. I reminded him that the judge had once amended the child safety zone, allowing me to live at my grandmother's house, which was within a 1,000-foot radius of several schools and daycares. That was a violation, too, but the judge allowed it, understanding my situation. After three and a half years of no violations and 100% compliance, I found myself here again.

I submitted petitions asking for permission to work and was still waiting for a response. I prepared myself to testify, ready to present the facts. My lawyer assured me he was still fighting for me, but it felt like I was in a fight I couldn't win.

The day of the trial, I waited in the holding cell behind the courtroom, on edge. If I couldn't convince the judge to see the facts and use logic, I was going to prison. I noticed that I was waiting longer than usual. My lawyer came back to tell me that the judge was running late due to a flat tire. I remember praying that God would send an angel to help him change it, hoping that would put him in a good mood.

My lawyer also explained that the judge had never answered my petitions, even though they were in my file, stamped and dated by the court clerk. Somehow, the judge had never read them. Despite this, he was still adamant about starting the trial. My lawyer relayed the judge's reasoning: "Your client should have quit the position, submitted his petition, and waited for my response before returning to work."

That didn't make any sense. How could you quit a job you just started and then ask for it back weeks later? What company would allow that? It was ridiculous, but my lawyer said the court was now offering me six years. He also warned that if I went to trial and lost, the judge would likely give me no less than 20 years. He left me to think about my options. I asked him to speak to my parents for their input.

I prayed for guidance. "God, please give me a sign. Should I take the six years, or go to trial?" As soon as I finished my prayer, the lights in the courtroom flickered. It was as if God had answered me directly. But wait! I wasn't sure what the sign meant. Was it to take six years, or to go to trial? Now, I was even more confused.

When my lawyer returned, I asked him if he had seen the lights flicker. He had, and I told him about my prayer. He handed me a handwritten note from my mom, telling me that whatever I decided, they would support me. I started crying. I made the decision. I would take the six years.

Minutes later, the bailiff led me to stand before the judge. There were two cases before mine. The first was a young white man who had violated his probation for the third time. The judge was unusually calm with him. "I see your parents are here," he said, "and I know they love you and support you. I'm going to give you one more chance. Don't make me regret this."

I couldn't believe it. Here was a young white man, facing his third violation, yet the judge was willing to give him another chance simply because his parents were there. Meanwhile, I had the support of my parents, grandmother, treatment provider, and thirteen of my friends, and it didn't matter. I couldn't understand why the judge showed so much leniency in that case.

The following case was a white woman who had violated her probation on a DWI charge. She had been pulled over, failed a sobriety test, and had pills in her car that weren't hers. The judge sympathized with her, saying, "I know life is hard and you're under a lot of stress, but you need to find a better way to cope than with alcohol and prescription drugs." He reinstated her probation.

Again, I was floored. If I'm lying, I'm frying. How could this judge be so sympathetic to others while being so harsh with me? When the bailiff called my docket number, I saw the judge's entire demeanor change. Everyone in the courtroom noticed it, too. The hate in his eyes was unmistakable. I turned to look at my parents and friends, and they silently confirmed it; his bias was evident.

I stood there, staring at him, hoping he could feel the disdain I had for him. I don't remember a word of what he said. After he finished speaking, my lawyer handed me a sheet of paper to sign and thumbprint.

Six years for simply working. I signed the court documents, agreeing to a six-year sentence-six years for working. The reality of it slammed into me, and a rush of emotions flooded my chest. Six years.

My whole life, trapped in a number. How could this be happening? Six years' punishment for trying to do something as simple as earn a living. My heart dropped, and the bitterness of it all left a sickening taste in my mouth. I had fought so hard to rebuild my life, and now, this. I couldn't wrap my head around it. How was it that something so seemingly innocent, holding a job, had led me to this point? I tried to keep my composure, but I could feel the tightness in my throat, the rising frustration threatening to break through. Six years. It felt like my life was slipping through my fingers, and I couldn't stop it.

As the bailiff led me back to the holding cell, I smiled at my mother and waved at my grandmother and friends behind me. When I looked at my probation officer, we made eye contact. She dropped her gaze, not able to meet my eyes.

In the holding cell, I cried. I cried until there were no more tears left. I did the math in my head: 27, 28, 29, 30, 31, 32. I'll be 32 years old when I'm released. The thought hit me like a ton of bricks. My nieces and nephews would grow up without their uncle. I had failed them. I had broken my promise, and I felt like I had let everyone down.

My lawyer came back to see me. He noticed my tears and said, "You did the right thing. Six years is better than 20." He tried to reassure me, "Besides, prison is so packed.

You'll be home in no time. If you and your parents want, I'll represent you at your parole hearing for free."

I wiped my eyes and looked up at him, trying to steady my breathing. My chest felt hollow, like everything inside me had already been emptied out. I wasn't bargaining anymore. I wasn't strategizing. I was done running.

I took a slow breath, the kind you take before telling the truth even when it can't save you.

"I still drank. I still went to clubs. I used the internet for work and school. I spent time with my family… even my nieces and nephews. I even went out of town." I paused, then added quietly, "But I never got caught."

The words felt like a confession and a funeral at the same time. He studied me through the thick glass partition, said nothing for a moment. Then, calmly, almost gently, he said, "It doesn't matter. It's all over now."

APPENDIX A

PROBATION TERMS AND CONDITIONS

CONDITIONS OF COMMUNITY SUPERVISION

THE STATE OF TEXAS

VS.

NORMAN BERNARD HARRIS, II

IN THE 351ST DISTRICT COURT OF

HARRIS COUNTY, TEXAS

CAUSE NUMBER ▮▮▮▮▮

On this the 11TH day of JANUARY, 2005, you are granted 7 years community supervision for the felony offense of SEXUAL ASSAULT OF A CHILD 14-17 in accordance with section 5 of Article 42.12, Texas Code of Criminal Procedure, in the 351ST District Court of Harris County, Texas, by the Honorable MARK KENT ELLISJudge Presiding. It is the order of this Court that you abide by the following Conditions of Community Supervision:

(1) Commit no offense against the laws of this or any other State or of the United States.

(2) Avoid injurious or vicious habits. You are forbidden to use, possess, or consume any controlled substance, dangerous drug, marijuana, alcohol or prescription drug not specifically prescribed to you by lawful prescription. You are forbidden to use, consume, or possess alcoholic beverages.

(3) Avoid persons or places of disreputable or harmful character, specifically: _________.

(4) Report immediately in person, to the Community Supervision Officer for the 351ST District Court on the 11TH day of JANUARY, 2005 and continue to report to the Community Supervision Officer on the 11TH of each month thereafter or as directed by the Community Supervision Officer for the remainder of the supervision term unless so ordered differently by the Court

(5) Permit a Community Supervision Officer to visit you at your home, place of employment or elsewhere.

(6) Abide by the rules and regulations of the Harris County Community Supervision and Corrections Department (hereinafter referred to as HCCS&CD). Refrain from disorderly conduct, abusive language or disturbing the peace while present at any HCCS&CD office or facility.

(7) Work faithfully at suitable employment and present written verification of employment (including all attempts to secure employment) to your Community Supervision Officer on each reporting date. You must notify HCCS&CD within 48 hours of any change in your employment status.

(8) Remain within a specified place, to wit: Harris County, Texas. You may not travel outside of Harris County, Texas unless you receive prior written permission from the Court through your Community Supervision Officer. You must notify HCCS&CD within 48 hours of any change of residence.

(9) Support your dependents as required by law. Provide your Community Supervision Officer with a certified copy of all Court orders requiring payment of child support.

(10) Submit to random drug/alcohol analysis by authorized personnel of HCCS&CD, including any department having courtesy supervision jurisdiction. Provide proof of any medication legally prescribed to you prior to submitting a specimen.

(11) Participate in the HCCS&CD Community Service Restitution Program (CSRP). **waived**

CONDITIONS OF COMMUNITY SUPERVISION

FOR: <u>NORMAN BERNARD HARRIS, II</u>   CAUSE NUMBER: ██████

(12)   Pay the following fees through HCCS&CD as specified herein. All payments MUST be in the form of a money order or cashier's check. Personal checks will not be accepted.

    12.1   Pay a **Supervision Fee** at the rate of <u>$25.00</u> per month for the duration of your community supervision beginning <u>MARCH 11, 2005</u> to HCCS&CD.

    12.2   Pay a **Fine** of <u>$0</u> and **Court Costs** of <u>$448.00</u>. You are given credit for <u>9</u> days.

    12.3   Pay a <u>$12.50</u> fee for an **Offender Identification Card** by <u>MARCH 11, 2005</u> to HCCS&CD.

    12.4   Pay <u>$50.00</u> to **Crime Stoppers of Houston** by <u>FEBRUARY 11, 2005</u> through HCCS&CD. _[handwritten: 65 in Feb. 11th]_

    12.5   Pay a <u>$15.00</u> fee for **DNA Testing** by <u>FEBRUARY 11, 2005</u> through HCCS&CD.

    12.6   Pay **the costs of providing notice for Publication to a newspaper** as required by law through HCCS&CD.

    12.7   Pay **Sex Offender Sign Fee(s)** for <u>FOUR (4)</u> **sign(s)** at the rate of <u>$30.00</u> per **sign** for a total of $<u>120.00</u> by <u>JUNE 11, 2005</u> to HCCS&CD.

(13)   ✓ Report in person to HCCS&CD by <u>JANUARY 13, 2005</u> for the purpose of creating and obtaining your **Offender Identification Card.** You are to carry this identification card on your person at all times.

(14)   ✓ Submit to an **alcohol/drug evaluation** by <u>JANUARY 13, 2005</u>, and at anytime thereafter as directed by your Community Supervision Officer. Attend treatment and aftercare as recommended or as designated by the Court, including but not limited to **the STAR Drug Court Program.** Comply with all program rules, regulations and guidelines until successfully discharged or released by further order of the Court. On each reporting date, submit written verification of your enrollment, attendance and/or successful completion of the program to your Community Supervision Officer, to be retained in HCCS&CD's file.

(15)   ✓ Participate in the HCCS&CD **Maximum Supervision Program** any time that you are assessed by HCCS&CD to require maximum supervision. Comply with all program rules, regulations and guidelines until successfully discharged or released by further order of the Court.

(16)   ✓ Submit to an evaluation of your **educational skill level** by <u>MARCH 11, 2005</u>. If it is determined that you have not attained the average skill of students who have completed the sixth grade in public schools in this State, you shall participate in the HCCS&CD program that teaches functionally illiterate persons to read.

(16)   ✓ Provide proof of your **High School Diploma or participate in a General Educational Development (G.E.D.) program** beginning <u>MARCH 11, 2005</u>. Comply with all program rules, regulations and guidelines until successfully discharged or released by further order of the Court. On each reporting date, submit written verification of your enrollment, attendance and/or successful completion of the program to your Community Supervision Officer, to be retained in HCCS&CD's file.

(17)   ✓ Comply with **sex offender registration** procedures as required by the laws of this or any other State in which you reside beginning <u>JANUARY 11, 2005</u> and at anytime thereafter as directed by your Community Supervision Officer. Verification upon completion of registration must be provided to a Community Supervision Officer, to be retained in HCCS&CD's file.

(18)   Participate in **Sex Offender Treatment** beginning <u>MARCH 11, 2005</u>. Attend treatment and aftercare with a State of Texas registered Sex Offender Provider as recommended. Comply with all program rules, regulations and guidelines until successfully discharged or released by further order of the Court. <u>**Assume responsibility for your offense.**</u> On each reporting date, submit written verification of your

CONDITIONS OF COMMUNITY SUPERVISION

FOR: <u>NORMAN BERNARD HARRIS, II</u>   CAUSE NUMBER: ███

enrollment, attendance and/or successful completion of the program to your Community Supervision Officer, to be retained in HCCS&CD's file.

(19) ✓ Submit to any program of **psychological and physiological assessment** at the direction of your Community Supervision Officer, including the **plethysmograph and/or polygraph**, to assist in treatment, planning and case monitoring.

(20) You are **not to contact the complainant,** ███ , in person, in writing, by telephone, via the internet, a third party or any other means for any reason except as specifically permitted by the Court.

(21) ✓ You are **to have no contact with any minor under the age of seventeen (17)** beginning <u>JANUARY 11, 2005</u> for any reason except as specifically permitted by the Court. **FOLLOWING TREATMENT PARTICIPATION, INPUT FROM S.O. COUNSELOR, AND COMPLETION OF A CHAPERONE PROGRAM BY A RESPONSIBLE ADULT, THE COURT *MAY* MODIFY THIS CONDITION FOR CONTACT .**

(22) *A.* **You are not to reside, go in, on or within *<u>1000</u>* feet of a premises where children commonly gather, including, but not limited to, schools, day-care facilities, playgrounds, public or private youth centers, public swimming pools, or video arcade facilities. The measurement of the distance between the residence of the offender and the premises where children gather shall be measured using the shortest, direct, straight line from the property line of the offender's residence to the property line of the premises where children commonly gather. The measurement of distance from the person of the offender to the premises where children gather shall be made using the shortest, direct, straight line between the person of the offender and the property line of the premises where children gather.**

B. You are ordered to reside for the next ten days following the signing of this order at *<u>(501 GREENS RD. #901 HOUSTON, TX, 77060 HARRIS COUNTYy)</u>*, **unless otherwise directed by the Court. After that time, you may not reside on or within 1000 feet of a premise where children commonly gather as described in paragraph 22 A above unless the terms and conditions of your community supervision have been amended.**

(23) ✓ **You are not to supervise or participate in any program that includes participants or recipients persons who are seventeen (17) years of age or younger and that regularly provides athletic, civic or cultural activities** beginning <u>JANUARY 11, 2005</u>for any reason except as specifically permitted by the Court.

(24) Report in person to HCCS&CD to submit a blood sample to the Department of Public Safety at the direction of and through HCCS&CD for the purpose of creating a **DNA Record/Database** by <u>MARCH 11, 2005</u>.

(25) ✓ You are **not to accept or maintain employment** which will bring you into direct contact with minor children unless approved by the Court.

(26) ✓ You are not to **work, frequent or patronize places where pornographic materials are sold**. You may not own or possess pornographic materials or frequent sexually oriented establishments beginning <u>JANUARY 11, 2005</u>.

(27) ✓ You may not have **access to the internet** through any manner or method, beginning <u>JANUARY 11, 2005</u> for any reason unless specifically ordered by the Court. You may not view, receive, download, transmit, or possess pornographic material on any computer. You are not to possess pornographic software images or material on any hard drive, floppy disk, Disk, Diskette or magnetic tape. **THE DEFENDANT MAY HAVE ACCESS TO A COMPUTER *HOWEVER*, THAT COMPUTER MAY NOT HAVE ACCESS TO THE INTERNET IN ANY WAY.**

CONDITIONS OF COMMUNITY SUPERVISION

FOR: <u>NORMAN BERNARD HARRIS, II</u>   CAUSE NUMBER: ███████

(28) You will **report in person** to the HCCS&CD Sex Offender Unit located at 600 N. San Jacinto **within 24 hours or the following working day by 10:00 a.m.** for the purpose of completing your **sex offender registration** and **Static 99**.

(29) Permit a Community Supervision Officer to search your residence, any vehicle to which you have access, and any of your possessions for **sexually explicit materials** or items or firearms prohibited by these conditions of probation. If the officer finds such materials, you will permit the officer to seize these materials. Seized materials shall be considered property of the Court and the Community Supervision Officer shall safely keep these materials until the court requests them.

(30) You shall **display a sign(s)** on all exterior doors of your residence/home by __FEBRUARY 11, 2005__, or when sign(s) are prepared, stating in **English and Spanish, "BY ORDER OF THE 351ST DISTRICT COURT NO ONE UNDER 17 YEARS OF AGE IS PERMITTED ON THESE PREMISES."** This sign(s) will be prepared through H.C.C.S.C.D. Should you change your place of residence, the sign(s) will be displayed at the new residence within seven (7) days of that change.

APPENDIX B

COLLEGE ADMISSION DENIAL LETTER

January 27, 2005

Mr. Norman Bernard Harris
501 Greens Road, Apt. 901
Houston, TX 77060

Mr. Harris,

The Texas Code of Criminal Procedure 62.03 (h) requires each person who has been convicted of and has completed his or her sentence for specific sexual offenses and who intends to attend classes at an institution of higher education to register with the campus police department within 7 days of class registration. The North Harris Montgomery Community College District Board Policy CED establishes procedures for reviewing the petitions of individuals who are registered as Sex Offenders as designated by the Texas Legislature, and to make recommendations regarding the attendance options for those individuals at an NHMCCD location or site.

The NHMCCD Review Committee and appropriate campus administrator have reviewed your petition to attend NHMCCD classes for the spring semester, 2005, and made the following decision:

1) *You are denied admission based on the information provided to us by you, your probation officer, and our review of the facts. Our review of your file found it incomplete and lacking the necessary information need to make a decision at this time. It is our best judgment that your enrollment at NHMCCD is not in the best interest of the students, employees, or community.*
2) *Under the NHMCCD Policy, you have the right to appeal this decision to the appropriate NHMCCD College President.*
3) *You may reapply for consideration at the next enrollment period.*

If you have any questions or if your status changes, you should notify your college dean/vice president of student services or the NHMCCD Police Department.

Sincerely,

Executive Vice Chancellor
NHMCCD Police Commissioner

APPENDIX C

APPEAL LETTER SUBMITTED TO THE COLLEGE

March 11, 2005

█████████████

5000 Research Forest Drive
The Woodlands, Texas 77381

█████████████

My name is Norman Harris and I am writing this letter to appeal the campus decision to deny my enrollment at North Harris. I do not feel that I was properly presented to the district board or yourself. Perhaps the district board heard sexual assault of a child and pre judge me to be a child molester, pedophile, or sexual predator but I am not. Before December 24, 2004 (night I was arrested) I was a full time assistant manger at a retail store, part time college student, uncle, son and friend; now I feel as though I have been robbed of my true identity. I know that society only sees a person over the age of 18 engaging in sexual conduct with someone under 18 and automatically assumes the situation to be like all prior cases. However in my case this is not true. I am not a sexual offender, I have no desire what so ever to seek sexual pleasure in young children. ████ ████I was lied to, I was deceived and used to gratify another person lust. I am no way declaring myself totally innocent since no one forced me to go to my "victim's" house. However I am saying that if my "victim" would have been honest about his age, I would have never pursed any type of relationship with him. I met my "victim" on an internet dating site, a site where you have to be 18 and over to even enroll as a user. On my "victim's" profile it clearly states that he is 18. I have lost my job, my car, 18 days of my life that I spent in jail, hundred of dollars, all because I was lied to, please don't make me loose out on my education.

Upon your approval I would like to enjoy another semester at North Harris in fact as a soon as the 1st summer semester. All my "sex offender registration" is current and I am able to provide the campus with any information that will satisfy campus law as well as the state of Texas. Thank you for allowing me to voice my concern considering this matter I look forward to hearing from your office.

Sincerely,

Norman Harris
P.O.BOX ████████
Houston, Texas 77267
(281) 591-██████hm.
(832) 724-████cell

APPENDIX D

CONDITIONAL ACCEPTANCE LETTER

NHMCCD

Learning without boundary...

NORTH HARRIS MONTGOMERY COMMUNITY COLLEGE DISTRICT
District Services and Training Center
5000 Research Forest Drive
The Woodlands, Texas 77381-4356
832.813.6500

May 4, 2005

Mr. Norman Bernard Harris
501 Greens Road, Apt. 901
Houston, TX 77060

Mr. Harris,

The Texas Code of Criminal Procedure 62.03 (h) requires each person who has been convicted of and has completed his or her sentence for specific sexual offenses and who intends to attend classes at an institution of higher education to register with the campus police department within 7 days of class registration. The North Harris Montgomery Community College District Board Policy CED establishes procedures for reviewing the petitions of individuals who are registered as Sex Offenders as designated by the Texas Legislature, and to make recommendations regarding the attendance options for those individuals at an NHMCCD location or site.

The NHMCCD Review Committee and appropriate campus administrator have reviewed your petition to attend NHMCCD classes for the summer semester 2005, and made the following decision:

1) *You are conditionally admitted based on the information provided to us by you, your probation officer, and our review of the facts.*
2) *You are to have NO CONTACT with anyone under the age of 17 years of age.*
3) *You are not allowed to volunteer in any capacity at any NHMCCD site.*
4) *You must notify the NHMCCD Police Department each semester that you attend prior to the start of classes.*
   A hold has been placed on your records that will prevent you from registering pending that notification.
5) *Any violation or deviation of the terms of admissions will result in immediate review of your situation and may result in your immediate dismissal from NHMCCD.*
6) *Under the NHMCCD Policy, you have the right to appeal this decision to the appropriate NHMCCD College President.*

If you have any questions or if your status changes, you should notify your college dean/vice president of student services or the NHMCCD Police Department.

Sincerely,

Executive Vice Chancellor
NHMCCD Police Commissioner

NORTH HARRIS COLLEGE   KINGWOOD COLLEGE   TOMBALL COLLEGE   MONTGOMERY COLLEGE   CY-FAIR COLLEGE   THE UNIVERSITY CENTER

APPENDIX E

RESTITUTION RECEIPTS

293

APPENDIX F

POLYGRAPH LETTERS SUBMITTED TO THE COURT

H P I HENDRICKS POLYGRAPH, INC. ▉

CONFIDENTIAL POLYGRAPH REPORT
[Monitoring]

▉

Harris County CS & CD
49 San Jacinto, 5th Floor
Houston, Texas 77002

COPY

September 5, 2006

Norman Bernard Harris

At your request on September 5, 2006, I administered a Clinical Monitoring polygraph examination to Mr. Harris. The following is an accurate account of his interview and examination.

Mr. Harris entered the polygraph office at 2:48 p.m. on September 5, 2006 for a Monitoring polygraph examination. The time of the events that took place during the polygraph examination were as follows:

Pre-Test		In-Test		Post-Test	
Begin	**End**	**Begin**	**End**	**Begin**	**End**
3:12 p.m.	4:00 p.m.	4:10 p.m.	4:22 p.m.	4:22 p.m.	4:35 p.m.

A short break was offered at 4:00 p.m. to allow Mr. Harris to use the restroom. The Post-Test ended at 4:35 p.m. and Mr. Harris was released following a short conversation.

During the Pre – Test interview, Mr. Harris provided the following background information and personal data:

Personal Data							
Name:	Norman Bernard Harris		**Address:**	▉ Houston, Texas 77086		**Phone:**	▉
Alias:	None			**Sex:** M	**Date Of Birth:**	06/09/1981	**Age:** 25
Race:	Black	**Ht:** 5-08	**Wt:**	190	**Hair:** Black	**Eyes:**	Brown
Birthplace:	Houston, Texas		**Marital Status:**	Single	**SS No.**	▉	
Education:		College Student	**DL or ID:**		TX DL ▉		
Identifying Marks:	None						
Children:	None						
Next of Kin:	▉ Father		**Address:**			**Phone:**	▉
SPN:	▉						
Employment Data							
Company:	▉		**Title:**	Finance Associate	**Phone:**		

Examinees Demeanor

Mr. Norman Harris arrived fifteen minutes early for his appointment dressed in a black pullover short sleeved shirt and dress slacks. This examinee is clean and neat in appearance and is clean shaven. He is alert, verbal and upbeat.

Examinees Personal Background and Comments

Mr. Harris graduated from Nimitz High School in 1999 and has currently attending North Harris Community College as a Business Major. He has completed thirty three hours of college credit.

Examinees Health and Physical Condition

This examinee is not currently under a doctor's care and is not taking any medication. He states that he feels "pretty good" about himself. Mr. Harris considers himself to be mentally, emotionally and physically stable at this time.

Examinees Drug and Alcohol Use

This examination subject states that he never had a problem with alcohol and that before probation, he consumed about three drinks on the weekends. He denies consuming alcohol while on probation. He denies any illegal drug use.

Examinees General Lifestyle Behavioral Patterns

Mr. Harris has never been married and has no children. He lived with ███████████ from April 2003 to August 2003.

Examinees Arrest and Conviction History

Instant Offense is Sexual Assault of a Child filed in the 351st District Court of Harris County, Texas / Cause Number ███████ filed on December 25, 2004. He pled for seven years deferred adjudication probation on January 11, 2005. The victim is ███████ age sixteen and they met through a chat line and met for sex. He found out that ████ was sixteen and not eighteen like he claimed when ████ mom got home. He denies any other crimes.

Clinical Monitoring Polygraph Examination

Norman Bernard Harris
September 5, 2006

I administered a Monitoring polygraph examination to Mr. Harris, using the Texas Department of Public Safety's Modified General Question Test (TX DPS MGQT), which utilizes Relevant (R), Sacrifice Relevant (SR), Irrelevant (I), and Comparison (C) questions. The TX DPS MGQT technique was conducted using the standard sequence in charts one and three. The second chart was conducted using a mixed series sequence. The examination was administered using an Axciton computer polygraph instrument which has the capability of recording the thoracic and abdominal respiratory activities; Galvanic Skin Resistance (GSR) and relative blood pressure, pulse rate and blood volume of the cardiovascular system.

PRE-TEST REVIEW AND ADMISSIONS

His first examination was Full Sexual History Disclosure on July 2005 and today's examination will cover Maintenance and Monitoring areas from day one of probation:

- Mr. Harris claims no Major Life Events.
- This examinee denies having any improper thoughts or fantasies.
- This examinee masturbates one time a week to thoughts of past adult lovers
- He has not had sex or sexual contact with anyone.
- Denies viewing any pornography.
- Mr. Harris denies going to any Sexually Oriented Businesses, using sex toys and he denies paying for sex or being paid for sex.
- This examinee denies being alone or unsupervised with anyone younger than 17.
- Harris denies any direct contact with anyone younger than 17.
- He denies any victim contact.
- Child Safety Zone violations – none.
- He denies any alcohol or illegal drug use.
- He denies any unauthorized travel.
- He denies having any contact with the police.
- Mr. Harris states that he will be paid up on his fines and fees in two days.
- He has no community service.
- This examinee denies possession of any firearms.
- His signs are displayed as ordered.
- He denies targeting, isolating, grooming or stalking anyone younger than 17.
- This examinee denies any other violations of his Conditions of Community Supervision.

EXAMINATION QUESTIONS:

The following is the format and listing of all questions asked on the TX DPS MGQT administered to Mr. Harris:

Type	No.	Question	Answer
(I)	1	Irrelevant	Yes
(SR)	2	Sacrifice Relevant	Yes
(C)	3	Comparison	No
(R)	4	During probation, have you isolated anyone younger than 17?	No
(R)	5	Since January 2005, have you committed any sex crime?	No
(C)	6	Comparison	No
(R)	7	In the last 21 months, have you had any sexual contact with anyone younger than 17?	No
(C)	8	Comparison	No

EXAMINATION RESULTS

The numerical evaluation of these charts revealed **"NO DECEPTION INDICATED"**

Question Number	Numerical Evaluation
4	+ 7
5	+ 4
7	+ 6

SCORING:

Numerical Evaluation	Indication
Each Numerical Evaluation +3 or Greater	No Deception Indicated

H P I   HENDRICKS POLYGRAPH, INC.

POST-TEST INTERVIEW

This examination was videotaped and is subject to quality control review.

The examination results were reviewed with Mr. Harris and he left after a brief conversation

This report will be submitted to █████████ at Harris County Community Supervision and Corrections Department and to the ██████ Clinic.

Respectfully,

Kelly B. Hendricks
Polygraph Examiner
766

CONSUMER INFORMATION: Board of Polygraph Examiners, P.O. Box 4087, Austin, TX 78773
(512) 424 - 2058

CONFIDENTIAL POLYGRAPH REPORT
[Maintenance]

COPY

Harris County CS & CD
49 San Jacinto, 5th Floor
Houston, Texas 77002

December 5, 2007

Norman Bernard Harris II

At your request on December 5, 2007, I administered a Clinical Maintenance polygraph examination to Mr. Harris. The following is an accurate account of his interview and examination.

Mr. Harris entered the polygraph office at 8:50 a.m. on December 5, 2007 for a Maintenance polygraph examination. The time of the events that took place during the polygraph examination were as follows:

Pre-Test		In-Test		Post-Test	
Begin	**End**	**Begin**	**End**	**Begin**	**End**
9:05 a.m.	9:40 a.m.	9:45 a.m.	10:20 a.m.	10:20 a.m.	10:38 a.m.

A short break was offered at 9:40 a.m. to allow Mr. Harris to use the restroom. The Post-Test ended at 410:38 a.m. and Mr. Harris was released following a short conversation.

During the Pre – Test interview, Mr. Harris provided the following background information and personal data:

Personal Data								
Name:	Norman Bernard Harris II	**Address:**		Houston, Texas 77086		**Phone:**		
Alias:	None		**Sex:**	M	**Date Of Birth:**	06/09/1981	**Age:**	26
Race:	Black	**Ht:**	5-08	**Wt:**	210	**Hair:**	Black	**Eyes:** Brown
Birthplace:	Houston, Texas	**Marital Status:**	Single	**SS No.**				
Education:		College Student	**DL or ID:**		TX DL			
Identifying Marks:	None							
Children:	None							
Next of Kin:	Father	**Address:**			**Phone:**			
SPN:								
Employment Data								
Company:	Unemployed		**Title:**			**Phone:**		

300

Examinees Demeanor

Mr. Norman Harris arrived early for his appointment dressed in a blue pullover knit short sleeved shirt and blue and gray pinstripe pants. He has facial hair around his mouth and he is otherwise clean shaven. This examinee is alert and verbal.

Examinees Personal Background and Comments

Mr. Harris graduated from Nimitz High School in 1999 and has currently attending North Harris Community College as a Business Major. He is currently a student at North Harris Community College.

Examinees Health and Physical Condition

This examinee is not currently under a doctor's care and is not taking any medication. He states that he feels "great" about himself. He has never been suicidal. Mr. Harris considers himself to be mentally, emotionally and physically stable at this time.

Examinees Drug and Alcohol Use

This examination subject states that he never had a problem with alcohol and that before probation, he consumed about three drinks on the weekends. He denies consuming alcohol while on probation. He denies any illegal drug use.

Examinees General Lifestyle Behavioral Patterns

Mr. Harris has never been married and has no children. He is currently single and lives with his grandmother, █████████████ and his cousin ██████████████████ He has someone new to him of (love) interest – ████████████   He lived with ██████████ age 22 from April 2003 to August 2003.

Examinees Arrest and Conviction History

Instant Offense is Sexual Assault of a Child filed in the 351st District Court of Harris County, Texas / Cause Number ██████████ filed on December 25, 2004. He pled for seven years deferred adjudication probation on January 11, 2005. The victim is ██████████ age sixteen and they met through a chat line and met for sex. He found out that ████ was sixteen and not eighteen like he claimed when ████ mom got home. He denies any other crimes.

Clinical Maintenance Polygraph Examination

Norman Bernard Harris II
December 5, 2007

I administered a Maintenance polygraph examination to Mr. Harris, using the Texas Department of Public Safety's Modified General Question Test (TX DPS MGQT), which utilizes Relevant (R), Sacrifice Relevant (SR), Irrelevant (I), and Comparison (C) questions. The TX DPS MGQT technique was conducted using the standard sequence in charts one and three. The second chart was conducted using a mixed series sequence. The examination was administered using an Axciton computer polygraph instrument which has the capability of recording the thoracic and abdominal respiratory activities; Galvanic Skin Resistance (GSR) and relative blood pressure, pulse rate and blood volume of the cardiovascular system.

PRE-TEST REVIEW AND ADMISSIONS

Since his last polygraph on September 5, 2006 to now:
- Mr. Harris claims the following Major Life Events: 1. He changed jobs and got fired from his new job. 2. He is currently unemployed.
- He states that he has been out of work since September 5, 2007 and is still looking for new employment.
- He claims his signs are displayed as required.
- This examinee denies having any improper thoughts or fantasies.
- This examinee masturbates three times a week to thoughts of past adult relationships.
- He has not had sex or sexual contact with ███████ and with ███████
- Denies viewing any pornography.
- Mr. Harris denies going to any Sexually Oriented Businesses, using sex toys and he denies paying for sex or being paid for sex.
- This examinee denies being alone or unsupervised with anyone younger than 17.
- Harris denies any direct contact with anyone younger than 17.
- He denies any victim contact.
- He denies being on any Child Safety Zone properties.
- Mr. Harris denies any alcohol or illegal drug use.
- He denies any unauthorized travel.
- Police Contacts – he had one traffic ticket that was dismissed.
- Mr. Harris is behind by one month on his fines and fees.
- He has no community service.
- This examinee denies possession of any firearms.
- He denies targeting, isolating, grooming or stalking anyone younger than 17.
- He has not been carrying his Sex Offender Registration card with him.
- This examinee denies any other violations of his Conditions of Community Supervision.

302

EXAMINATION QUESTIONS:

The following is the format and listing of all questions asked on the TX DPS MGQT administered to Mr. Harris:

Type	No.	Question	Answer
(I)	1	Irrelevant	Yes
(SR)	2	Sacrifice Relevant	Yes
(C)	3	Comparison	No
(R)	4	Since your last test, have you viewed any pornographic image in any medium?	No
(R)	5	Have you had any direct contact with anyone younger than 17 since your last polygraph?	No
(C)	6	Comparison	No
(R)	7	Have you physically been on any Child Safety Zone properties since your last test?	No
(R)	8	Since your last polygraph, have you accessed the Internet in any way not admitted?	No
(C)	9	Comparison	No

EXAMINATION RESULTS

The numerical evaluation of these charts revealed "**NO DECEPTION INDICATED**"

Question Number	Numerical Evaluation
4	+ 3
5	+ 3
7	+ 3
8	+ 4

SCORING:

Numerical Evaluation	Indication
Each Numerical Evaluation +3 or Greater	No Deception Indicated

HENDRICKS POLYGRAPH, INC.

POST-TEST INTERVIEW

This examination was videotaped and is subject to quality control review.

The examination results were reviewed with Mr. Harris and he left after a brief conversation.

This report will be submitted to ████████ at Harris County Community Supervision and Corrections Department and to the ████ Clinic.

Respectfully,

Kelly B. Hendricks
Polygraph Examiner
766

CONSUMER INFORMATION: Board of Polygraph Examiners, P.O. Box 4087, Austin, TX 78773
(512) 424 - 2058

APPENDIX G

PETITION LETTERS SUBMITTED TO THE COURT

Judge Mark Kent Ellis
Harris County Criminal Justice Center
1201 Franklin, 14th Floor
Houston, Texas 77002

Dear Judge Ellis

Greetings:

It has been a little over three years since I stood before you, terrified facing 2-99 years for Sexual Assault of a Child. I sure was relieved when I found out that probation was an option instead of being sentenced to prison. However, the terms and conditions of my probation was no walk in the park either. When I first started my probation term I didn't know how I was going to make it. It was so overwhelming trying to meet the deadlines, making sure I didn't miss any appointments or overlook any of my conditions. With the help of my family and friends things began to ease up a little and before I knew it, I had completed my first year. One thing I am certain of is that a successful completion of a probation sentence doesn't come without challenges, and that is why I am writing you today.

I lost my job in September 2007 and now it has been five months since I've worked. I exhausted every available resource there is. I daily visit the Texas Workforce, I have been to several job fairs, and even passed out my resume to formal co-workers and friends. I applied at Harris County several times and the City of Houston since it is a proven fact that they employ those with criminal records. I also attended the Bi-Saturdays job fairs that are administered by David Mills with Community Supervision, and still haven't been successful in gaining employment. I should clarify something, there have been job offers until a criminal background check is performed and the offers are withdrawn. I have tried second chance agency like Eagle Pro, Staff Force and Labor Ready and once interviewed I am turned down because "this isn't the type of work for me" or "with your financial background and experience I am sure you can do better". Judge Ellis, I have even applied at gas stations and fast food restaurant but because of my previous experience I am constantly being turned down. Every bill I have is past due, up until recently I was behind in my monthly probation fees (I used my 1st check to get caught up), The balance in my weekly Sex Offender Treatment Program is way over $800. With the help of my unemployment I was able to pay on my balance, however my unemployment benefits balance is now at zero. I haven't been able to pay my monthly rent to my grandmother, which puts her in a bind since she is on a fixed income. My parents have been able to offer some financial assistance with books, food and toiletries but for the most part I am broke.

There is some good news; I have been offered a position as a Billing Associate at 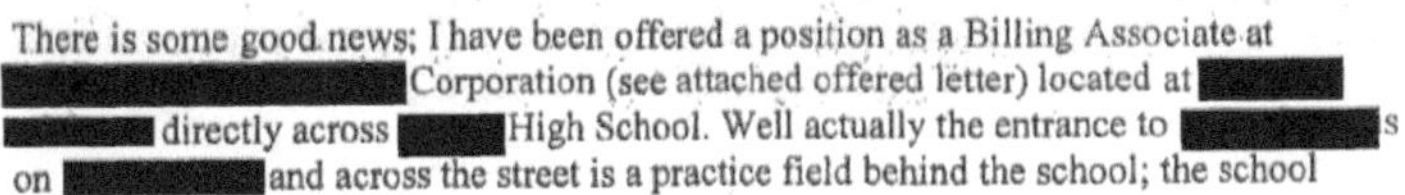 Corporation (see attached offered letter) located at ▮▮▮▮ ▮▮▮▮ directly across ▮▮▮▮High School. Well actually the entrance to ▮▮▮▮s on ▮▮▮▮ and across the street is a practice field behind the school; the school entrance is on Westhimer. I am fully aware that I have a 1000ft child safety zone and an amended 700ft child safety zone for my residence, which is why I am asking for your permission to work at ▮▮▮▮▮▮▮

I know that distance is very high risk; however I feel that I have demonstrated rehabilitation and earned the trust of your court. I have successfully completed the first three out of seven years of my deferred adjudication. I haven't had a "dirty" urinary analysis, and I have passed all three of my annual polygraph test. Minor or major I have been compliant with all of my conditions. In my Sex Offender Treatment classes I have approximately three assignments left in Phase III before I am voted into Phase IV which is a monthly maintenance. I am still enrolled in college at Lone Star College Systems (formerly North Harris Montgomery College) and this summer I will graduate with my Associates Degree and then transfer my credit hours to the University of Houston to finish my degree in Management.

Judge Ellis, I am asking your permission to work at ▮▮▮▮▮▮▮ I still remember how you made it clear that "you are the only person who can amend my conditions". A major advantage of deferred adjudication is I have the opportunity to make restitution without serving prison time and that is all I want to do. An assignment in Phase II of my treatment was called Impact Essay. The purpose of this assignment was to identify areas like finances, employment, family, leisure a total of 18 different essay had to be written to show me how my choices not only effect me but the people around me. Prior to attending group I thought since I didn't have any children I was free to live my life how I please. I thought as long as I went to work and paid my bills everything will be fine in life. However, through the Impact Essay I saw how my parents had to sacrifice their time and money as well. I see the burden and stress I am causing my grandmother not being able to contribute to our household. This job at ▮▮▮▮▮▮▮ will allow me the chance not only to catch up on my obligations but also sustain in life.

I appreciate you for reading my plea, and I look forward to your decision. Hopefully, it will be in my favor, if not at least I tried. Thank You, sir.

Over the last month I have work at ▮▮▮▮▮▮▮ I ride to work with mother, I eat at my desk, I don't leave out of this building until 5pm at which my mom is outside already waiting on me. My desk is located on the opposite side of ▮▮▮High School which means I don't see any minors or the school if I look out of the window. I have no contact with any minors at this job.

At your mercy,

Norman Harris

SPN#▮▮▮▮▮▮

Honorable Judge Ellis
Court 351
1201 Franklin Street
Houston, Texas 77002

Dear Judge Ellis,

   I am writing on behalf of my son Norman Harris (spn # ███████ requesting your approval of his employment because of the job's location. You approved his place of residency when the distance did not quite meet the standards of the required qualification and he has abided by your rules every since you permitted him to live with his grandmother. Judge Ellis you said only you can change your decisions concerning Norman's probation. Norman is in college and being productive in society by attending college and taking care of himself. Please allow Norman to work at this job. As a mother I am asking this of you because Norman is doing what's required to display behavior of confirming to his probation. He has been able to pay his fees and other bills and his college tuition; without a job Norman cannot take care of himself and his obligations as a man. His grandmother can provide him a place to stay but she cannot feed and clothe him. I am able to drop him off and pick him up. He doesn't have to come out of the building because he can take a lunch. The school this job is near has a fence around it; there are no stores or restaurants around it and Norman doesn't have to come out the building until he gets off; He can take his lunch and eat there. Judge consider the benefits of Norman having this job-it's proving to the society one can be rehabilitated and community-based corrections is profitable and does work for Norman whose an offender you chose to grant probation because he appeared to be a good prospect for avoiding future criminal violations. Thank you for your considerations.

Sincerely,

████████████

Dear Judge Ellis,

   I am Norman's Harris ██████████ father writing you to ask you to consider all the efforts Norman and this family have put into following your guidelines for his correctional program when you allowed him to live in society instead of behind bars and give him permission to work at this job. Norman sent his resume to over 205 companies, until this company contacted him in February. Judge Ellis, he has a life sentence having to register as a sex-offender. He needs to work in order to bear his own burdens. He is in school and he has to pay his probation, tuition and take care of himself. Please have mercy in Jesus Name and let Norman have this job. Sir I would like to come talk to you. How can I have a meeting with you? Judge only you can help us with this matter; this is a good job with an Engineering Company, Norman is a Billing Specialist. We work hard as a family to keep up with these conditions.

Sincerely,

██████████

APPENDIX H

JUDGE'S COMMENTS (ARTICLE EXCERPT)

Click2Houston.com

Houston Rapper Gets 45-Year Sentence
Prosecutors Asked For Life In Prison

POSTED: 11:59 am CDT May 30, 2002
UPDATED: 4:56 pm CDT May 30, 2002

HOUSTON -- A jury handed down a prison sentence of 45 years for Houston rapper Carlos Coy Thursday morning.

The same jury that convicted Coy, 31, who is known as "South Park Mexican," on May 18 of sexually assaulting the girl at his southeast Houston home back in September, reached its verdict shortly after 11 a.m.\

Coy was also sentenced to pay a $10,000 fine.

The rapper showed no emotion as Judge Mark Kent Ellis read him his sentence. He turned to his family and mouthed, 'I'll be all right.'

Then, Ellis asked him to approach the bench so that he could address him.

"Mr. Coy I have spent 17 years in this courthouse, and in that time I have seen more sex offenders than I wish to remember," Ellis said. "But one thing that I have found over (time) is that sex offenders have one trait in common, and that is that they all are liars — and you are no exception to that rule."

Ellis told Coy that there was no excuse for his conduct, and that contrary to his testimony that he is also a victim in this case, because he is a rapper, that just isn't so.

"Well, the fact is that there is only one victim in this case, and it is a 9-year-old girl," Ellis said. "Now that is reality, and you need to deal with it.

"It's time for you to face the music," he said.

The sentence could have been a minimum of five years probation or a maximum of life in prison.

Prosecutors were hoping to send Coy to prison for life and brought in eight women who testified that they had sex with him when they were 12, 13 and 14 years old.

Defense attorney Chip Lewis maintained that his client was innocent, and that there was never any proof that Coy committed any of these crimes, just hearsay.

Despite objections by his attorney, Coy took the stand in his own defense Tuesday and testified that he never sexually assaulted the girl.

Coy said that the eight women who testified last week lied to the jury when they claimed that they had sex with him.

Previous Stories:

- May 29, 2002: Jury Begins Deliberating Rapper's Fate
- May 28, 2002: Houston Rapper Takes The Stand
- May 24, 2002: Tempers Flare Outside Rapper's Trial
- May 23, 2002: State Psychologist: Rapper Should Be Locked Up
- May 21, 2002: Women Testify Of Sex With Rapper As Young Girls

9/22/2008

APPENDIX I

VICTIM PROFILE

Can I Keep It Truthfull?!?!?!?

18, 5'11 (1.8m), 170lb (77kg), 32w, Average build , Black hair, Smooth, Black, Looking for Friendship, 1-on-1 Sex, Relationship

Location: Houston, North Houston
Last Activity: 2 weeks ago